ACTING IRISH IN HO[...]

ACTING IRISH
IN
HOLLYWOOD
FROM
Fitzgerald to Farrell

RUTH BARTON
University College, Dublin

Foreword by
LUKE GIBBONS

IRISH ACADEMIC PRESS
DUBLIN • PORTLAND, OR

First published in 2006 by
IRISH ACADEMIC PRESS
44 Northumberland Road, Dublin 4, Ireland

and in the United States of America by
IRISH ACADEMIC PRESS
c/o ISBS, Suite 300, 920 NE 58th Avenue
Portland, Oregon 97213-3644

Website: **www.iap.ie**

British Library Cataloguing in Publication Data
An entry can be found on request

ISBN 0-7165-3343-X (cloth)
ISBN 0-7165-3344-8 (paper)

Library of Congress Cataloging-in-Publication Data
An entry can be found on request

Typeset in 11pt on 13pt Sabon
by FiSH Books, Enfield, Middx
Printed by MPG Books Ltd., Bodmin, Cornwall

For Willie

Contents

List of Abbreviations/Acronyms

AMPAS   Academy of Motion Picture Arts and Sciences
BFI   British Film Institute
FCOI   Film Company of Ireland
HUAC   House Un-American Activities Committee
IMDb   Internet movie database
LA   Los Angeles
MGM   Metro-Goldwyn-Mayer
PCA   Production code administration
RTÉ   Radio Telefís Éireann
RUC   Royal Ulster Constabulary
UCLA   University of California, Los Angeles
USC   University of Southern California
UCD   University College Dublin
vhs   video home system

List of Illustrations

Acknowledgements

THIS BOOK WAS written under my tenure as O'Kane Senior Research Fellow at the Centre for Film Studies (now the School of Languages, Literatures and Film) at University College Dublin (UCD). I am most grateful to Frank and Rosaleen O'Kane for their generous support both of my work and the work of Film Studies at UCD. I would also like to acknowledge the support of the then Faculty of Arts at UCD in awarding me a travel grant that enabled me to carry out research in the archives of the University of Southern California (USC), UCLA and the Academy of Motion Picture Arts and Sciences, Margaret Herrick Library in Los Angeles. My trip there was facilitated by the efficiency and enthusiasm of Ned Comstock and Hayden Guest at USC, both of whom generously shared their enormous knowledge of their materials with me. I would also like to thank Anne Gilliland at UCLA for making my visit to their archives run so smoothly and Barbara Hall and Janet Lorenz at the Margaret Herrick Library for helping me get through so much material in so little time. My thanks too to Pam and Mike for showing me a little more of life in LA.

I have also plundered the libraries of the British Film Institute, the National Library of Ireland, NUI Galway and Trinity College Dublin, and thank their staff as well as those in UCD, along with Antoinette Prout and Sunniva O'Flynn in the library and archive of the Irish Film Institute. I have, as usual, taken advantage of my colleagues, Tony Fitzmaurice's and Harvey O'Brien's, remarkable video collections and impossibly obscure books and our administrator, Rowena Kelly's, dedication to carry out this research. Thanks too to Christopher Morash for initial suggestions about the contents of this book.

Many people helped me with anecdotes and memories of the actors discussed in the pages that follow, although here I can mention but a few. Most particularly, in researching the life of Constance Smith, I would like to thank Paddy and Jody McGhee and Pat Grimes, formerly of Mountpleasant Flats, and the customers of The Hill in Ranelagh for sharing their memories of those years with me. Declan McLoughlin of the Limerick Film Archive supplied much of my background material for this chapter and facilitated my viewing needs. Many thanks to him and to Robert Kruger and his wife, Joan, for their hospitality, time and recollections.

The encouragement I have enjoyed from my editor, Lisa Hyde, has made working with the Irish Academic Press a pleasure. Finally, but most importantly, I would like to thank my family for going along with all this. My parents-in-law, John and Clare, have repeatedly stepped into the breach and enabled me to take time away from home; I have escaped to my mother's house in Donegal when I could and, of course, Conal, Eoin and Paddy (the latter particularly) have carried out essential research on my behalf into representations of Irishness in popular American television culture. Willie takes a principled stand on not reading what I write and I dedicate this book to him.

Foreword

During his final illness, according to what may be an apocryphal story, Richard Harris had to be rushed to hospital from his suite of rooms at the Savoy Hotel in London. Finding no ready access to the emergency exits, the ambulance team dashed through the main dining room with their ailing patient, to the consternation of its discerning clientele. Seizing the moment, Harris sprang up in his stretcher, arms akimbo and drips flailing: 'It's the food!!,' he shouted, 'It's the food!!!!.' Grandstanding to the bitter end, it was as if Harris had kept his best lines until last.

In Ruth Barton's fine new study, Harris is among the leading players in the story of the Hollywood Irish, bringing with him the larger-than-life persona that has often passed for the inherent theatricality of Irish character. 'Call the Irish imaginative', wrote a British commentator at the turn of the last century: 'They are actors, and they know they are actors; and each man knows that the man to whom he is talking is not only playing a part, but knows that he knows that he is playing a part.' This was not meant as praise, of course, but as an indictment of the stage-managing of the self under colonialism; yet it was also fitting for a society embarking on a Cultural Revival through the establishment of a national theatre, the Abbey, founded by W. B. Yeats and Lady Gregory. In one of the most compelling turns in her argument, Barton suggests that the experience of emigration and exile added another layer to the Irish facility for wearing masks. Under pressure of assimilation in the United States, the Irish had to impersonate a newly acquired identity, often becoming more American than the American themselves, but in Hollywood they also found – most notably Barry Fitzgerald and Maureen O'Hara – that they had to impersonate Irishness as well. Even when their background was not flagged, or when they are not cast explicitly as Irish characters, the possibility remained that popular images – the fighting Irish, the sentimental Celt, the loquacious Gael – were somehow watermarked into performances. As is brought out in the discussions of the gangster and thriller genres, the role of 'the hood with a heart' points to a residue of the Celtic 'Jeykll and Hyde', the killer played by Stephen Rea in *The Crying Game* (Neil Jordan, GB, 1992) or Gabriel Byrne in *Miller's Crossing* (Joel Coen, USA, 1990) who can't go through with shooting someone in cold blood, especially if it happens to be in the woods. Though not featured in a central role in Barton's discussion, Michael Collins, as played by Liam Neeson (*Michael Collins*: Neil Jordan, USA, 1996), or the General as played by Brendan Gleeson (*The General*: John Boorman, Ireland/GB, 1998), also fits this billing. At the other end of the social (though not necessarily moral) scale, the casting of Pierce Brosnan as the suave, debonair James Bond belies centuries of stereotypes of the uncouth Irish or sex-shy Catholics, not to mention terrorists who took up arms against Her Majesty's Service in film after film dealing with the Troubles.

One of the recurrent themes in Barton's study is whether Irish actors ever throw off a stage-craft honed in theatre itself, the capacity to realize a dramatic persona before a live audience. Walter Benjamin once suggested that the close-up was fashioned in cinema to compensate for the absence of live presence, but the close-up, with its intimations of a psychological depth, has not really been the forte of Irish movie stars. In a work on 'the psychology of the Gael' published during the hey-day of the Abbey Theatre, Sophie Bryant suggested that the Irish bring complexity to self-expression, not by drawing on the resources of some inner life within, but through presenting an alternative public expression at the same time. Hence a certain instability of expression typified in Stephen Rea's hang-dog intensity, Gabriel Byrne's Heathcliff good looks, Pierce Brosnan's sly urbanity, or Colin Farrell's agitated eyes, all of which could provide an alibi for a killer. In the explosive opening sequence of *inter*Mission (John Crowley, Ireland/GB, 2003) Colin Farrell sweet-talks an enamoured check-out girl at a shop counter, only to smash her face suddenly with a punch. In a fascinating discussion of the contrast between the acting styles of Marlon Brando and Richard Harris, Barton point out that Harris' physical presence did not lend itself to the 'method acting' of the Actor's Studio, even if he was trained in its protocols at Joan Littlewood's Theatre Workshop. In his powerful depiction of Machin, the miner turned rugby player in Lindsay Anderson's *This Sporting Life* (GB, 1963), Harris gives very little away of his character's inner life but while there are no secrets, there are irresolvable complexities or even contradictions in the qualities he brings to the screen. As Barton comments (in terms that could equally be applied to Colin Farrell's volatile screen persona): 'In no sense is this a portrayal of a man with whom the audience is intended to sympathise or who could be labelled with a romantic loner tag of a Brando or [Jimmy] Dean character... If the film's final moments come closest to the representation of an inner moment, overall Harris's performance is less naturalistic than theatrical, drawing attention to the actor as performer. The effect is not so much Brechtian distancing as biographical layering (heightened, for an audience attuned to nuances of accent, by Harris's easily detectible Limerick tones).' Likewise, Neil Jordan's *The Crying Game*, which is indeed about masquerade: it is not only the characters but viewers who are denied access to the enigmatic inner lives of Fergus (Stephen Rea) and Dil (Jaye Davidson). What is missing psychologically, however, is often more than compensated for by *intellectual* depth, as exemplified by Rea himself, or another remarkable Irish actor, Dan O'Herlihy (1919–2005), a favourite with Orson Welles, Luis Buñuel and Douglas Sirk.

More than any other attribute, it is through the voice – the idioms of accent, the intonations of speech – that Irish actors bring the cadences of their culture to the screen. Re-negotiating his role in *Miller's Crossing*, Gabriel Byrne transformed his character into Tom Reagan, an Irish mobster, thus allowing Byrne to speak in his own distinctive voice. But even when Irish accents are not overt, the soft-spoken voice of characters played by Irish actors such as Byrne, Rea, Liam Neeson, Brendan Gleeson or Colm Meaney adds an oblique ethnic dimension to the character, often providing unstated 'explanations' for actions where psychological motivations leave off. At times – and this is perhaps an attribute derived from Irish theatre itself - it is as if speech and language are invested with a sematic intensity of their own, leaving Irish actors in an ungainly relationship with their bodies – not to mention the bodies of others. Sometimes, the body acquires an 'accent' of its own, as in the farmer's gait of Liam Neeson in *Michael Collins*, the swagger of Charlo (Sean McGinley) in Michael Winterbottom/Roddy Doyle's television drama *Family* (1994), Benny Brady's (Stephen Rea) rubbery walk at the beginning of *The Butcher Boy* (Neil Jordan, USA/Ireland, 1998), or the straightening of the shoulders which has become almost the signature of Brendan Gleeson.

Perhaps the most ground-breaking aspect of Ruth Barton's study lies in its treatment of female stardom, exemplified by the careers of Maureen O'Sullivan, Maureen O'Hara and – a triumph of original archival research and oral history – the tragic life of the now almost forgotten Constance Smith. One of the questions raised by the current high profile of Irish leading males in Hollywood is why no female stars have attained similar success? It is certainly not due to an absence of charisma or performative ability, as is clear from the notoriety of the rock star Sinead O'Connor, or the powerful stage presence of Fiona Shaw. Historically, it may have been the cultivation of acting styles that eschewed the close-up and negated the allure of the body that placed Irish actresses in a quandary, particularly in the empire of the gaze for which anatomy became destiny in the case of female stars. As Barton points out, though Maureen O'Hara became the quintessential face of Mother Ireland – flaming red hair, pale skin, tearful eyes – she excelled in swashbuckling roles that transferred a dynamism to the female body, as well as questioning voyeurism in her direct address to embarrassed male spectators in Dorothy Arzner's *Dance, Girl Dance* (USA, 1940).

Over ten years ago, I was involved in researching a book and television series on Irish leading players in Hollywood with the late Aine O'Connor, and while six leading males were easily chosen – Patrick Bergin, Peirce Brosnan, Gabriel Byrne, Liam Neeson, Aidan Quinn, Stephen Rea – no similar female stars presented themselves, apart from Fionnuala Flanagan, whose best Hollywood work still lay ahead. Ironically, it has been the advent of a new cast of male stars, exemplified by the deranged dreamer quality of Cillian Murphy, or the smouldering bad-boy persona of Colin Farrell, that has brought a newly-found eroticism to the Irish body on the screen. More recently, younger actresses, such as Eva Birthistle in Ken Loach's *Ae Fond Kiss* (GB/Germany/Italy/Spain/France, 2004), have also brought a belated sexual openness to Irish female characters, without losing anything of the cultural layers or the way with words of their predecessors. Starting out from the mists of the Celtic Twilight, Irish actors have best served Hollywood when they have de-misted the silver screen.

Luke Gibbons
April 2006

Acting Exile

I think anybody who leaves Ireland and who
goes abroad...a strange thing happens you
because in a weird way you never really belong
again in the place that you've left and you never
really belong in the place that you go to so that
you live in a kind of limbo world in between. It
has tremendous advantages and it has also
certain drawbacks. Liam [Neeson] and I often
talk about that, could you ever go back to live in
Ireland, and there are so many reasons why I
would love to come back here but I would miss
America an awful lot too.

Gabriel Byrne[1]

IF EMIGRATION AND EXILE remain two of the most potent narratives
of this and the previous century, it is in Hollywood that they have
found one of their most compelling narrators. The often-told story of
Hollywood is of an enterprise founded by immigrant entrepreneurs
and peopled by exotic talents whose Americanised names provided
scant cover for their alien, often eastern European identities.[2] These
immigrant individuals wove their collective pasts into the films they
made, populating American stories with mysterious foreigners and
setting them in far-off locations, Casablanca for instance, where
American values had little hold. The weight of these stories was born
by the actors who animated them, themselves often shoehorned into
roles that were quite at odds with their own ethnic backgrounds – as
Thomas Elsaesser reminds us, it was common for German Jews to be
cast as Nazi officers.[3] Elsaesser further notes that the Europe these
exiles recreated in Hollywood was one that corresponded to a New
World fantasy of the Old, of Viennese waltzes and Parisian romance,
rigid class structures and a decadent aristocracy.

Hollywood's romance with Europe and empire fed images of these highly fictionalised spaces not just back home but to Europe where they were consumed with equal warmth. The traffic in images was complemented by a traffic in personnel, particularly in the 1930s.[4] Directors, actors and other film workers moved between Europe and Hollywood, many eventually relocating for good in California where they formed their own communities in exile. It is within this narrative of emigration and exile that I wish to locate the many Irish actors who at different moments left Ireland for Hollywood, and chart their varying fortunes there.

Irish actors form only one part of the story of the Irish in Hollywood; Rex Ingram, born in Dublin in 1893, was one of the most influential of the silent film directors to work from Hollywood and was largely responsible for launching Valentino's screen career (in *The Four Horsemen of the Apocalypse* [USA, 1921]).[5] Irish writers in pre-war Hollywood included W.R. Burnett, Philip Dunne, John Meehan and John Patrick Goggan, while Irish composers and songwriters included Jimmy McHugh and Robert Emmett Dolan.[6] I have decided to focus on actors in this book for a number of reasons. Limitations of space dictate that, for the topic to enjoy depth of analysis, its scope must be restricted. The study of stars and screen actors is gaining increasing attention within academia, both from an analytical and a historical perspective. More than ever before, film actors define films and their significance as players within the Hollywood power game has increased exponentially. Cinemagoers remain fascinated by stars and the presence of certain actors in a film signal its content in advance ('What's the movie? Who's in it?'). It is timely, therefore, that this under-represented area in Irish film and theatre scholarship receives its due attention.

Academic writing on actors and stars has tended to focus on the latter. More visible, better known, more fascinating maybe, stars have been analysed for their significance within Hollywood's elusive dynamics of pleasure and for their status as national symbols. Richard Dyer's seminal scholarship has been hugely influential in articulating a semiotics of image and performance and providing a methodology for analysing what he termed the 'star text', itself based on textual analyses of star performances.[7] His writing reflects the early influence of cultural studies in his parallel discussion of the sociology of stars, questioning how they function in society. Christine Gledhill's edited volume of essays, *Stardom: Industry of Desire* picks up on feminist and psychoanalytic (primarily Lacanian) analyses of stars, incorporating to a greater extent methodologies derived from cultural studies but also questioning the notions of pleasure inherent in the consumption of star images.[8] It also has a strong historical bias, looking at stars from the silent period to the present. More recently, Ginette Vincendeau explored and analysed the history of French stars from Max Linder to Juliette Binoche, arguing that the French industry had produced a particular kind of star whose success was based on local rather than international appeal.[9] Geoffrey Macnab and Bruce Babington have written and edited corresponding books that locate British stars within the British industry but also as Hollywood imports.[10] Diane Negra, in turn, has explored the relationship between ethnicity, performance and spectatorship in her book, *Off-White Hollywood*.[11] That connection between stars and issues of national identity is further explored by the editors of another reader in the area, *Stars: The Film Reader*, who write that, 'the link between the star's image and screen roles has been intimately tied to questions of the national imaginary, of how the star embodies and also alters characteristics associated with questions of political identity, value, and attitude'.[12]

Another approach has been to analyse film acting as performance, paying particular attention to voice, gesture and movement. James Naremore laid down the parameters for such studies in his *Acting in the Cinema*.[13] Here, he explores the intersection between the connotative power of the star's image and the conventions of gestural acting with particular emphasis on the legacy of the melodrama in realist acting. Through a series of detailed case studies, he demonstrates how acting styles contribute to meaning creation. Roberta Pearson's *Eloquent Gestures* focuses on acting at one particular historical moment (1905–13) as film made its transition from the melodramatic mode of early cinema to the realist style of what is now understood to be conventional Hollywood production practices.[14] In their edited collection of essays on screen acting, Peter Krämer and Alan Lovell somewhat controversially criticised existing scholarship on the grounds that, 'many analyses of film acting are in fact discussions of a fictional character (whose creation is the work of a writer) rather than analyses of how that character is embodied (the work of an actor)'.[15] The essays that follow in that reader build on Naremore and Pearson's work by discussing actors' interpretations of scripts and the influence of acting schools, in particular the Actors' Studio, and by examining individual performances in detail.

Criticising an article in *Sight and Sound* on Antonio Banderas, Alan Lovell wrote in a letter to that journal that:

At the root of many of the problems in the discussion of (star) acting is the concept of 'persona', which suggests that an actor's performance is always marked by his/her own personality. It encourages a view that acting is predominantly a form of self-expression, that the actor is an auteur in the same way as a director is supposed to be. And because, in most cases, there's a lack of substantial evidence about personality, critics seize on details to bolster their case [...] I suggest there's a need for a new framework for the discussion of acting that would show a greater awareness of the existence of scripts. How can you properly assess actors' performances without knowing what they had to work with?[16]

Lovell and Krämer's scholarship is informed by what might be termed an empiricist approach to criticism; in other words, if you cannot prove it, then leave it out. It also rather anachronistically ignores the role of consumption in meaning-creation. In my experience of studying many of the scripts on which the star performances in this book are based, there is often a disparity between the written word and the screen performance, yet little to indicate who influenced that metamorphosis – director, producer, actor, all or other.

In his essay, 'Methodological reflections on the study of the émigré actor', Dana Polan recognises the importance of the émigré actor to diasporic studies, suggesting that analyses of these actors in Hollywood would benefit from understanding them as part of a mode of production. The analyst would then include in their argument: 'first, the activity of production (the province of political economy); second, the structure of the produced thing itself (the province, in the case of actors, of image-analysis, iconographic analysis, textual analysis, semiological commutation tests, and so on); third, the reception/consumption of the produced thing'.[17] My own approach adopts many of these methodologies, borrowing both from star studies and performance theories to create a framework that allows for an exploration of the Irish experience of stardom. The primary determinants of that framework are as follows:

- The actor as symbolic emigrant.
- The actor as returning emigrant.
- The economy of acting.
- The construction of the Irish star image in studio publicity and media discourse.
- The related practices of 'passing' and 'performativity' as strategies of integration, and resistance to integration.

- The place of accent as a marker of authenticity.
- Irishness, ethnicity and 'whiteness'.
- Irish traditions of performance and the performance of ethnicity.
- The role of biography in star performances.

Irish actors, stars or otherwise, I will be arguing, have enjoyed enormous symbolic importance as embodiments of the emigrant dream. At the same time, they have provided a link between the Irish 'at home' and abroad, between the indigenous and diasporic Irish communities. They have populated Hollywood, American cinema with Irish characters, all the while reminding their viewers, through their biographies, that they are 'authentically' Irish. This is not to suggest that Irish-American actors, or those Irish born in America, lack authenticity; indeed Hollywood and local Irish coverage in the classic era seldom discriminated between the two. So, for instance, when Maureen O'Hara and Pat O'Brien visited Ireland in 1946, no distinction was made in news reports of the event between the two members of the 'Irish in Hollywood', notwithstanding the fact that this was O'Brien's first time in Ireland. The Irish press and the Los Angeles Gaelic Association regularly claimed newsworthy actors for Ireland; these included Ann Blyth, Bing Crosby, Veronica Lake and Ginger Rogers as well as more obvious names such James Cagney, Errol Flynn and Spencer Tracy. Rather, those actors who arrived in Hollywood brought with them, through accent, behaviour or style, a renewed discourse on Irishness. These stars' ethnic allegiances were widely proclaimed in secondary publicity material as Hollywood reached out to the massive Irish-American audience and those in sympathy with Irish screen personalities and stories. We will also be looking at how studios fashioned images for their stars through the machinery of studio publicity, press interviews, biography and autobiography, with Irish women being promoted as fiery but pure colleens (Maureen O'Sullivan, Maureen O'Hara) and men as romantic rebels (George Brent). Taking this into the present day, we will see, with specific reference to Colin Farrell, how stars have used the media to construct images of themselves. In Farrell's case, this has meant drawing on multiple connotations of Irishness from hell raiser and rebel to 'Mammy's boy'.

My study of Irish actors does not concentrate solely on aspects of stardom, though most of those actors whom I shall be discussing in greater detail enjoyed star status, if only in some instances, on a transient basis. Rather it seems to me that the Irish actor in Hollywood typifies the complexities of emigration. Successful actors generated, and continue to generate, an enormous level of national pride, returning home to civic and private receptions organised to celebrate their achievement. In doing so, they have perpetuated a fantasy of the immigrant who, through hard work and good fortune, makes good. Some (Constance Smith) fell by the wayside, overwhelmed by an unforgiving system for which their background had left them little prepared. Others (George Brent) are now largely forgotten. Many (Richard Harris) disdained the hand that fed them, reserving their best work (also Stephen Rea) for indigenous Irish films. More recent actors (Gabriel Byrne, Pierce Brosnan) move easily between Hollywood and Ireland, using their star status to garner funding for local Irish projects.

Acting, we could argue, is an analogy as well as an embodiment of the emigration process, requiring the individual to pass themselves off as 'other' in terms of accent, attitude and behaviour while retaining traces of their original identity. Hamid Naficy writes of what he terms the 'accented filmmaker' who reproduces their own identity formation through their fictional subjects. Distinguishing between 'mimicry' and 'imitation', he argues that:

> imitation involves identification with the other to the point of producing whole, identical subjects, where the original and the copy match [...]. Mimicry, on the other hand, involves the kind of overimitation or underimitation of the other that, in its surplus or deficit and in its irony, produces partiality of identity, where there is a slippage between the original and its copy. It is in this slipzone of unfitting that the critical tensions of exilic mimicry and irony can be deciphered [...]. In exilic situations, especially for first-generation exiles, born in one country and reared in another, there is a prior identity, an original sense of self at home, that they compare themselves with and to which many of them long to return. The juxtaposition of the originary self and the new evolving self creates hybridized performances [...]. In such performances, the homeland is often the source of the true original identity to which exilic identity is a poor imitation.[18]

This concept of performativity, of the slippage between the original and its copy seems to me crucial in understanding the importance of the Irish actor to Irish and Irish-American identity formations. It is precisely in that phrase, 'an accented cinema' that we can retrieve from such performances the traces of an 'original' identity. In other words, in accent we detect ethnicity. Further, such traces are more readily identified by members of that ethnic group. The screen actor is thus an ideal of assimilation – apparently performing under the guise of their new identity but actually retaining decodable signifiers of their real ethnicity. There is, however, a problem with Naficy's formulation in so far as it presupposes that the originating identity is the ideal. Intrinsic to the Irish emigrant experience is the sense, evidently not shared by all emigrants, of escape, and a memory of the homeland as the site of an old trauma. In this case, the adoption of a new identity may be seen as a strategy of effacement, a voluntary participation in the masquerade of performance. To complicate Naficy's formulation further, the equation of authenticity and the originary self is not always a given. Certainly, as we shall see in the case of Pierce Brosnan, the members of that originating society may not view the exile as an authentic member of their community. National identity, we need to bear in mind, is a fabrication not a given. As Naficy further reminds us, 'national identity [is] not a fixed edifice but [...] a shifting, performing strategy'.[19] Any study such as this runs the danger of veering into essentialism, with national symbols, the film stars, invoked to prove the existence of an all-encompassing Irishness. This cannot be done and, anyway, leads to reductiveness. What I hope will emerge from the chapters that follow is a series of engagements with aspects of a performative Irishness as it has been encountered, enacted and embodied by the stars in this study.

Issues of accent are crucial to this argument – how an Irish identity is diffused through accent and how local Irish audiences may read character differently through accent recognition. For many Irish actors, it became a necessity to adopt a kind of generalised mid-Atlantic intonation in order to escape the limitations that attached to a strongly inflected Irish voice. In the present, we will see how performers such as Gabriel Byrne have re-inflected Hollywood dramas with their ethnic accents. Wordiness, as much as accent, has long been a significant factor in distinguishing the Irish actor in Hollywood and British cinema. The presumption of Irish eloquence, even prolixity, is one of the recurrent themes of this book, and it will be argued, central to that triangular structure – Irish actor, British stage, Hollywood screen – that supports many, though by no means all, of the performances discussed in the following chapters.

Another important defining feature of the Irish émigré actor was colour, specifically whiteness. Noel Ignatiev's seminal publication,

How the Irish Became White, explains the history of Irish immigration into the United States during the nineteenth century as a
(primarily) symbolic process of becoming white, of the Irish
rendering themselves distinct from the Negro labourers with whom
they were initially closely associated.[20] While most commentators
agree that this practice was complete by the time span covered here,
its traces remain evident in the discourse that surrounds the early
Irish stars in Hollywood and are very provocatively evoked in their
casting, particularly in the cases of Maureen O'Sullivan and
Maureen O'Hara. We only have to pause and consider the opening
moments of *The Story of Seabiscuit* (David Butler, USA, 1949) to see
just how potent this discourse remained even in post-war
Hollywood. In this sequence, Barry Fitzgerald (as Shawn O'Hara)
and Shirley Temple (his niece, Maggie), arrive off a train in America,
ready to be taken to the stud where Shawn will train Mr Milford's
(William Forrest) racehorses. They are greeted by an African-
American called Murphy, played by Sugarfoot Anderson:

Murphy   (raising his hat): Is, uh, you folks, uh . . . ?
Maggie: Could you be after telling me, is a certain Mr Milford,
             the horse breeder, about?
Murphy: I don't rightly know what you is saying, Missy. I'm
             here to pick up some folks who are going out to Mr
             Milford's farm.
Shawn: What language is this strange person talkin', Maggie?
Maggie: I'm not sure.
Murphy: Don't you all speak the English language?
Maggie: Yes, we do. Now, you listen carefully. This is Mr
             Shawn O'Hara. I'm his niece. We have come all the
             way from Ireland. Mr Milford's expecting us. *Mr
             Milford.*
Murphy: Yassum. You is which I'm looking for. I'm Mr
             Milford's boy.
Shawn: His boy, you say?
Murphy: Yessir. Murphy's the name, sir.
Shawn: Murphy? Did he say 'Murphy'?
Maggie: I think he did, Uncle Shawn. Did you say 'Murphy'?
Murphy: Yes. They call me 'Walkin' Murphy'. Most of us
             Murphys down here just sit. I walk.
Maggie: Well, that's fine.
Shawn: Murphy, well what part of Ireland are you from?

Murphy:	I don't rightly know sir. Us Murphys down here only got a casual acquaintance with Irish.
Maggie:	Come on, Murphy. Take us to Mr Milford.
Murphy:	I nearly forgot what Mr Milford said. Welcome to Kentucky, the Blue Grass state.
Maggie:	Thank you, Murphy. Now get walking.

'They call me Walkin' Murphy'. Barry Fitzgerald, Shirley Temple, Sugarfoot Anderson in *The Story of Seabiscuit*

As Diane Negra has carefully demonstrated, the ideal of beauty for Hollywood actors shifted during the twentieth century from the kind of shimmering whiteness and pure sexuality embodied by Colleen Moore to the more sultry skin colour of the mixed-race actor.[21] This initially benefited, and later disadvantaged, Irish female actors with what might be termed classic Irish looks, a very white skin and dark or red hair. It also had repercussions for Irish male actors, although for somewhat different reasons. As I will be suggesting, with the increasing visibility of a new generation of such actors, it could be argued that the Irish in Hollywood are in the process of renegotiating their whiteness, if not becoming black again.

Skin colour is a less specific determinant of national identity than accent, and the latter seems to me to be the most consistent mode of identification for Irish émigré actors. Dudley Andrew, on the other hand, has proposed that we can identify a distinct Irish acting style – in an argument influenced by Fredric Jameson, he suggests that actors within a national cinema feed off a set of gestures inherited from their national theatre; this is not to be confused with the output of playwrights, but comprises:

> the gait, the inflection, the facial grimaces which 'national actors' put into play, no matter what roles they take on. These physical habits comprise an inventory of national expression. [...] Home audiences instinctively experience as their own the movies in which their actors express things in just this Irish way.[22]

Is this so? The question hangs over the chapters that follow. There seems to have been, in its early days, an identifiable Abbey acting style, but we may ask how much of that was transferred to screen and whether it survived the influx of Abbey actors into Hollywood. How did the Abbey acting style fit with the evolving modes of performance of early American cinema? Can we talk of a Field Day or Project Theatre acting style? Can we talk of a 'national troupe'?

That there were overwhelming commercial reasons, on both sides of the bargain, for importing the Abbey actors into Hollywood is discussed below and in Chapter 1, on Barry Fitzgerald. That the Abbey acting methods fused with an older performance tradition, inherited from the American popular stage, and became absorbed into Hollywood performance styles is also almost certain. Threaded through both styles, and perhaps their most potent legacy, is the comic figure of the Stage Irishman, an inheritance that was to become the benchmark for judging most subsequent performances of Irish masculinity. In a useful history of this persona, Maureen Waters has traced its genesis from 'omadhawn' or primitive peasant simpleton of the mid-nineteenth century to Brendan Behan's performance of his own identity as 'wild Irish boy' for the benefit of the English and American media:

> Although the [Irish] clown shares some of the features of the folk fool, the humor which he generates is largely based on cultural differences. In the early nineteenth century he is a blundering, often hot tempered

but benevolent buffoon, ignorant of the modern world and incapable of speaking English properly. A second type, brought to perfection by Somerville and Ross, is the cunning clown who seems bent on dissolving the foundations of Anglo-Saxon civilisation.[23]

The other stock character bequeathed by Anglo-Irish writing to the dramatis personae of Irish fiction is the rogue, often a disinherited nobleman, but later any kind of outsider figure whose disregard for legality is often a comment on the very nature of the system of which he is, it is suggested, justifiably dismissive. From the writings of Samuel Lover, through Synge, Boucicault and O'Casey, the rogues 'flourish because they break through the conventional boundaries or the usual domestic ties. Unlike the peasant who subordinates himself to family, community or some higher authority, the rogue is characterised by self-interest and by a desire for freedom and autonomy.'[24]

Gifted with a high degree of verbal felicity, the stage Irishman as he emerged into the twentieth century was as prone to critiquing his own society and its pieties as he was to undermining Anglo-Saxon probity. Such was the function of Christy Mahon in Synge's *The Playboy of the Western World* and of the parts played by Barry Fitzgerald in O'Casey's plays. Yet, at the same time as these characters were entering the contested spaces of the Irish stage, audiences were continuing to enjoy their less subversive predecessors:

> They were a regular feature of music hall entertainment in Dublin and London where Irishmen themselves laughed at clowns with a thick brogue and a shillelagh, who for all their misadventures, invariably landed on their feet. Their laughter probably expressed ambivalence toward that old Gaelic world; affection mingled with contempt for what seemed outmoded, clumsy, primitive.[25]

This performance style, in turn, owed much to the American tradition of vaudeville, which itself was indebted to Irish-American negotiations of the figure of the stage Irishman. Most writers agree that it was with Dion Boucicault that Irish characters became the subjects rather than the objects of representation. Prior to then:

> For Anglo-Americans, the Irishman may have been perceived to be as Yankee Doodle was to the prewar colonizing English – a provincial whose narrow self-interest, colloquial speech, and overall ineptitude allow the dominant type to display cultural superiority through satire.

In turn, this identification would have provided theatre-going
Americans with a tacit, if not too overtly stated, alignment to English
culture, allowing them, like their London cousins, to make the Teague
a perpetual outsider – fit for service in a limited way, but certainly
unfit to lead.[26]

Boucicault has been much written about in Irish studies as the key
to the transformation of the stage Irishman in the nineteenth
century; for now I would direct the reader to William H. Williams'
invaluable *'Twas Only an Irishman's Dream*.[27] In this study of Irish-
American popular songs in the period 1800 to 1920, Williams writes
that: 'unable to escape the stereotype that preceded them, the Irish
gradually remolded it into something with which they could live –
and eventually something they could use to express pride in themselves. In the process, the Irish had to "negotiate" the nature of their
image and identity within a largely Anglo-American culture.'[28] In
part, they achieved this by flooding American popular culture with
sentimental ballads that associated Irishness with a sense of loss and
longing. Then they offered the American public a rendition of the
comic stage Irishman that became a promise of easy and effortless
entertainment. As Williams notes, the first great Irish peasant role
was played by Tyrone Power, the progenitor of a long theatrical line
that stretched into Hollywood cinema, and with Tyrone Guthrie,
into American theatre.[29] As Samuel Lover's Rory O'More, in the play
of the same name, Power reinvented the Irish Paddy as the star of the
evening's entertainment, thus inaugurating a tradition of performing
ethnicity, of reconciling the wider American public to the peasant
Irish immigrant by rendering that figure a symbol of good-
humoured entertainment while simultaneously signalling its
constructedness. In the aftermath of the Civil War, Boucicault, a
near-permanent exile from Ireland, where he was born around 1820,
reprised this tradition, further transforming the traditional stage
Irishman 'from a mindless buffoon into a comic hero'.[30] Performing
in his own plays – *The Colleen Bawn* (1860), *Arrah na Pogue*
(1865), *The Shaughraun* (1874) – Boucicault popularised Irish sentimentality and the figure of the charming rogue within a format, the
melodrama, that provided audiences with a highly performative
representation of Irishness. In the same period, the development of
vaudeville as the pre-eminent form of popular entertainment opened
up a space for the new Irish stage act, usually a comedic duo
performing slapstick routines. This had the effect of speeding up the

delivery of the entertainment, substituting the gag and the put-down for the slowly developing story. Vaudeville, in its heyday, was the locus for 'a celebratory, performative ethnicity that operated, at least in part, outside of the narrative of assimilation [...], that paid lip service to progressive notions of moral and social edification and advancement'.[31] In vaudeville, 'to be Irish was to dance'.[32] To be Irish was now, also, to be Irish-American and these dancing, singing, joking, naïve Irish-American figures formed the basis for the representation of the Irish character in early American cinema, a medium in which the Irish themselves played little part other than as performers and thus wielded little influence.

The early Abbey acting style, by contrast, was deliberately minimalist and distinct from the prevailing melodramatic mode of performance.[33] As developed by the brothers Frank and Willie Fay, effect was achieved through vocal projection rather than physical gesture, with the other performers drawing attention to the main speaker by fixing their eyes on him or her, creating sightlines for the audience to follow. Evenness of tone was insisted upon and histrionics in general were banished from the Abbey boards. The company did not encourage a star system although Sara Allgood and Arthur Sinclair emerged as the critics' favourites. The objective of this acting style was to create a new naturalism and to divert audiences' attention away from performance for the sake of it. Of course we cannot know how performances looked but some idea of the impression they gave is available from contemporary criticism.[34] Even still, reviewers were divided over whether this new naturalism was a cover for amateur performances or a radical departure; what does emerge most clearly was a presupposition that the portrayal of Irish character should be a comic one and a peasant one. The Players were at this time in transition from their amateur status, their authenticity achieved to an extent through their residual non-professionalism (in fact, actors began to receive salaries in 1906, and by 1908 the core performers – Sara Allgood, J.M. Kerrigan, Máire O'Neill and Fred O'Donovan – 'increasingly came to see themselves as professional actors rather than as cultural revolutionaries').[35]

The Players' understated, naturalistic style seems overall to have appealed more to metropolitan Dublin and London audiences, for whom it bore the charm of novelty and freshness, than to rural Irish audiences who found it dull and lacking in humour when compared to the broad farce and melodrama that were regularly toured by amateur and other 'traditional' performers.[36] In the eyes of the outside world, however, the Abbey Actors, by virtue of their positioning as part of a National Theatre, became the voice of an authentic Ireland, whether or not they conformed to that nebulous identity.

The frequency with which the company toured America brought them in contact with American audiences and critics from their first engagements in 1911. The first Abbey tour attracted some considerable attention as a result of the riots that greeted their staging of Synge's *Playboy of the Western World*. This response, like that of the earlier Dublin audiences, was in part provoked by commonly perceived slurs on Irish womanhood. William H. Williams further remarks that the Irish-American audiences did not wish to acknowledge the dismal rural Ireland portrayed by Synge. Instead, they wanted narratives that would reflect their new status as urban bourgeoisie, or 'lace curtain Irish', and an image of Erin that was amenable to nostalgic yearning.[37] Henceforth, Irish characters and narratives would have to conform to that idealised image if they were to succeed. Alternatively, they would have to play up the national character for comic effect – as the tours demonstrated, the most popular representation of Irishness was the stage Irishman, played as buffoon:

> What began as an improvised self-mocking, meta-theatrical, exaggerated performance style as part of the dramatic events during the American tours, gradually became a standard attribute of a night at the Abbey Theatre in Dublin. As critics increasingly noted a relaxing of artistic standards, this mode of comic self-reflexive representation shifted from the spontaneity of the performance to being written into the dramatic text.[38]

In this period, American filmmaking was in transition from a splintered, experimental entertainment form to becoming hierarchically organised. From around 1908 film acting began to be recognised as an art and by 1913, 'with the emergence of the star system, the press began to discuss actors' private lives, the people they "really were" off the silver screen'.[39] Performances relied less on melodramatic gesture and became increasingly marked by a shift to a new, restrained style of interpretation, very suitable, therefore, for those trained on the Abbey boards.

At this point, few of the Abbey actors were tempted to cash in on their reputations and try their luck in the new entertainment medium of cinema. However, as early as 1904 several, including Dudley Digges and Maire Quinn, had left the Irish National Theatre Society for stage and subsequently screen careers in America. In any case, from 1916, following the establishment of the Film Company of Ireland (FCOI), actors had the opportunity to try their hand at film acting without having to travel any distance. The founder of the FCOI, Irish-American James Mark Sullivan, had been involved in protests against the Abbey's 1911 American production of *The Playboy of the Western World* and seemed intent on establishing a popular entertainment form that would not emulate either the acting style or the controversial agenda offered by Yeats' and Lady Gregory's theatre. Audiences for the new Irish films were largely drawn from the class that was accustomed to melodramatic fare, comedy and farce. Even though film was eventually to displace all but the most gritty of such live acts, in the beginning both media managed to co-exist and, indeed, to adapt to each other. The revue *Charlie Chaplin Mad* promised a stage full of Charlie Chaplins, and the Royal and Gaiety Theatres booked plays (*The Cinema Star* and *The Girl on Film*) that held out the promise of incorporating the new entertainment form.[40] Actors also managed to move between stage and screen and very soon two of the Abbey's most cherished actors (if pay packages are to be the measure of recompense), Fred O'Donovan and J.M. Kerrigan, were working on the films of the FCOI.[41] The use of amateur actors was also to be a feature of early indigenous Irish filmmaking and one of the reasons why it exported so badly.

By the 1920s, the impetus for an Irish film industry had petered out and it was obvious that fortunes in the film industry were only going to be made by leaving Ireland. This J.M. Kerrigan did in 1922, trading most likely on his film experience as well as his name as an Abbey actor. The Abbey acting style did not remain in stasis, and by the 1920s increasingly involved 'hamming it' and playing to the gallery. Certain actors gained such a reputation as comic personae that audiences automatically laughed when they performed, regardless of their role. In a sense, this moved them closer to the kind of character acting in which many were to become involved in Hollywood; at the same time, it militated against the creation of the kind of star persona that was needed for the dominant modes of Hollywood narratives – the melodrama, the detective film, the Western.

With the introduction of sound and the opportunity for audiences, particularly in America, to hear 'genuine' Irish accents, the Abbey accent, as the voice of Ireland, was to become an important selling point for aspirant exiles. Dooley describes how Paramount studios sent the entire cast of *Irish Luck* (Victor Heerman, USA, 1925) to Ireland to perfect their accents and that the Abbey players were announced as participating – 'though no recognizable names appear in the cast'.[42] Conversely, films such as *Top O' The Morning* (David Miller, USA, 1949) were singled out for praise as a consequence of the presence of Abbey actors.[43]

If the 1920s witnessed a slow leeching of Irish talent to Hollywood, it was in the 1930s that this became a remarkable phenomenon. What provoked the Abbey and other actors to leave Ireland for California? Obviously they were drawn by the promise of money and opportunity. Throughout its life, Yeats' and Lady Gregory's theatre was remarkable for its insolvency. Actors were paid pittances and were never guaranteed a steady source of income. Rumours of contractual differences accompanied the actors on tour but these remained their best chance of making something like a decent living. Differences between the actors and the directors appointed by the company were also frequent and the notion of performance being a collaborative exercise between performer and director was replaced by a more autocratic style of management.

The wider picture was even less inspiring with Ireland lurching from civil war (1922–3) to a prolonged period of cultural and economic depression that saw many thousands of Irish people of all walks of life forced into emigration. The Church–state alliance that oversaw the development of the new state in the years after independence was, as has been thoroughly documented, utterly opposed to the development of a native film industry.[44] The closer alternative, of seeking employment in the British industry, was a less attractive option in the early part of the century primarily because of that industry's own parlous state, although this, as we shall see, was later to change. The Irish in America, by contrast, were part of the national narrative and, as we shall be returning to throughout this book, models of assimilation. As such, they figured largely in Hollywood fictions, a guarantee of roles, therefore, for Irish actors. They were also an important audience and one that liked to see its own actors on screen.

The crucial link between Irish actors and Hollywood was John Ford. Committed from his early days in silent cinema to making Irish-themed films, the outstanding success of *The Informer* (John Ford, USA, 1935 – it won four Academy Awards and only lost out on one nomination for Best Picture) encouraged the Irish-American director to develop his ambition to make films with Irish political themes. *The Informer* had included in support roles a number of ex-Abbey actors, now resident in California, notably Una O'Connor (in her fifteenth Hollywood film) and J.M. Kerrigan (in his twenty-seventh). The film's central role was, however, reserved for Ford's acting troupe stalwart, Victor McLaglen. By now familiar with the Abbey actors in person, Ford proceeded to negotiate for their temporary contractual release for *The Plough and the Stars* (USA, 1936). After dealings with the then director of the Abbey, Hugh Hunt, Ford came to an agreement that five Abbey actors would be made available for shooting in return for the theatre receiving 10 per cent of their takings.[45] The five actors were: Barry Fitzgerald, F.J. McCormick, Eileen Crowe, Denis O'Dea and Arthur Shields.

Although only Fitzgerald remained on in Hollywood, we may well regard this moment as crucial to the realisation that not just fame but fortune were waiting for Irish actors in Hollywood. Arthur Shields and Sara Allgood were also to make their homes in America, the latter in 1940, though Eileen Crowe and her husband, F.J. McCormick, were unhappy out of Ireland and turned down lucrative offers of film work to stay on the stage. Later, Siobhán McKenna was to recollect that when she and her husband, Denis O'Dea, were offered contracts in Hollywood, he was tempted by the thought of having their own swimming pool. She, however, 'had heard the stories about Sara Allgood and Barry Fitzgerald, of how they had gone out for one picture and found the life so comfortable that they had not come back. Apart from Barry Fitzgerald, the great ones settled down to playing little parts.[46]

Great actors playing little parts – here lay the future for many of the Irish actors in Hollywood. Certainly, they would earn more in California than they could dream of with the Abbey, and they could indeed enjoy houses with swimming pools, but John Ford was only part of a tradition that saw Irish performers restricted to minor roles and as character actors. These roles – the mammy, the colleen, the priest, the trooper – perpetuated a set of national stereotypes and, with the inner-city gangster, became the mainstay of Irish-American characterisation and the Irish actor's repertoire.

To break that mould, to challenge that typecasting, it took actors of exceptional talent and the resilience to refuse to conform to studio expectations. The ten actors that I will be discussing in detail in the following ten chapters are those who have, one way or another, negotiated the expectations of the Irish actor in Hollywood. They are: Barry Fitzgerald, George Brent, Maureen O'Sullivan, Maureen O'Hara, Constance Smith, Richard Harris, Stephen Rea, Gabriel Byrne, Pierce Brosnan and Colin Farrell. I know that names have been omitted or treated in less detail than will please everyone; Liam Neeson's absence is, I fully realise, particularly regrettable. Nor, for the purposes of this book, have I included Irish-American actors, such as James Cagney or Pat O'Brien. The proposition is that each of the actors dealt with here represents more than an individual biography – they also illustrate aspects of the history and academic arguments outlined in this and the following chapters.

There is, also, an element of biography in this work. Part of my motivation for writing the book was recuperative – to retrieve from historical oblivion performers whose reputations have waned with the passing of time; hence, the inclusion of a chapter on George Brent and one on Constance Smith. I have drawn on a number of biographies and autobiographies as part of this exercise. As research sources, these evidently need to be regarded with caution, as do studio biographies and star interviews. Actors invent and re-invent their life stories according to necessity; George Brent is, as we shall see, a prime example of this process. Yet biographies and autobiographies can often afford us a sense of their times and mores as well as providing insights into studio structures and the processes of filmmaking. Actors' lives do, in various ways, spill over into screen performances and into the narratives they animate, and knowing more about their lives can enhance our analyses of their on-screen characterisations. More problematically, biographies and autobiographies form the kernel of an ongoing narrative of success and failure rendered in the terminology of excess. Star biographies thrive on tales of rags-to-riches lives shadowed by the threat of penury and the lure of titillating accounts of misbehaviour; stars are thus both 'real' people and fictions, constructed for and by us.

The writing of standard biographies of these actors I will leave to others. My guiding principle here has been less celebratory than inter-rogatory. Taking as my starting point that sense of liminality expressed by Gabriel Byrne in the quotation that opens this 'Introduction', in the chapters that follow I want to explore the in-betweenness of the émigré actor, the modes of production and consumption that define their identities and the concept of performance that lies at the heart of assumptions about national identities. At the same time, I do not want to reduce the actor to a mere symbol, but to allow for some measure of agency in the processes of identity construction. Over and above all that, I hope to have retained some reminder of the pleasures of watching star performances, particularly by those talented individuals who are the subjects of this book.

NOTES

1   Gabriel Byrne interviewed by Mike Murphy, *The Arts Show*, RTÉ Radio One, 15 February 1995.
2   See for instance J. Baxter, *The Hollywood Exiles* (New York: Taplinger, 1976); M. Davis, *City of Quartz, Excavating the Future in Los Angeles* (New York: Verso, 1990); G. Petrie, *Hollywood Destinies: European Directors in America, 1922–31* (London: Routledge & Kegan Paul, 1985); G.D. Phillips, *Exiles in Hollywood: Major European Film Directors in America* (London: Associated University Presses, 1998); and J.R. Taylor, *Strangers in Paradise: The Hollywood Emigrés, 1933–1950* (London: Faber & Faber, 1983).
3   T. Elsaesser, 'Ethnicity, Authenticity, and Exile: a Counterfeit Trade? German Filmmakers and Hollywood', in H. Naficy (ed.), *Home, Exile, Homeland* (New York and London: Routledge, 1999), pp. 97–123, p. 120.
4   A. Higson and R. Maltby, *'Film Europe' and 'Film America' Cinema, Commerce and Cultural Exchange, 1920–1939* (Exeter: University of Exeter Press, 1999).
5   L. O'Leary, *Rex Ingram, Master of the Silent Cinema* (Pordenone/London: 12th Pordenone Silent Film Festival/British Film Institute, 1993; first published 1980).
6   J.M. Curran, *Hibernian Green on the Silver Screen* (New York, Westport, CT, London: Greenwood Press, 1989).
7   R. Dyer, *Stars* (London: BFI, 1998 new edition; first published 1979); R. Dyer, *Heavenly Bodies* (London and New York: Routledge, 2004 2nd edition).
8   C. Gledhill (ed.), *Stardom: Industry of Desire* (London: Routledge, 1991).
9   G. Vincendeau, *Stars and Stardom in French Cinema* (London and New York: Continuum, 2000).
10 G. Macnab, *Searching for Stars: Stardom and Screen Acting in British Cinema* (London and New York: Cassell, 2000); B. Babington (ed.), *British Stars and Stardom* (Manchester and New York: Manchester University Press, 2001).
11 D. Negra, *Off-White Hollywood* (London and New York: Routledge, 2001).
12 L. Fischer and M. Landy, *Stars: the Film Reader* (London and New York: Routledge, 2004), p. 1.
13 J. Naremore, *Acting in the Cinema* (Berkeley, Los Angeles, CA, London: University of California Press, 1988).
14 R. Pearson, *Eloquent Gestures* (Berkeley, CA and London: University of California Press, 1992).
15 P. Krämer and A. Lovell (eds), *Screen Acting* (London and New York: Routledge, 1999), p. 5.
16 A. Lovell, 'Sensitive to technique', *Sight and Sound*, 15, 4 (April 2005), p. 88.
17 D. Polan, 'Methodological reflections on the study of the émigré actor', *Screen*, 43, 2 (Summer 2002), pp. 178–86, p. 179.
18 H. Naficy, *An Accented Cinema* (Princeton, NJ and Oxford: Princeton University Press, 2001), p. 285.
19 Ibid., p. 284.
20 N. Ignatiev, *How the Irish Became White* (London and New York: Routledge, 1995).

21 Negra, *Off-White Hollywood*.
22 D. Andrew, 'The theater of Irish cinema', in D. Andrew and L. Gibbons (eds), *Yale Journal of Criticism*, 15, 1 (2002), pp. 23–58, p. 28.
23 M. Waters, *The Comic Irishman* (Albany, NJ: State University of New York Press, 1984), p. 27.
24 Ibid., p. 40.
25 Ibid., p. 79.
26 J.H. Richards, 'Brogue Irish take the American Stage, 1767–1808, *New Hibernia Review/Iris Éireannach Nua*, 3, 3 (Autumn 1999), pp. 47–64, p. 53.
27 W.H.A. Williams, *'Twas Only an Irishman's Dream* (Urbana and Chicago, IL: University of Illinois Press, 1996).
28 Ibid., p. 3.
29 Ibid., pp. 66–8.
30 Ibid., p. 98.
31 N. Sammond and C. Mukerji, '"What you are...I wouldn't eat", ethnicity, whiteness, and performing "the Jew" in Hollywood's golden age', in D. Bernardi (ed.), *Classic Hollywood, Classic Whiteness* (Minneapolis, MN and London: University of Minnesota Press, 2001), pp. 3–30, p. 25.
32 Williams, *'Twas Only*, p. 120.
33 C. Morash, *A History of Irish Theatre* (Cambridge, New York: Cambridge University Press, 2002), p. 140.
34 For easy access to these reviews, I am indebted to the work of Robert Hogan, Richard Burnham and Daniel P. Poteet whose published documents of this period are an invaluable resource for researchers. See R. Hogan, R. Burnham, and D.P. Poteet, *The Abbey Theatre: The Rise of the Realists, 1910–1915* (Dublin: Dolmen Press, 1979).
35 Morash, *A History*, p. 143.
36 Hogan *et al.*, *The Abbey Theatre*, p. 199.
37 Williams, *'Twas Only*, pp. 200–36.
38 B. Monahan, 'Deconstructing the nation: the Abbey Theatre and stage-Irishness on screen, 1930–1960', unpublished PhD thesis (Trinity College Dublin, 2003), p. 96.
39 Pearson, *Eloquent Gestures*, p. 16.
40 Hogan *et al.*, *Abbey Theatre*, p. 404.
41 The highest paid Abbey actor in 1914 was Arthur Sinclair who earned £4 per week. Fred O'Donovan and J.M. Kerrigan came next at £3.10.0 (W.B. Yeats, quoted in Hogan *et al.*, *The Abbey Theatre*, p. 369).
42 R.B. Dooley, 'The Irish on Screen I', *Films in Review*, 3, 5 (1957), pp. 211–16. p. 214. Given that the film predates sound, this is a particularly startling detail. Certainly the film was shot in Ireland; see K. Rockett, *The Irish Filmography* (Dublin: Red Mountain Media, 1996), p. 317.
43 R.B. Dooley, 'The Irish on Screen II', *Films in Review*, 3, 6 (1957), pp. 259–79, p. 265.
44 R. Barton, *Irish National Cinema* (London and New York: Routledge, 2004). L. Pettitt, *Screening Ireland* (Manchester and New York: Manchester University Press, 2000), K. Rockett, L. Gibbons and J. Hill, *Cinema and Ireland* (London: Routledge, 1987).
45 For a good account of Ford's negotiations to take on the Abbey actors, see A. Frazier, 'Barry Goes to Hollywood', *Dublin Review*, 15 (Summer 2004), pp. 68–86.
46 Quoted in E.H. Mikhail (ed.), *The Abbey Theatre, Interviews and Recollections* (London and Hampshire: Macmillan Press, 1988), p. 210.

1

Barry Fitzgerald

From the Abbey to Hollywood
(1888–1961; film career: 1930–59)

IN A POIGNANT closing sequence in Paul Rotha's otherwise unexceptional documentary on the Abbey Theatre, *Cradle of Genius* (GB, 1958), Barry Fitzgerald is reunited with Sean O'Casey in the latter's Devon home. By now old men both, O'Casey leans forward to Fitzgerald and says, 'You had that particular poetical touch in you that was denied so many others.'[1]

After his death, obituary writers were unanimous in eliding Fitzgerald's national identity and his stage persona – 'The Man Whose Wrinkles Spelled Ireland' ran the headline to the tribute in Britain's *Daily Express*.[2] The *Express* article proceeded to pronounce Fitzgerald's voice to have been 'thick and Irish as the bog'. Another obituary opined that, 'If the newborn Ireland had used artists like him as they should have been used, she might be the leading theatrical nation in Europe today.'[3]

Barry Fitzgerald's early career in the newborn Ireland is synonymous with the birth pangs of the state and the maturation of the Abbey Theatre, spanning as it does the move from amateurism to professionalism, from innovation to repetition and from enthusiasm to disillusionment. As the consummate stage Irishman, his acting recalls a performance history that reached back through vaudeville into the past of Anglo-Irish literature and was reinvigorated, if briefly, by the new playwrights of the emerging state. His close association with Sean O'Casey, another Protestant, gave him his defining roles, ones that were created for him and that he developed to the extent that those actors such as Cyril Cusack, who subsequently played them, were always compared, and not necessarily favourably, with Fitzgerald's prototype. Moving to Hollywood satisfied the yearning for financial security that Eileen O'Casey noticed in Fitzgerald but left him more exposed than ever to the prevailing winds of commercialism and the conservatism of popular taste.[4] His is the history not just of the Abbey actor, but of Irish-American cinema; it is also the story of an extraordinarily gifted comic performer, whose talents may well have been incompatible with the newborn Ireland, with American cinema and on which even the mature state of the 1950s failed to capitalise. Cinema has archived his best and his least innovative performances in a way theatre cannot; looking back at them, we can trace his rise from character actor to leading player and, with it, his evolution as a performer.

When Fitzgerald first appeared at the Abbey, he was still working as a civil service clerk under his real name of William Joseph Shields. In later life, he claimed that he based his character parts on the people he encountered while in the Department of Employment: 'You don't get to be an actor by studying acting. You do it by studying character. Three and four hundred people a week used to come through the Labour Exchange. I studied them.'[5] Fitzgerald rehearsed during his lunch break and in the evenings, swiftly gaining stage roles. His debut performance was in Lady Gregory's *The Dragon* (1919). In 1924, Sean O'Casey's first play, *Juno and the Paycock*, was performed at the Abbey, launching, as Robert Welch reminds us, 'a new master', who relocated Synge's corrosive comic vision of Ireland from the Aran islands to Dublin's tenements.[6] Fitzgerald was cast as Captain Boyle (the 'Paycock') although the part went to Edward Chapman in Hitchcock's 1930 film version, apparently because Fitzgerald failed his screen test.[7] F.J. McCormick played Joxer Daly and such was the play's popularity in Dublin that Lady Gregory was convinced that at last the Abbey had become a 'People's Theatre'.[8] Fitzgerald had played in many parts at the Abbey before and after *Juno* but this and his subsequent performance in *The Plough and the Stars* (1926) remain his defining stage roles. Along with Maureen Delaney, Fitzgerald was widely regarded as the Abbey's pre-eminent comic actor.

Also appearing on stage at this time was Fitzgerald's brother, Arthur Shields, who too made a career in Hollywood, although his persona – bookish and precise – was quite different from his brother's. The brothers acted alongside each other in several films, most notably John Ford's *The Quiet Man* (USA, 1952), where Fitzgerald played Michaeleen Óg Flynn and Shields, the Reverend Playfair. Shields was highly regarded as a director, and directed Fitzgerald at the Abbey and later on Broadway. He was also hired as technical advisor on a number of Hollywood's Irish films, including *Top O' The Morning* in which Fitzgerald featured.

Sean O'Casey insisted on having Fitzgerald cast as Fluther Good in the Abbey's 1926 production of *The Plough and the Stars*, writing in his autobiographies that he 'held firm for Fitzgerald, knowing in his [O'Casey's] heart that he, and he alone, could get the arrogant, boozy humour from the character'.[9] Both Arthur Shields and Barry Fitzgerald were on stage when the audience rioted in response to O'Casey's play. Famously dubbed by Yeats as O'Casey's 'apotheosis', the fracas was instigated by UCD members of *Cumann na mBan* and, as Christopher Murray notes, was an expression of a sense of betrayal, a feeling that Easter 1916 and the civil war were being swiftly forgotten: 'When Republican women turned out in force at the Abbey on the fourth night of the Plough, then, they carried into the stalls with them the discontent of a failed revolution.'[10] Later Arthur Shields recalled the evening:

> One night when I wasn't playing, I looked out from the wings and saw three people on the stage where only two should have been. I reached out, took this female by the neck, dragged her back into the wings, up a flight of stairs and into the alley. I dusted my hands, came back, looked out, and there was *another* strange one there. One night Barry met the situation by knocking a man back into the orchestra pit when he tried to climb on the stage. Great days, great days![11]

This incident was followed by a kidnap attempt on Barry Fitzgerald. On the final day of the play three young men arrived at his mother's home in Clontarf in north Dublin, announcing that they intended to kidnap him to prevent him from going on stage that night. Alerted to what might happen, the actor did not return to the house that evening and the men departed without their intended victim.

Fitzgerald resigned temporarily from the Abbey players and permanently from the civil service to appear as Sylvester Heegan in O'Casey's London performance of *The Silver Tassie* (1929). After the Abbey's notorious rejection of O'Casey's play, Charles Cochrane funded a London production with Charles Laughton in the part of Harry Heegan; he also hired Fitzgerald to play a number of comic roles in the revue that he was touring around Britain. For this the actor received £25 per week.[12] According to O'Casey, Fitzgerald had planned to make a career in Britain but failed to do so, though he and other of the Abbey actors continued to appear in productions of Irish plays there.[13]

Fitzgerald returned to the Abbey, sailing in 1931 for New York with a roster of plays from the company's repertoire. The actors were paid double their Dublin salaries during the tour, which was planned primarily to alleviate the theatre's chronic indebtedness. In his letter to Sean O'Casey written on board ship, Fitzgerald was clear that he did not intend to return to Dublin:

> The theatre has been running at a pretty heavy loss, particularly during last winter. I will say without being too cocky that things improved a wee bit when I went back. I fancy, however, I'm not as popular as I used to be; perhaps I haven't as much vigour as I had or perhaps people who go away as I did are disapproved of by Dublin people. I found it frightfully hard to get used to Dublin again & I was generally pretty unhappy when I got back there, but I'm hoping that I may, by some good fortune, be able to stay away for good & all this time.[14]

In fact, on this occasion, Fitzgerald did not stay in the United States and in 1935 was back in Dublin from another tour, writing to O'Casey that: 'I'm home again and utterly miserable, I should do anything to get back to the United States – it's the only live vital country I know of.'[15]

Did the 'newborn Ireland' squander Fitzgerald's talents? Certainly, when he left the country finally in 1936, Fitzgerald seems to have believed so. His friend and mentor, Sean O'Casey, had already left for England and 'many were glad to see him go'.[16] As we have seen in the 'Introduction', the Abbey actors were chronically underpaid; their relationship with the Abbey management was an unhappy one and the country's artistic climate was becoming increasingly circum-scribed by petty bourgeois Catholic morality. The players may have been critiqued for playing to the audience's taste in unsophisticated comedy, but, as Barry Monahan has demonstrated, the Abbey management was equally culpable in abandoning artistic integrity for easy box-office income and, beyond that, the government was implicated too, consistently refusing to offer the theatre anything but the most meagre of subventions.[17] Adrian Frazier has suggested that 'the audience only wanted Fitzgerald to make them laugh; they would laugh even before he had done anything to make them do so. When he took serious roles, critics complained that he was miscast.'[18] Of course, he may have been miscast, or to have struggled with non-comic roles; an unsigned review of Lennox Robinson's *All's Over Then?* suggests that by 1932 the Abbey acting style itself was the problem:

Unfortunately the traditional acting at the Abbey Theatre is not able to cope with this type of play, and the acting last night was indifferent. The tense scene in the third act, between Henry and Eleanore, was under-acted by Mr. Barry Fitzgerald and Miss Eileen Crowe; but in the second act Miss Crowe and Miss Shelah Richards got enough out of the play to hint at its power.[19]

'I do hope Hollywood won't kill his exquisite artistry in humor,' O'Casey mused on hearing of Fitzgerald's departure.[20] In fact, as I will be suggesting below, Hollywood offered the actor the opportunity to stretch his range, establishing a type for him and then, in his more interesting roles, requiring him to play against it. On the other hand, it is certainly true that he was often required to do little more than repeat a performance that sailed close to whimsicality. Did Fitzgerald achieve his potential in America? Certainly, he made more money there, rising from a salary of $450 per week for *Ebb Tide* (James P. Hogan, USA, 1937) to $2,500 for *Stork Club* (Hal Walker, USA, 1945) and, following his Academy Award for Best Supporting Actor in 1945, $10,000 per week for *Miss Tatlock's Millions* (Richard Haydn, USA, 1948).[21] Nor was he limited to screen-acting, taking numerous Broadway roles, primarily in Irish plays. In interview, he insisted on his indifference to his success, to his profession and to fame when it came. He remained unmarried, sharing his bungalow in Los Angeles with his stand-in and valet, Gus Tallon, until the latter's death, and stayed close to Arthur Shields. In later life, he moved between Los Angeles and Dublin, and between Hollywood, British and Irish filmmaking.

Once in Hollywood, Fitzgerald became established as a character actor:

a minor player, usually over the age of forty, with a face and voice so vividly eccentric that it saves writers and directors a good deal of trouble. Performers of [this] sort usually specialized in humorous or sinister overplaying; in the era of studio moviemaking, they gave the screen a more brilliant stylization than anyone since the Sennett clowns.[22]

Stylisation was the key to the actor's many screen performances, invoking as it did both the tradition of the stage and the history of the stage Irishman. Fitzgerald, himself, delighted in vaudeville and regularly attended performances while he lived in Dublin; he was, as O'Casey and others recognised, an artist, a physical performer in the mode of Chaplin, Mack Sennett and the early comedians of silent cinema. His cocky swagger belied a nimbleness that allowed him to caper around his more rooted and solid co-performers. Even in his later films, the now distinctly corpulent Fitzgerald moved gracefully within the frame. In *The Big Birthday* (aka, *Broth of a Boy*, George Pollock, Ireland, 1959), Fitzgerald's final screen appearance, the actor is evidently ailing but still manages to end the film dancing a jig. He often performed entire scenes in mime; for instance, in *The Plough and the Stars*, as Fluther, he emerges from church at the end of the service and walks down the steps with the other churchgoers. At the bottom he encounters the sick child, Mollser (Bonita Granville) and wordlessly performs sleight of hand tricks to amuse her. This brief scene tells us as much about Fluther as do the dialogue-heavy passages; having been already introduced to us as the 'arrogant, boozy' charlatan of the slums, he now shows us his other side. Then again, when playing a role that required a less performative Irishness, Fitzgerald exchanged his capering dance-like movements for a stiller presentational mode. In Clifford Odets' strangely expressionistic *None But The Lonely Heart* (USA, 1944), Fitzgerald plays Henry Twite opposite Cary Grant's Ernie Mott. Set in London's East End, the film follows Mott's various encounters with a gallery of local characters as he tries to be true to his bohemian, artistic sensibilities (he has perfect pitch and can name any note) and to care for his dying mother, Ma Mott (Ethel Barrymore). Soon he becomes embroiled with the petty crook, Jim Mordinoy (George Coulouris) and finds himself part of a raid on a jeweller, Ike Weber (Konstantin Shayne), who has been his and his mother's protector. Fitzgerald's Twite is a kind of nebulous *deus ex machina*, appearing in an unexplained manner at various moments in the plot. Like so many of the characters, he has an unearthly quality that in his case sees him cast as a benevolent spirit, there to guide Mott out of trouble. Twite is not identified by his Irishness (indeed many of the slum characters are from non-English back-grounds), and is not required to entertain the audience by acting out stage Irish qualities. Instead, he often sits or stands quite motionlessly in the frame, allowing Grant to draw the eye of the camera towards his own restless, uncomfortable physicality. Twite seems to move with ease between the film's various locales, slipping in and out of rooms, materialising suddenly and unexpectedly at Mott's side, sitting often just above and to the side of him as if about to whisper in his ear. Here, Fitzgerald's character is integrated into the plot, rather than functioning as straight entertainment and he plays it without the exhibitionism that marks out other of his performances.

Most memorable of all Fitzgerald's traits was his vocal delivery. His voice was so distinctive that the camera did not need to identify the speaker; articulating his lines through a slight rasp in his throat, his dialogue often seemed to ride on a wave of laughter. As the laughter threatened to overwhelm the words, so his vocal pitch rose an octave, ending on a squeak as he made it to the end of the line. He stressed unexpected or incongruous vocabulary, creating a hiatus between a persona that was often ill-educated or socially ignorant and a command of English that was rich and knowing. One of his repeated gags was to screw up his face and, surveying an outburst of mayhem, pronounce on it from above: 'Drink? Preposterous!' he exclaims in John Ford's *The Long Voyage Home* (USA, 1940) as the assembled sailors of the SS *Glencairn* mob the London trickster who offers them free liquor. Many years later, in *The Quiet Man*, he repeats much the same facial gestures as, on the morning after Mary-Kate Danaher's (Maureen O'Hara) and Sean Thornton's (John Wayne) wedding night, he utters his verdict on what appears to be the wildly disarrayed bedroom, 'Impetuous...Homeric!'

This delight in incongruity was part of Fitzgerald's subversive comic talent, a play with words that in their rolling delivery and unexpected lexical range destabilised assumptions of class and national identity. To say that he was the classic stage Irishman is to say very little; the term is a fluid one, bearing connotations that are both negative and positive. Joep Leerssen reminds us that, 'What makes a character Stage Irish is not the degree to which its characterization is stereotyped [. . .] but the variable degree to which a changeable audience chooses to accept the stereotype as sympathetic or obnoxious', a comment that holds as good today as it did in Fitzgerald's.[23] What is relevant here is to remember the sensitivities and sympathies that Barry Fitzgerald had to negotiate when he took his clown/rogue persona to Hollywood. He had emerged as the Abbey's most famous comic actor, his persona finely honed in the O'Casey plays but also in an array of performances designed simultaneously to recall and undermine earlier representations of the stage Irishman. Now he was playing to a global audience comprised of those who were familiar with his character as it had developed on the Abbey stage, and many others who were accustomed to seeing versions of the stage Irishman on screen. As I have discussed elsewhere and in the 'Introduction', early American cinema abounded in Irish characters, many drawn from the tradition of the music hall. The simplistic and, to many, offensive, depiction of 'Paddy' and 'Bridget' in early and silent farces was soon superseded by more nuanced race comedies, many staged between Jewish and Irish families, as organised groups such as the Ancient Order of Hibernians protested against the excesses of cultural stereotyping.[24]

Fitzgerald's Hollywood was an institution with one eye fixed on its core ethnic working-class audience, and the other on the political establishment and the power groups who controlled its access to that audience. With assimilation the dominant orthodoxy of American political thinking, films therefore had to be both ethnic and assimilationist. They had to appeal to, and certainly not offend, those diverse interests. They were also ruthlessly targeted at the key English-speaking territories, primarily Britain. Comedy, particularly ethnic comedy, was a staple of that cinema's output and a successful comedian could command large audiences and concomitant earnings. The comedian could also pose a challenge to the status quo:

> The greatest comedies throw a custard pie (sometimes literally) in the face of social forms and assumptions. The greatest film comedians are antisocial, but in this antagonism they reveal a higher morality. Ironically, these iconoclastic comedies are products of a commercial system that depended on the support of mass audiences composed of anything but iconoclasts. Perhaps the enjoyable silliness of a comedy muted the underlying attack; perhaps comic iconoclasm provided the audience with a useful emotional release, an opportunity to indulge their own antisocial urges without damaging the social fabric; perhaps the iconoclast was free to speak against social and moral values because he [sic] used the entertaining comic form – a traditional privilege of comedians since Aristophanes.[25]

The fate of Sean O'Casey's *The Plough and the Stars,* Fitzgerald's first American film, is just one indication of the limits of representation Hollywood imposed on its artists. The actors participating in *The Plough* seemed to believe that John Ford's empathy with Irish material would lead to a production that was not reliant on the kind of stereotyping that had marked earlier filmic versions of Irish characters. As Eileen Crowe declared in interview shortly after her return to the Abbey, 'We were very lucky, I thought, in having a man who understands Ireland – because if the Director decided that he wanted a "stage-Irish" play he'd have to get it!'[26]

In the event, the play was restructured to replace its deliberately haphazard and serendipitous portrayal of the events of 1916 with a conventional linear narrative of cause and effect. As in Ford's earlier version of *The Informer*, the Rising is rendered as a simple confrontation between British might and Irish right, a far cry from O'Casey's jaundiced, acerbic exploration of the futility and corruption of conflict, and more in tune with America's history of independence. With Barbara Stanwyck and Preston Foster imposed on the director as Nora and Jack Clitheroe, and the Abbey actors scooping up the main character parts, we are confronted with a film that seems to be playing against itself.[27] Stanwyck's Nora Clitheroe is a classic Hollywood tragic victim; shot in lingering soft-focus, she relies on the device of looking mistily into the middle-distance to indicate longing and despair. Her movements are ponderous, as befits the bearer of so much tragedy, while Foster's presence is negligible. The Abbey actors, by contrast, invest their performances with an energy and a feel for ensemble playing that recalls descriptions of the classic Abbey style. The five actors imported from Dublin – Eileen Crowe (Bessy Burgess), F.J. McCormick (Captain Brennan), Denis O'Dea (the Covey), Arthur Shields (Irish leader/Padraic Pearse) and Barry Fitzgerald in his old role as Fluther Good – were joined by J.M Kerrigan (Uncle Peter) and Una O'Connor (Mrs Gogan). Between them they swagger, brawl and brag their way through the plot, only coming to a halt with the death of Mollser and the need to shield Jack Clitheroe (in this new version of the play) from the marauding British troops. Where O'Casey kills off the hapless Clitheroe, Ford has him take an heroic stand at the film's end, declaiming: 'We'll live to see Ireland free and go on fighting till we do!' 'And we'll go on weeping', Nora chimes in, as Dublin burns in the background.

Fitzgerald's Fluther survives the transition from O'Casey to Ford relatively intact. Capering around the set, he is alternatively cunning and brazen; his first key scene takes place in what was originally Act 2 but is relocated in the film to the beginning. The crowd has just witnessed the Irish leader/James Connolly (Moroni Olsen) speaking from a platform and Clitheroe is filled with the passion of revolution. Turning to Langon (Neil Fitzgerald), he reminds him: 'You have a mother, Langon.'[28] The reply comes back: 'Ireland is greater than a mother,' and then again: 'And you have a wife, Clitheroe.' Clitheroe's reply is heard over a close-up of Nora's

agonised face: 'Ireland is greater than a wife.' From here the scene
moves to the pub and to a table where Fluther is sitting with Uncle
Peter. After declaiming 'Up the Rebels', he sits down with Uncle
Peter, who opens up the conversation with: 'Well that was a grand
meeting, a grand meeting!'[29] So moved is Fluther with enthusiasm
that he slams down his half drunk pint, spilling the drink. With a
look of bleary transcendence, he turns to Uncle Peter, who is dressed
in full imperial regalia, and declaims: 'The memory of all things that
was done and all the things that was suffered be the Irish people
was boomin' in me brain.' Uncle Peter comes back quickly to outdo
his eloquence: 'You know, every nerve in me body was quivering to
do something desperate.' Pulling himself slightly back and looking
up from under his hat, Fluther is warm now to this theme; a happy
expression across his face, he comes back with another contribution
to this celebration of alcohol-fuelled nationalism: 'I listened to th'
speeches pattherin' on th' people's head, like rain fallin' on the corn;
every derogatory thought went out o' me mind, an' I said to meself,
"You can die now, Fluther."' Rolling back his sleeve, he produces
his trump card: 'Here, d'you see them veins? Well, the blood was
boilin' in them!' This is a war of words, each participant fighting to
outdo the other in loquacity and posturing; in another moment the
pub will break out in uproar as Bessie Burgess and Mrs Gogan tear
into each other, finally being thrown out of the pub, each one
smashing a window as they go, the regulars crowded at the
doorway behind them.

Very shortly afterwards, Fluther is back at the bar, this time facing
off against the Covey. As both men ready themselves for a fistfight,
Fitzgerald circles Denis O'Dea, his arm bent at the elbow, his face
contorted with a sense of outraged dignity, turning in circles but
never landing a blow on the younger man, who himself is soon
evicted from the pub leaving Fluther to brush himself off after the
imaginary victory, put on his coat and demand, with the confidence
of the victor, that his hat be passed to him by the admiring Rosie
(Erin O'Brien-Moore), now transformed from O'Casey's prostitute
to Hollywood's preferred comely Irish lass in a shawl.

In the extended looting sequence that sees the tenement dwellers
make the most of the chaos of the city under fire, Fluther and Covey
dance off in search of a bar to ransack. Fitzgerald gambols along, his
chest out and his legs high-kicking and leaps onto the counter of his
local, smashing his tab as he goes. After making the most of his
treasure trove, he returns to the tenements, clad in a long polka-dot

dressing gown and a top hat, singing, 'Fluther's a jolly good fellow
... Up the rebels!'

The talent O'Casey and others recognised in Fitzgerald shines
through what was widely recognised, particularly by Irish critics, as
a travesty of *The Plough*. Fluther drinks and declaims his way
through the Easter Rebellion as do the other Abbey actors in
performances that must be close to those of the original stage
production. It seems that these were directed by Arthur Shields,
which accounts for their greater fidelity to the original play.[30] Yet,
with Ford's heavily sentimental depiction of the conflict and Barbara
Stanwyck's cloying rendition of Mrs Clitheroe, the tragedy of
O'Casey's original is lost. No more does Nora lose her unborn child
and fall into insanity, illustrating the purposelessness of the conflict
that Fluther Good and his cronies parody. With the Rising now
rendered as heroic, its comic undermining is meaningless, so that the
film now works against itself not only via its conflicting acting styles
but also in terms of its message.

Louisa Burns-Bisogno has detailed the censorship issues Ford
encountered before *The Plough* had even gone into production;
faced with concerns from the Production Code administrator, Joseph
Breen, who was already aware of the reputation of the stage play for
inciting riot, and from Colonel Hanna, of the British Board of Film
Censors, RKO insisted on the removal of a number of contentious
lines and scenes from the screenplay.[31] The effects of this, and of the
studio's interference in his casting choices, discouraged Ford from
pursuing his interest in Irish nationalism. Irish characters were to
recur in his work after *The Plough*, but it was not until 1952 that he
returned to Irish subject matter with quite a different production,
The Quiet Man. The response of the American critics to *The Plough*
may also have had some influence on his change of direction. On
both sides of the Atlantic, it was widely recognised that the only
performances of note in the film were those of the Abbey actors,
with Fitzgerald singled out for particular praise: 'It is the Abbey
Players who give the picture its chief vitality. Principally the film can
boast of Barry Fitzgerald who, as the strutting, drunken Fluther,
injects rich humor into the proceedings and generally manages to
walk off with all the acting honors.'[32]

Many of Fitzgerald's subsequent roles saw the actor do little more
than play a roguish, twinkly-eyed Irish buffoon with a terrible thirst
on him. In one of the earliest of these, as the gardener, Gogarty, in
Bringing Up Baby (Howard Hawks, USA, 1938), he is introduced

with a half-empty bottle of whiskey in his hand and proceeds to add to the general mayhem in a genre, the screwball comedy, to which his ongoing re-negotiation of reality made him amply suited. Similarly, as O'Doul in *Tarzan's Secret Treasure* (Richard Thorpe, USA, 1941), he makes his first appearance in the jungle driving a truck through a horde of attacking natives, only to faint at the wheel of his truck. When brandy is called for, he comes to enough to request Irish whiskey. Laying eyes on Tarzan (Johnny Weissmuller), he is quick to recognise the king of the jungle's antecedents: 'He's the spitting image of the Irish giant, Finn McCool . . . I'll wager you have some Irish in you.' Tempting as it might be to read into this comment recognition of a representational history of simianising the Irish, it is more the case that Fitzgerald functions here as the converse of the white British imperialist class from which the films habitually disassociate themselves.[33] As we shall see in Chapter 3, the O'Sullivan/Weissmuller films naturalise the presence of their central couple in the jungle on the basis of their peace-loving version of colonialism; the opposite of this is British venality, practised by the representatives of the imperial class. By virtue of being Irish, O'Doul, like the working-class Rawlins (Herbert Mundin) in *Tarzan Escapes* (Richard Thorpe, USA, 1936), is located on the wrong side of the power fault line. Both bring elements of comic relief to plots that otherwise rely on anthropomorphising the apes for laughs – in films that place animals above native Africans in the social order, it is a compliment when Boy pronounces O'Doul a good man 'like Cheetah'. Indeed, like Cheetah, the ape, O'Doul is a simple but good and ultimately resourceful soul, who helps save Tarzan when the crisis hits. Most importantly, as cameraman he connotes entertainment, emphasised in the scenes when he projects films in the tent for the amusement of the travellers.

If Fitzgerald had continued to play good-hearted clowns in Hollywood, then he would indeed have had little to show for a career that spanned twenty years. Just as he was in danger of becoming the 'old Irish ham' that Raoul Walsh was once reported to have called him, Fitzgerald reworked his own screen image in a series of performances that enabled him to move from the sidelines to the centre, from comic character actor to star.[34]

One of the earliest manifestations of Fitzgerald's ability to transform his persona is in his playing of the cook (Cookie) in Michael Curtiz's *The Sea Wolf* (USA, 1941). A much reworked version of the Jack London novel, the film is set aboard *The Ghost*, whose captain,

'Wolf' Larsen (Edward G. Robinson) is a malicious tyrant wracked by headaches that leave him temporarily blind. Embracing Milton's dictum, 'Better to reign in hell than to serve in heaven', he surrounds himself by men too broken to oppose him. Yet, he longs to be remembered as other than the cruel man he is and orders the writer he has rescued, Humphrey Van Weyden (Alexander Knox), to record his experiences of the ship and his impressions of the men he meets on it. 'A brutal, callous and inhuman lot, cast in the same mould as their captain,' is Van Weyden's response. Also on board are the fugitive Ruth Brewster (Ida Lupino) and George Leach (John Garfield), kidnapped by Larsen as the ship set sail. *The Sea Wolf* is shot, like Ford's earlier *The Long Voyage Home*, as a film noir, with the casting of Edward G. Robinson recalling his classic gangster roles. Dramatically, Curtiz's film is much tighter than Ford's and his use of Barry Fitzgerald, cast in similar roles in both films, could be seen as a comment on the earlier production. Where Ford had Fitzgerald play 'Cocky' as a drunken but genial crew member, Walsh transforms him into a degenerate lackey. There to echo and mock Larsen's spiteful rages, Cookie serves his master by betraying Leach to him when the latter plots a mutiny. 'That's his profession, being a stool pigeon,' Larsen explains to Van Weyden. Scuttling across the cabin floor, his laughter and rasping voice combining to thicken the gothic atmosphere of the ship's interior, Cookie never suggests for a moment that he shares his master's potential for redemption. Nor does he subscribe to any code of loyalty – when he finally notices that Larsen suffers from temporary onsets of blindness, he responds by tripping him up so that the captain falls across the deck.

In Fitzgerald's performance we can see the alter-ego of the stage Irishman; where his other roles present subversion as an antidote to the dominance of a hegemonic order that masks its control through the veil of social etiquette, here we are presented with the consequences of an untrammelled id. The message, that when society breaks down, evil becomes uncontrollable and innocence utterly corrupted, prefigures Curtiz's later *Casablanca* (USA, 1942), a less allegorical exploration of Nazi occupation. Where Larsen represents the duality of that evil, Cookie is its irredeemable agent, the guileless spontaneity of Fitzgerald's earlier performances replaced with an equally impulsive cruelty. Yet, the character is recognisably that of Fitzgerald in his comic roles, just slightly altered in order to strip it of its innocence. In fact, in the original script, Cookie was a Cockney; Fitzgerald, however, famously could or would not alter his accent. A

memo from Hal Wallis to Curtiz makes it clear that the studio was
not entirely enthusiastic about one of their more highly paid actors'
enunciation (Fitzgerald earned $125,000 per week for the film): 'It is
almost impossible to understand Fitzgerald, and besides his being so
hard to understand, he spoke several of his lines with a cigarette in his
mouth, and then it is only a jumble. You don't know what the hell it
is all about. [...]You must have him enunciate more clearly.'[35]

Fitzgerald's opportunities to play against type were limited within
mainstream Hollywood and *The Sea Wolf* remains one of the most
interesting reworkings of his comic persona (another is his Judge
Quincannon in the greatly inferior *And Then There Were None*
[René Clair, USA, 1945]). Thoroughly evil Irish characters were few
and far between in Hollywood of the war era, committed as the
studios were to illustrating the homogeny of American society. Irish-
Americans as a group had proved themselves reluctant to support
America's intervention in the First World War and, again, at the
outbreak of the Second World War, their by now well-positioned
politicians were unwilling to declare themselves pro-war: 'Irish-
Americans were fond of pointing out that a small country, nestled in
one corner of the British Isles, had found neutrality workable. Was
this not an example for the United States, separated by 3,000 miles
of water from the blood baths of Europe?'[36] As popular anxieties
about fascist infiltrators and enemy agents grew, so official insistence
on the loyalty of the country's ethnic minorities and reminders of the
good lives they had acquired since arriving in America were filtered
through the media and entertainment. In, for instance, March of
Time's newsreel, *Americans All!* of February 1941, the thrust is to
emphasise America's welcome for political refugees from fascist
countries as well as the loyalty of its existing ethnic communities.
Following footage of a Jewish religious celebration, the voice-over
continues over the inspection of a line of New York policemen:
'Merged into the life of the nation today are its Irish-Americans,
descendents of the millions who came to America in the first great
wave of nineteenth-century immigration.' The film cuts to an Irish
club where young couples are dancing a jig. Then, over shots of
priests walking together out of a seminary, it continues: 'Once
strangers in a strange land, the Irish are now among the nation's
leaders and they are the backbone of the Roman Catholic Church
whose many institutions they generously support.' The next ethnic
group to be celebrated are the Germans; the newsreel proceeds to
warn against fifth columnists and other potential spies.[37]

In terms of dominant and, therefore Hollywood, representation, the preferred view of the Irish was as hard working, integrated members of long-established, working-class communities, with the priest and the policeman acting as guarantors of that group's stability and conformity. Fitzgerald ultimately made his name playing both those roles, appearing most famously as Father Fitzgibbon in *Going My Way* (Leo McCarey, USA, 1944) and Detective Lieutenant Dan Muldoon in *The Naked City* (Jules Dassin, USA, 1948). After being nominated both for Best Actor and Best Supporting Actor in *Going My Way*, and winning in the latter category (with his co-star, Bing Crosby, taking the award in the former), he became the only member of the Abbey actors to achieve star status. This in turn meant that the minor character parts were replaced with a series of dramatic roles that required Fitzgerald to cast in his lot with the hegemonic order that he had so consistently undermined in his seminal theatre and cinema performances.

Figure 1.1 A study in resigned old age. Barry Fitzgerald in
Going My Way

Going My Way is set in the inner-city parish of St Dominic's. Its most prominent parishioners are elderly Irish women, but the area is multi-ethnic and held together by its Catholic ethos and ageing but much loved Catholic priest, Father Fitzgibbon. As the film opens, his church is under threat from the Knickerbocker Savings and Loan Company, who want their loan repaid. Arriving to sort out the parish's problems is Father O'Malley (Crosby), a young but sensitive cleric from Illinois who has the ear of the bishop. O'Malley soon rounds up the neighbourhood's Dead End kids and forms them into a choir; he also befriends a runaway, Carol James (Gene Heather), whose singing voice he nurtures. Faced with these changes Father Fitzgibbon complains to the bishop, only to discover that Father O'Malley is in fact his superior. The old priest packs his bags and himself runs away from 'home' but later wanders back, soaked to the skin and is nursed by Father O'Malley who sings him the Irish lullaby Father Fitzgibbon remembers his own mother singing.

The crisis is resolved when Father O'Malley and the choir sell one of their compositions to a record company and, in the same manner, he funds the rebuilding of the church after it has burnt down. In the film's final moments, he reunites Father Fitzgibbon with his ninety-year-old mother whom he has brought over from Ireland before he himself slips off to his next parish.

Going My Way won a total of seven Academy Awards including best picture; it was also a multiple award winner at the Golden Globe awards and in numerous competitions. The critical reviews from trade papers and press alike of the period were unanimous in their praise for McCarey's film, many of them focusing on the acting partnership of Bing Crosby and Barry Fitzgerald. This, according to Crosby, was founded on mutual regard and McCarey's willingness to let the two improvise and play off each other, and was reprised in *Welcome Stranger* (Elliot Nugent, USA, 1947) and *Top O' The Morning*.[38] All three films establish similar personae for their two leads; Fitzgerald is the crusty old Irishman who resists change and is losing the authority he has held in a small community; Crosby is a moderniser who must learn to win over the trust of the older man as he solves the crisis his old-fashioned leadership has been unable to prevent. The films balance change against continuity, reserving their most sentimental moments for depictions of the 'old ways' while still insisting on the need for some limited modernisation. The huge critical and commercial success of *Going My Way* (it took

$6,500,000 in the USA), suggests that this message was welcomed by the film's audiences, so much so that Paramount effectively remade the film over and again, not just in the plotting of the other two Crosby–Fitzgerald films but also in the sequel to *Going My Way*, *The Bells of St Mary's* (Leo McCarey, USA, 1945) in which Crosby played opposite Ingrid Bergman.[39] That the parish is saved through capitalist enterprise rather than renewed spiritualism further echoes the dominant ideological thrust of the wartime era; such films 'labeled as subversive a counternarrative of American identity in which citizens grounded in regional or ethnic communities were critical of monopoly capital'.[40]

Barry Fitzgerald's Father Fitzgibbon is a study in resigned old age; gone are the balletic movements of the past, their place taken by a reverent demeanour and a slight suggestion of defeatedness. Despite a plot device that sees Father O'Malley's composition, 'Going My Way', rejected by the impresario on the grounds that it is sentimental schlock, McCarey revels in moments of high sentimentality, most particularly around Father Fitzgibbon. As in *The Naked City*, there is also a hard edge to Fitzgerald's screen character. He is firm on his opinion of Carol James: 'Being a good wife and a mother is a good enough start for you, just like you own mother,' he tells her, with more than a hint of menace in his voice. Similarly, in *The Naked City*, there is a sense that Muldoon enjoys the power he has access to as head of the homicide division, and relishes exercising it.

Although Irish-American McCarey was best known as a director of comedies, amongst them the Marx Brothers' *Duck Soup* (USA, 1933), *Going My Way* is better seen as a straightforward drama, with undertones of melodrama. Having a Protestant play the most traditional of the two priests does not seem to have impinged on its overall effect, which was, as Lawrence McCaffrey has argued, two-pronged. It presented the Catholic Church as humane, enlightened and unthreatening, and its success bolstered the morale of the Irish-Catholic population (as well as providing for a generation and more of vocations).[41] We could add that, in the relationship between the two priests, that community was able to work through its own ambivalences around the shifting values that generational change entailed. Via Barry Fitzgerald, they could celebrate but also take their leave of an old-fashioned adherence to principles of austerity and selflessness, embodied in a performer who came from the 'old country', while Bing Crosby represented the acceptability of a new Irish-American identity that could combine religious principles with hard-nosed commercial exploitation, specifically of the residue of that shared heritage.

In Hollywood, Fitzgerald's awards and the commercial and critical success of *Going My Way* led him to being offered leading, occasionally starring, roles in a succession of films that made much of his 'old codger' persona. Many of these performances see Fitzgerald simply rehashing his act – in *Top O' The Morning*, his Briony McNaughton is the Irish policeman at home, a bumbling, well-intentioned but ineffectual figure, much loved within the small community who wake up one morning to find that the Blarney Stone has been stolen. Reuniting Fitzgerald with Bing Crosby, the film reprises the relationship of the previous films, while allowing for Crosby to pursue a romantic interest, played by Ann Blyth as McNaughton's daughter, Conn. The robbery is partially solved through the intervention of the elderly soothsayer, Biddy (Eileen Crowe), who can unravel the old prediction that determines the events of the action. Although technically far inferior to *The Quiet Man*, the Paramount production anticipates Ford's film in many ways.

Top O' the Morning makes no pretence of depicting a 'real' Ireland. Instead, it delivers a highly performative version of Irishness enhanced by the inclusion in the cast of two of the Abbey's former actors (Fitzgerald and Crowe). It knowingly plays nostalgia off against comedy, inviting its audience to enjoy and recognise its sentimental vision (and to buy its soundtrack). Just as *The Quiet Man* was to do, it celebrates Ireland as it has been constructed by the emigrant imagination, as a country far removed from America by time and space.

The Quiet Man, as so many writers have noted, is the consummate articulation of that vision.[42] As a comedy, it is also self-consciously performative and non-realist, hence the now standard reading of the film as foregrounding its own fantasy. Michael Patrick Gillespie warns against a simplistic reading of Ford's film by reminding us that 'either/or' binaries (Ireland in the film is either modern or pre-modern, etc.) needlessly limit the parameters of interpretation.[43] Bearing this in mind, we may best appreciate Fitzgerald's inter-pretation of Michaeleen Óg Flynn as both stage Irish and a commentary on the stage Irishman. He is a 'real' character in so far as he has a place within the plot, as the garrulous matchmaker and intercessor between the key players; he is also a representation of the stage Irishman as theatrical device in so far as his acting style is 'excessive', that is, it breaks the boundaries of conventional cinematic representation, reaching out beyond the frame to the imaginary audience. Further, he is timeless – his dress code belongs to no recognisable era – and allusive – by referring to himself as the 'shaughraun', he summons up the ghost of Boucicault and his reworking of the stage Irishman.

Michaeleen Óg Flynn is a leery, almost supernatural figure, with a touch of the malign about him. In reviews of his films, Fitzgerald was often referred to as a leprechaun, and in *The Quiet Man*, this is in part what he is, a figure from Ireland's mythical past, come to intervene and interfere in human affairs. Fitzgerald also plays him, as he did many of his better comic roles, with a touch of knowingness. To take one example, in the scene where Sean Thornton and Mary-Kate are taking their first ride in the horse and trap together, Michaeleen Óg, as the jarvey, is placed firmly between them. 'I don't get this,' Thornton complains, 'Why do we have to have you along? Back in the States, I'd drive up, honk the horn, the gal would come a running up...'.

'Come a runnin'?' Mary-Kate is outraged, 'I'm no woman to be honked at and come a runnin'.'

'America?' their driver cuts in with a dismissive snort. 'Pro-hib-ition! Hup, hup!' This last to the pony, Michaeleen Óg has exposed American mores for a sham, and one that, if it concerns a shortage of drink, is quite contrary to the Irish temperament.

Yet, as the film's viewers, particularly those in Ireland, would have been well aware, Sean Thornton was not *The Quiet Man's* only returning emigrant. For Maureen O'Hara, Barry Fitzgerald and Arthur Shields the making of the film was a figurative journey home, and in the case of the latter two, a return to the kind of performance style that had defined their careers as Abbey actors. The sense of communality that so identifies Ford's Ireland is reliant on the largely indigenous cast playing as an ensemble; as I will be arguing later in this book, such is the ease with which these actors work together, each one playing to the other's strength, comfortable with their mutual comic timing, that we could argue for the troupe as substituting for the national. Although *The Quiet Man* is a film with two identifiable stars in its lead, it is not a star vehicle; in other words, Ford does not repeat his mistakes of *The Plough and the Stars*, of having two acting styles and traditions coming into conflict with each other. Where, however, the Abbey acting style at its most authentic presumed a metropolitan and sophisticated viewer, here the actors draw on the American tradition of vaudeville and slapstick to give their performances just that kind of mass appeal that Lady Gregory's and Yeats' theatre never quite attained.

The centrality of the ensemble, even if by now it was becoming virtually impossible to include the original Abbey actors, to Irish-made and Irish-themed films of the 1950s reinforces this sense of the local and the communal; it is particularly noticeable in the so-called Abbey films, those productions filmed at Ardmore Studios using Abbey plays and a cast largely composed of Abbey actors.[44] Fitzgerald's roles in his last Irish-themed films, Grandfather O'Flynn in *Rooney* (George Pollock, GB, 1958) and Patrick Farrell in the Abbey film, *The Big Birthday*, recall his Michaeleen Óg Flynn while his part as Thady O'Heggarty in *Happy Ever After* (Mario Zampi, GB, 1954) is a virtual reprise of his previous role. Even as Uncle Jack Conlon in *The Catered Affair* (Richard Brooks, USA, 1956), Fitzgerald seems to be delivering on an expectation that he would portray a curmudgeonly but ultimately good-hearted old duffer with a twinkle in his eye and a bottle of whiskey under his arm.

By the end of his life, Fitzgerald had taken the stage Irishman to its limit, and finished by pastiching his own performances. Arguably, he left political engagement behind him when he parted ways with O'Casey and decamped to Hollywood; yet when we see him play the old rogue, Patrick Farrell, in *The Big Birthday*, we need to acknowledge that it is perhaps more the case that Ireland abandoned Fitzgerald. By the late 1950s, most critics were agreed that the Abbey had long since lost its edge; now with the construction of Ardmore Studios (opened in 1958), it seemed that at long last the country was to have its own film industry. That this should be built upon the reputation of the Abbey actors and the repertoire of the Abbey Theatre was unfortunate timing. Although recent scholarship has revised earlier and more dismissive accounts of the Abbey films (particularly by contemporary film reviewers), of the productions initiated by Emmet Dalton under his holding company, Emmet Dalton Productions, *The Big Birthday* has always been considered one of the weakest. In common with *This Other Eden* (Muriel Box, Ireland, 1959), the film concerns the encounter between an Englishman and a canny, close-knit Irish community. Here a television producer, Tony Randall (Tom Wright), arrives in Ballymorrissey to find that they are about to celebrate Patrick Farrell's 110th birthday. Thrilled that he has come upon an event that will revive his own flagging career, Randall phones his television station to secure funding for an on-the-spot exclusive. His superior is unconvinced but

Randall presses ahead, assuring the community that they will be on television. As they prepare for the arrival of the media, Farrell continues to go about his day, poaching trout with his own ageing son, Wee Willie (Harry Brogan). When contact is finally established with the birthday celebrant, he reveals that there is in fact an older man in the world, living in Turkey. All is resolved with the news of the death of the Turkish centenarian and, after much ballyhoo, the show goes ahead. Directed by George Pollack, who had also directed Fitzgerald in *Rooney*, and adapted from a play by Hugh Leonard, the film allows the troupe of Abbey actors to perform to the invisible gallery in a manner that could hardly be termed innovatory. Fitzgerald plays Farrell as a grouch who cares little for the wider interests of Ballymorrissey, and nothing for Wee Willie. It was to be his last screen performance and with it he all but announces the death of the stage Irishman. Of course, such a remark is only possible with hindsight, but there is something absolutely final about Fitzgerald's Farrell, as if he had run out of patience with his own comic creation.

Barry Fitzgerald died on 4 January 1961. After his death, Eileen O'Casey discovered that she and Sean had been left 'some money' in his will, and 'a letter that arrived in confirmation contained Barry's praise of Sean as the man who had realised his talents and inspired his work.'[45] It turned out, according to Christopher Murray, to be $15,000.[46]

NOTES

1 For a description of the making of the documentary, see C. Murray, *Seán O'Casey* (Dublin: Gill & Macmillan, 2004), pp. 408–10. Fitzgerald was now in the advanced stages of Parkinson's Disease and physically and mentally debilitated.

2 Express staff reporter, 'The man whose wrinkles spelled Ireland', *Daily Express*, 5 January 1961 (British Film Institute, Barry Fitzgerald microfiche).

3 L. Maloney, 'The twinkling actor', *Daily Herald*, 5 January 1961 (British Film Institute, Barry Fitzgerald microfiche).

4 E. O'Casey, *Sean* (London: Gill & Macmillan, 1971), p. 105.

5 K. Crichton, 'The Actor Who Doesn't Care', *Picturegoer*, 14, 625 (1945), pp. 8–9, p. 9.

6 R. Welch, *The Abbey Theatre 1899–1999* (Oxford and New York: Oxford University Press, 1999), p. 87.

7 G. Fallon, *Sean O'Casey* (London: Routledge & Kegan Paul, 1965), p. 134.

8 D. Krause (ed.), *The Letters of Sean O'Casey, 1910–41* (London: Cassell, 1975), p. 222.

9 S. O'Casey, *Autobiographies 2, Inishfallen, Fare Thee Well* (London: Pan Books, 1980), p. 104.

10 Murray, *Seán O'Casey*, p. 174.
11 Crichton, 'The Actor Who Doesn't Care', p. 9. For a detailed account of the riots, see R.G. Lowery (ed.), *A Whirlwind in Dublin* (Westport, CT and London: Greenwood Press, 1984).
12 Krause, *Letters of Sean O'Casey*, p. 397.
13 Ibid., p. 438. *The Silver Tassie* eventually opened in Dublin in 1935, with Barry Fitzgerald again in the role of Sylvester and F.J. McCormick as Harry Heegan. Hostile press reviews (excepting the *Irish Times*) and opposition from religious representatives saw it close within a week; see Murray, *Seán O'Casey*, pp. 242–3.
14 Krause, *Letters of Sean O'Casey*, p. 437.
15 Krause, *Letters of Sean O'Casey*, p. 575.
16 Welch, *Abbey Theatre*, p. 97.
17 Monahan, '*Deconstructing the Nation*'.
18 Frazier, 'Barry Goes to Hollywood', p. 77.
19 'All's Over, Then?', *The Times*, 28 July 1932, p. 10.
20 Krause, *Letters of Sean O'Casey*, p. 634. After he had moved to Hollywood, Fitzgerald failed to keep in touch with O'Casey to the latter's increasing chagrin.
21 All figures from the Paramount contract files, AMPAS.
22 Naremore, *Acting in the Cinema*, p. 249.
23 J. Leerssen, *Remembrance and Imagination* (Cork: Cork University Press, 1996), p. 173. For a discussion of recent screen stereotypes of Irish identity, specifically in the *Leprechaun* films, see R. Barton, 'It Came From Glocca Morra!' *Film Ireland*, 97 (March/April 2004), pp. 28–31.
24 Barton, *Irish National Cinema*, pp. 60–4.
25 G. Mast, *The Comic Mind* (London: New English Library, 1973), p. 21.
26 'Hollywood, seen by Miss Eileen Crowe', *Woman's Life*, 28 November 1936, pp. 5–6.
27 Preston Foster was in fact Irish-born but as Joseph McBride comments, 'there was little resonance of his ethnic background in his bland personality'. J. McBride, *Searching for John Ford* (London and New York: Faber & Faber, 2001/2003), p. 242. Barbara Stanwyck also came from an Irish-American family but never looked at ease in her part.
28 Although the film credits name neither Shields nor Olsen as Pearce or Connolly, the two actors were widely understood as occupying those parts.
29 This line is not in the original stage play and recalls more the language of *Juno*.
30 I am grateful to Alicia McGovern for drawing my attention to this in her talk at the 'Abbey and Film' seminar at the Irish Film Institute, 7 November 2004. The comments of the panel of John Lynch, Lelia Doolan and John McDevitt, regarding the Abbey acting style have also influenced my own interpretation of this issue.
31 L. Burns-Bisogno, *Censoring Irish Nationalism* (Jefferson, NC and London: McFarland, 1997), pp. 79–84.
32 R. Pelswick, 'Abbey Players augment Hollywood cast in film from O'Casey play', *New York Evening Journal*, 29 January 1937, p. 18.
33 For more on the Tarzan films, see Chapter 3. According to Robert Welch, Séan MacLahraidh played Tarzan on US television and spoke Irish as his jungle language, see Welch, *Abbey Theatre*, p. 147.
34 Bryan Forbes quotes Walsh's comments in his memoirs, B. Forbes, *A Divided Life* (London: Heinemann, 1992), p. 41.
35 *Sea Wolf* file. Warner Bros' Archive, USC. Fitzgerald also played an Irish cook, Dooley, in *Two Years Before the Mast* (John Farrow, USA, 1946).

36 S. Adler, *The Isolationist Impulse* (London and New York: Abelard-Schuman, 1957), p. 291.

37 This newsreel can be viewed on-line at http://xroads.virginia.edu/~MA04/wood/mot/html/amall.htm (consulted 12 April 2005).

38 C. Thompson, *Bing, The Authorised Biography* (London: Star Books, 1976), pp. 100–3.

39 Rental figures for *Going My Way* taken from the Internet Movie Database (IMDb). http://www.imdb.com/title/tt0036872/business, consulted 12 April 2005.

40 L. May, 'Making the American Consensus: The Narrative of Conversion and Subversion in World War II Films', in L.A. Erenberg and S.E. Hirsch (eds), *The War in American Culture* (Chicago, IL and London: University of Chicago Press, 1996), pp. 71–102, p. 72.

41 L.J. McCaffrey, '*Going My Way* and Irish-American Catholicism: Myth and Reality', *New Hibernia Review*, 4, 3 (Autumn, 2000), pp. 119–27.

42 For extended and complementary analyses of the film see L. Gibbons, *The Quiet Man* (Cork: Cork University Press, 2002); and M. McLoone, *Irish Film: The Emergence of a Contemporary Cinema* (London: British Film Institute, 2000), pp. 44–59.

43 M.P. Gillespie, 'The myth of hidden Ireland: the corrosive effect of place in *The Quiet Man*', *New Hibernia Review*, 6, 1 (2002), pp. 18–32.

44 For further reading on the Ardmore Studios and Abbey films, see Barton, *Irish National Cinema*, pp. 76–82; F. Farley, *This Other Eden* (Cork: Cork University Press, 2001); Monahan, 'Deconstructing the Nation'; K. Rockett, L. Gibbons and J. Hill (eds), *Cinema and Ireland* (London: Routledge, 1988), pp. 103–11.

45 O'Casey, *Sean*, p. 277.

46 Murray, *Seán O'Casey*, p. 410.

2

George Brent

Freedom fighter, film star
(1904–79; film career: 1930–78)

Mr George Brent, poised between the women, but
consistently inclining to Maggie, stands pleasantly
before the cameras but this is a film made for
women and acted outstandingly well by them.
The Times, 2 October 1941[1]

Brent's career at Warner Bros. typifies in many ways the
position of the contract player, even one in the lead category, in
the Hollywood studio system. The importance of the studio in
defining star roles cannot be under-estimated; MGM was the source
of costly glamour, often purveyed through lavish period films. Even
its Tarzan cycle, discussed in Chapter 3, was made to high production values and enjoyed a more generous shooting schedule than its
makers could have expected elsewhere. Columbia had a more varied
slate and, as a consequence, its contract players enjoyed a greater
potential range of roles. Under the three brothers, Jack, Harry and
Abe, Warners in the early 1930s was the epitome of the low-cost,
production line model of studio filmmaking organised under
patriarchal principals. Stars had minimal say in their casting and
tended to be tied to genres, allowing them meagre opportunities to
expand their range of character types. Equally, directors had little
influence over the finished product, handing over their films to
editors and producers for a final cut. Only a few of Warners' top
male stars were able to exploit their situations to demand higher
salaries – Edward G. Robinson had made *Little Caesar* (Mervyn
LeRoy, USA, 1930) without a contract and so was able to negotiate
his own terms on the back of that film's success, resulting in a two-
year, six picture deal at $40,000 per picture which he signed in 1931.
Cagney managed to raise his salary to $3,000 per week in 1932 after
refusing to perform and being put on indefinite suspension.[2] Neither

star gained any creative control over the films in which they played.

Female stars enjoyed even less autonomy within Warner Bros. Having lured Kay Francis and Ruth Chatterton from Paramount in 1931, Warners found few opportunities to exploit these stars, both of whom commanded high salaries, the former earning $3,000 per week in 1931–2 and Chatterton $8,000 for only three pictures a year in the same period.[3] Barbara Stanwyck moved between Columbia and Warners, having signed non-exclusive contracts with both studios. Schatz has detailed Bette Davis' struggle to be allowed to do outside work and so play in a wider range of roles during the 1930s when she was signed for Warners. Only after her success in *Jezebel* (William Wyler, USA, 1938) shot with (uncustomary for Warners but customary for Wyler) expense and attention to minute detail, did the studio shift its policy to include more women's pictures and hence better roles for its female stars.[4]

Stars at all studios worked regularly with the same directors and cinematographers, who over the years learned how best to photograph their players, and how to rehearse them so that filming could proceed as swiftly as possible. This intense relationship was, as so many biographies of the era attest, both exploitative and protective. A favoured star could enjoy extraordinary attention, particularly in the more lavish studios such as MGM. At the same time, they were regarded by the studio heads as property, an investment that had to pay off through round-the-clock filmmaking and ancillary publicity activities. Brent was just one of many actors who, when their contract expired, did not walk out of their studios, as they had so often threatened to do, but stayed on, cautious now of losing the security their status had achieved and reluctant to work with production teams unfamiliar with their requirements.

George Brent made his name in the 1930s as a contract player for Warners. In a studio better known for its 'tough guy' male leads, specifically James Cagney and Edward G. Robinson, and swashbuckling heroes played by Errol Flynn, he was most typically cast as a 'debonair', a stylish, somewhat effete and cynical urban sophisticate. Where the tough guys belonged to the streets and to the ethnic underworld, the debonair was most at home in society drawing rooms, or enjoying an evening at the theatre. The tough guy enjoyed the company of other men, the debonair of beautiful women. His was the decadence of the Old World, associated with a dwindling potency; his lineage that of the legitimate stage rather than the vaudeville boards that bred the ethnic tough guy. If he was not a native of the city streets, nor was he at home on the frontier, the other testing ground for American masculinity. Under such circumstances, it was more appropriate for him to be played by a non-American, and so such roles were most often taken by Europeans and particularly by English actors, amongst them Cary Grant, Rex Harrison and David Niven. During the 1930s and into the 1940s, Brent was one such import, recognisable for his immaculate dress style and his pencil-thin moustache, and now best remembered as being the stooge for Bette Davis' intrigues in a string of 1930s melodramas.

More often aspiring to, rather than being the possessor of, wealth, the debonair secretly shared an overriding ambition of the tough guy, the pursuit of a fortune through illegitimate means. Both held vicarious appeal to depression era audiences; where the tough guy took a stand against a social order that many of the working-class viewers of their films regarded with a shared antipathy, the debonair presented an alternative escapist fantasy:

> It was eminently reassuring to see on film the impeccably groomed debonair actor who seemed not to have a care in the world and had a perfect wardrobe for every situation. He was the possessor of a ready wit and a nimble brain, namely a man whose purpose was to have a good time in opulent settings beyond the reach of most of the audience. Often he was larcenous, and this aspect too had a kind of vicarious appeal for the have-nots of the period. What appealed most was his courage and style in meeting and conquering the seemingly insuperable obstacles placed before him in what appeared to be an easygoing manner.[5]

Pugnacious and agile, Cagney's Irish gangster was the opposite of Brent's society sophisticate and more typical of Warner's output in the post-Depression period, their 'fast-paced, fast-talking, socially sensitive (if not downright exploitive) treatments of contemporary stiffs and lowlifes, of society's losers and victims rather than heroic or well-heeled types'.[6] Cagney's ethnic roles played out issues of authority and defiance, increasingly moving towards a model of containable individualism, one that was regularly mediated by Pat O'Brien's representative of institutional conformity, the Irish priest. By contrast, Brent, who was, unlike Cagney, a first-generation immigrant, seldom played Irish roles, although both appeared together as Irish-American characters in *The Fighting 69th* (William Keighley, USA, 1940).

Most film historians agree that the immediacy of Warners' films created a studio output that was inseparable from the social conditions to which it responded:

> Warners both reflected and reflected on the society in which they operated, and their films contain many of the ideological features which characterised Roosevelt's first two terms of office. Above all, they contain many of the same contradictions. The strongest of these was the need to deny that there was anything fundamentally wrong. The Depression, it was implied, had been a passing malfunction in an otherwise efficient system, brought on, perhaps, by greed. There were lessons to be learned from this, but they were lessons of adjustment, not radical change. What this meant in terms of movies was that the same values which had caused the crisis in the first place – rugged individualism; economic incentive as a basis for general growth – continued to be asserted as ways of resolving the crisis.[7]

If the gangster film, later the crime movie, was the most obvious incarnation of the Warners' style, the studio was also noted for its backstage musicals and biopics. Yet it could not ignore the lucrative market of the women's film. By the early 1930s it had acquired the female leads needed for such films and was now on the lookout for corresponding male talent. This they found in George Brent. In fact, there was little in George Brent's background to suggest that he would become one of Hollywood's leading debonairs of the 1930s. Before looking more closely at that background, a word of caution needs to be sounded. Although most of the biographical articles written during the actor's career concur on the story of his early years, there is strong evidence to suggest that most of what was written about Brent was invented. George Brent was born George Patrick Nolan in Ballinasloe in 1904. Although his studio biographies describe his father as a journalist, John Nolan is listed on the registry of births as a shopkeeper. Brent's parents died young and he was brought up by his maternal grandparents in Dublin before being sent with his sister, in 1915, to live with an aunt in Manhattan. According to most accounts, he returned at the age of 18 to Dublin, meeting on board the ferry a man known as Father Dan who was an Irish patriot returning to aid the Republican movement. Brent is said to have attended university in Dublin where he took up amateur dramatics, although no record exists of his graduating either from Trinity College or the National University. Nor does the Abbey Theatre hold records that can substantiate his own claims to have been a member of the Players: 'It was the theatre at its best. And how we loved it, the good thing, the artistic. We were all a bit mad with the intensity of our endeavor, I guess. We believed in the splendor and the integrity of the Irish drama.'[8]

Father Dan apparently then reappeared in Brent's life, suggesting that he volunteer for Michael Collins as a despatch rider. This he did, criss-crossing the country with messages for Collins' various commanders until his own leader was assassinated. With the British forces closing in on Collins' active supporters, Brent escaped to Glasgow and from there to Plymouth, all the time aided by Father Dan. From Plymouth, Brent travelled to Canada where he changed his name from Nolan to Brent.

After a couple of years touring Canada in stock companies, Brent moved to New York, where he found work with a theatre group based in the Bronx. In 1925 he toured America playing the Jewish Abie in the stage version of *Abie's Irish Rose*. After several unsuccessful efforts to set up his own touring companies, Brent migrated to Los Angeles and, again after a first attempt that ended in failure, he signed with an agent, Minna Wallis, who is also credited with 'discovering' Clark Gable and Errol Flynn. In December 1931, she secured him a six-month contract at $250 weekly with Warner Bros.[9] Hired to compete with another debonair, MGM's Clark Gable, Brent launched a long career that saw him appear in a succession of roles (initially he was making a film a month) that earned him the reputation of being, as some saw it, a highly paid clothes horse who was there to refract the sheen of Warners' female leads. He starred in eleven films with Bette Davis, with whom he was rumoured to be conducting an off-screen affair and four with Ruth Chatterton, one of his five wives. Until the outbreak of the Second World War, Brent continued to play solid, urbane, unflappable leads, his career only waning in the post-war era when a new kind of male star came into demand. In any case, Brent was by this stage in his forties. His appearance in *The Spiral Staircase* (Robert Siodmak, USA, 1946) allows him to look unmistakeably middle-aged, as well as exploiting his character-casting by having the actor play against type as a serial killer.

The contrasts between Brent's on-screen persona and his off-screen 'history' as Irish freedom fighter form a tension that was explained in publicity materials and in the press as a world-weariness, a kind of combat fatigue, that fitted in with his debonair characterisation:

Success in pictures has meant the end of real adventuring, and the settling down to more or less routine life in the cinema capital. For Hollywood cannot offer Brent more excitement than he has already been through. The wildest Hollywood party – and they are not very wild any more – is a tame and uninteresting affair compared with the actor's adventures while working in the turmoil that was Ireland during the last revolt.

It is very doubtful if Brent will ever again feel the call of carefree, devil-may-care adventure in strange and far-away lands. He is content now to sit back in an easy chair by the fireside and let the past take care of itself.[10]

By the late 1930s, as an article in *Photoplay* attests, Brent's biography was beginning to compete with his screen persona as a fictional creation:

Father Dan's departing heels tapped a measured good-by [*sic*] on the road overhead, the sound fading into silence. George leaned against the base of the old stone arch, looking out of its shadow at fields chalk-white under Ireland's August moon, listening to the quiet that meant Michael Collins was dead, the rebellion over, the great plans shattered...

'*One hundred pounds on your head before morning.*' George passed his hand over his hair and swallowed hard against a rising lump of nausea in his throat. Somewhere in the swirl of panic a sane small voice said: You will get out of this. You have plenty of money, you've got that motorbike. Keep your head, you damn fool. [...]

At nine that evening George stood in a Glasgow alleyway, knocking on the kitchen door of a cheap café. He had bank notes ready in his hand – better than a gun. The man with the apron, and slits for eyes, gave him a slip of paper with an address on it. 'Hide at this place until tomorrow. There'll be a trawler steaming down the Firth and through the Irish Sea to Liverpool. You can get a freighter there.'

'Bound...?'

The man shrugged. 'You'll not be caring. America, probably.'[11]

The end of idealism and its sublimation into screen-acting, the pursuit of romance, expressed through multiple affairs and marriages, and a resignation to life's failure to live up to its early promise were essential qualities of the debonair. In marked contrast to Barry Fitzgerald's personification, Brent's Irishness and his revolutionary past were put to use to explain his aura of disappointed dreamer. Most news reporting of the star's life also insisted on his solitariness and his eschewal of the Hollywood social scene, further indication, certainly, of Byronic tendencies. The mystique of the Irish freedom fighter was a further hook to catch the Irish-American audience; it does, however, seem likely that the whole story was invented. Records show that Brent did indeed travel under the name of Nolan to America in 1915.[12] After that, there is no evidence of his return to Ireland and his involvement in any military activity, and his family has consistently disputed the veracity of this account of his early life. In a further biographical twist, it has been suggested that his brother, John James Nolan, was the infamous racketeer, Jack 'Legs' Diamond, another 'fact' that remains open to question.[13]

In his first years at the studio, Brent worked the routine hours of the contract player:

> You signed those seven-year contracts, and they had you. There was nothing on earth you could do about it. Nothing. For years I was working six days a week and until midnight on Saturdays if the film was behind schedule. It wasn't until a few years later when I was established that I could say no more night work and never again on Saturdays. And you never had any script options: you were sent a script on Thursday, you began rehearsals on Monday, you started shooting on Tuesday [...] You never saw daylight. You got up when it was dark, you spent the whole day on a soundstage, and you went home at night. At one point I made thirteen films in eleven months![14]

At the same time as they hired Brent, Warners also signed William Powell, another debonair. Powell made his name as a smooth, urbane detective, a role that he became best known for when he moved to MGM and starred in the *Thin Man* series. After Powell's defection to MGM, Brent assumed his mantle as 'Warner's Favourite Leading Man', a title bestowed on him by another of the studio's female contract players, Ann Dvorak.[15] By this time, Brent had developed a more assertive attitude with the studio, refusing to star in *Mandalay* (Michael Curtiz, USA, 1934) or *Heat Lightning* (Mervyn LeRoy, USA, 1934) both on the grounds of the types of character he was being expected to play and in an effort to increase his salary. The studio, who suspected that Ruth Chatterton was putting her new husband up to this, placed Brent on ninety-day suspension and wrote to all the other studio heads to remind them that he was under contract to them. When Brent travelled to Europe,

Warners circulated the British production companies warning them against employing him. In February 1934, Brent went to court against Warners but lost his case on the basis that he had no contractual right to select his roles. The actor had little choice but to return to work and in 1935 signed a new contract for $1,000 per week.[16] Even in these circumstances, the studio retained the upper hand: 'You couldn't even go to Europe and work. If they heard about it, they would bring an injunction against the production and the producer would lose his shirt. It was terrible. I just had to eat crow and go back to work. And they would laugh in your face. You were stuck, and you couldn't do anything about it.'[17] The war rumbled on between Brent and Warners, with, on one occasion, the studio deliberately sending him a contract they assumed he would balk at in order to suspend his salary. When the actor fell ill in 1941, the studio again threatened to reduce his salary to take into account his time in hospital.[18]

In 1934 Brent was lent out to MGM on two occasions, to play in *Stamboul Quest* (Sam Wood, USA, 1934) and with Greta Garbo in *The Painted Veil* (Richard Boleslawski, USA, 1934). In 1939, when Ronald Colman demanded too high a salary for the part, he was lent out to Twentieth Century-Fox to play Tom Ransome opposite Myrna Loy in *The Rains Came* (Clarence Brown, USA, 1939). Loaning out was a strategy routinely resorted to by studios in order to find work for actors for whom there were no obvious roles but who were costing money as contract players; it often suited actors equally, allowing them the opportunity to evade being typecast within the framework of their own studios' generic range.

Despite his differences with Warners, Brent chose to remain with them when his original contract expired in 1939 because: 'I wanted to work. I needed the dough, and no one offered anything better.'[19] At the end of this contract, Brent announced that he was quitting acting for the duration of the Second World War in order to work as a flying instructor at the Army Air Force base in Oxnard, California. In fact, he made one film a year during the war. In 1945 he signed a new two-picture contract with RKO at $17,500 per week, under the terms of which he made *The Spiral Staircase*. From this period onwards, Brent moved between studios and projects, now playing ageing playboy roles. In the late 1950s and early 1960s he reprised these roles on television but by the mid-1960s, his film career was over. In 1966, Brent announced that he was coming to live in Ireland. With his fifth wife, Janet Michaels, he rented a house in the wealthy Dublin suburb of Foxrock, bringing with him seven horses in training. He purchased three more in Ireland and planned to enter Irish racing. The Irish weather coupled with the Irish attitude, however, saw the couple return to California after a year: 'you couldn't get anybody to do anything, everything was mañana. I shipped my Rolls-Royce over and they scratched the doors; they thought it belonged to a British official. I had a helluva time getting it repaired.'[20]

Brent's effectiveness as romantic lead may have made him a career and, eventually, a name, largely forgotten as it now is; yet there is always something lacking in his Warners' performances, a hesitancy that opens up a space for stronger, usually female actors to step in and control the screen. Take, for instance, his starring role in *42nd Street* (Lloyd Bacon, USA, 1933). Here he plays Pat Denning, lover to the lead performer, Dorothy Brock (Bebe Daniels) in the show *Pretty Lady*. She in turn is being wooed by the elderly but wealthy and repellent Abner Dillon (Guy Kibbee), whose financing has allowed the tour to go ahead. The film pays its dues to its Depression-era setting, reminding us that money is hard come by these days; the resolution has the show's producer, Julian Marsh (Warner Baxter) convince Abner that if he exploits his position as financier and pulls the plug on the show, hundreds of ordinary men and women will lose their incomes.[21] Brock and Denning's love affair is carried on behind the backs of Abner and Marsh, who initially does not want Brock's loser of a guy to come between her and Abner. Denning is indeed a loser, with a waning career in vaudeville and not enough money to take Dorothy out to dinner. Brent plays him with a vulnerability that is markedly at odds with the wise-cracking showbiz characters who participate in the backstage musical. Even when he takes out the new chorus girl, Peggy (Ruby Keeler), who will eventually save the day and make her name in the show, he hovers over her in his apartment in a moment when it seems that no one in the room knows what he will do next. She falls asleep on his sofa and he leans towards her, as if to kiss her, and then just veers away and lifts her into his bedroom where he leaves her to sleep. In the closing moments of the film, Dorothy hands over her part to Peggy, wishing her well as replacement lead and, in tears, announces that she will take Pat and vaudeville – 'or whatever it is' – and that they are to be married the next day. It is hardly a moment of delirious epiphany, rather a recognition of a reality that lurks behind the show's precarious façade. Brent functions within the film as a reminder of the loss of esteem and of social position unemployment brings, a fate that will befall the chorus line, the technicians and many others if *Pretty Lady* does not go on.

Figure 2.1 Depression-era loser. Ruby Keeler and George Brent in *42nd Street*.

Pat Denning was an unusual role for Brent who more commonly played solid pillars of the wealthy community, playboys and single men who, at the moment the story opens, find themselves ready to abandon, or on the cusp of abandoning, bachelorhood for matrimony. His most durable films remain those with Bette Davis, whether as the Southern conservative, Buck Cantrell, in *Jezebel*, the paternalistic Dr Frederick Steele in *Dark Victory* (Edmund Goulding, USA, 1939)or unfortunate Peter van Allen, love object of two high society women, concert pianist, Sandra Kovak (Mary Astor) and Maggie Patterson (Bette Davis) in *The Great Lie* (Edmund Goulding, USA, 1941), a reprise of his earlier position in *The Old Maid* (Edmund Goulding, USA, 1939). When he appeared with Ruth Chatterton, Brent was slightly less shamelessly outmanoeuvred; *Female* (Michael Curtiz, USA, 1933), for instance, is an engaging pre-Production Code comedy in which Chatterton plays Alison Drake,

Managing Director of Drake Motors. The film's humour is derived from its role-reversal premise. Chatterton plays Drake as a man-eating tycoon, an office tyrant who lures innocent young male employees to her lavish mansion, there to be rendered malleable by copious doses of very strong vodka; moonlight swims and sex without commitment (on her part) follow, only for the young men to find themselves posted to remote parts of her business empire if they dare to think that they may express intimacy with her in the workplace. Inevitably, this all changes when the one man who does resist her, engineer Jim Thorne (Brent) takes up a contract with Drake Motors. To its credit, the film does not insist that Drake abandon her career for her man but ends with her realisation that love and a career are combinable lifestyle choices for the modern woman.

Allowed some greater acting leeway by both Chatterton and Michael Curtiz, Brent appears somewhat less solid and worthy than he does in the Davis vehicles. In all these productions, Brent does indeed stand pleasantly before the cameras, his solidity contrasting with the mobility of the Bette Davis character. His soft voice and expressive eyes commonly purvey tormented love and his person-ality is often associated in some way with loss – in *Jezebel*, it is the impending defeat of the American South, in *Dark Victory*, the death of his wife from a brain disorder he cannot operate on. Although he was not old at the time of the making of the films – in his thirties for most of them – he never seems young, but rather burdened by age, somewhat world-weary. This is further made evident by offsetting Brent's character against that of a younger, more passionate man, Henry Fonda as Preston Dillard in *Jezebel*, or the miscast Humphrey Bogart as Irish stable hand, Michael O'Leary, in *Dark Victory*. As women's pictures, as most of these were, the choices on offer are dependability versus excitement; or if those choices are not there to be made, equivalent tensions emerge, as in *The Old Maid* or *The Great Lie*, in the strong female relationships. The narratives and characters are those of the 1930s' melodrama – a world of broken engagements, mismatched love affairs, bitter spinsters, hidden illegitimacies and bitchy rivalries.

Having the correct type of male lead for these films was important to the production staff at Warners, who had a firm idea of what the contemporary female audience was in search of. For the role of Dr Steele in *Dark Victory*, for instance, both Spencer Tracy and Basil Rathbone were considered for a part that the scriptwriter, Casey Robinson, saw as crucial to the success of the film:

> It is, above all things, a tender love story between a Long Island glamour girl and a simple, idealistic, more-or-less inarticulate New England doctor. If we don't capture this feeling in the proper casting of Doctor Steele, I know we will wind up with a tragic flop instead of a truly great picture.[22]

In *The Old Maid* Brent was again argued to represent strength and personality, the kind of values two young women would fight over:

> In the present stress and with the general line-up, I do feel that the picture needs George [Brent] – because, as we all agreed, the picture is based on two girls falling in love with a man. That man must be important both in name, performance and appearance. He must be someone to remember throughout the play. That was why my first impulse was to suggest David Niven to you. Unless the man has the requisite strength and personality to be remembered – and this is a man whom the women in the audience will believe could have been this important to our two girls – the picture will lose something of what it requires...[23]

Clem Spender was, according to script notes, 'a woman's man. Reckless, impulsive, humorous, handsome and completely undependable...What more could a woman want? That is, what more could she want in her album of memories – Clem would not have made a good husband.'[24] Humphrey Bogart had started in the part but no one seems to have been satisfied that he was right for it. With feelings on set between the two female stars running high, it seems that a decision was made to bring in George Brent and shoot his scenes swiftly before he went to Fox on a loan out. This meant five days of retakes on a film that was already running behind schedule and bedevilled by its female stars' frequent bouts of illness as well as Miriam Hopkins' insistence on discussing her character before each take. The result was aptly summarised by one of the film's reviewers:

> George Brent has the role of Clem Spender. It is not his most attractive portrayal. It is not an easy task for two of the screen's foremost stars to introduce one of Hollywood's No. 1 leading men, dismiss him, and then carry on so successfully without him as to erase him from the mind of the audience, even though they frequently speak his name. But Miss Hopkins and Bette Davis have achieved it.[25]

Brent played out many of the contradictions that Roddick detects in the Warner Bros. films of the 1930s in his innumerable parts. On the one hand, he stands for an old-fashioned model of masculinity, long since outmoded by the Jazz age and the Depression; on the other, he offers a dependability and continuity with tradition that anchors the flighty female leads played by Warners' most highly paid stars. 'One of the attractive things about you and me has always been that you understood women,' Sandra Kovak tells Brent in *The Great Lie*, spelling out his appeal in the vocabulary of the melodrama. This appraisal echoes the recollections of the stars with whom Brent worked. Bette Davis, for instance, later recalled that Brent was one of the few lovers she remained friends with, and described him as 'an enchanting man with wit and beauty, and an excitement he rarely was in the mood to transfer to the screen'.[26]

In fact, not all reviews dismissed Brent's performances with Davis, particularly on the release of *Dark Victory*: 'Almost as surprising as Bette's own performance is that of George Brent, who plays the doctor. His tender sympathy, great kindness and appreciation of her mental struggle is not only one of the best things George has ever done, but one of the best things any actor has offered in a long time.'[27]

Figure 2.2 Tenderly sympathetic. Bette Davis and George Brent in *Dark Victory*

Although Brent made his name as romantic lead in the melodrama, he also worked in other genres. His least successful medium was the comedy and it is equally something of a surprise to find him in William Keighley's contribution to the war effort, *The Fighting 69th*, where he plays commanding officer, Wild Bill Donovan. In fact, this film is primarily a Cagney–O'Brien vehicle and a display of what Grant Tracey has identified as Cagney's ethnic simultaneity:

> As an Irish-American and a primarily New York City star, Cagney was an icon for immigrants because he represented a complex simultaneity: he was both a part of and apart from Anglo-Saxon society. The Irish were the older immigrants, largely mainstreamed, but their Catholicism kept them outside of Protestant America. In a series of vehicles, Warner Brothers presented Cagney as an outsider/insider figure, a character who didn't want to conform to the dictates of the collective, but through the love of a WASPish woman or the demands of the authoritative Pat O'Brien, harnessed his energies to communal good.[28]

Introducing himself in the early moments of Keighley's film, Cagney spits out his response to being identified as Irish: 'I don't work at it. I don't like those flannel mouth Micks going round singing Molly Malone all the time.' As Jerry Plunkett, he has to learn to quit the individualist ethnic behaviour that leads on two occasions to the deaths of his comrades in the celebrated Irish regiment of the film's title and to embrace a collectivity that wartime filmmaking demanded. Branded a coward and isolated within the troupe, Cagney is supported only by Father Francis Duffy (Pat O'Brien) who coaxes him towards the ultimate act of bravery that will lose him his life but save the regiment.

The Fighting 69th was a key film in Warners' rush to declare their wartime patriotism and the subject of an extended dispute with Fox, who believed that they held the film's rights. Warners made every effort to block Fox including persuading the real life prototypes of the fictional characters to sign over their right to be represented on screen to Warners. Donovan was Warners' main point of contact with the regiment and seems to have been the first to come on board and take sides in the battle with Fox. His correspondence with the studio suggests that he saw the film as a patriotic opportunity and was pleased with their depiction of him. Although Spencer Tracy had been mooted for the part, Donovan was happy that Brent was to portray him on film.[29]

As Plunkett's commanding officer, Brent represents the less malleable side of officialdom, indicated by his customary stiff demeanour. He is 'wild' in so far as he is brave but, in line with the new strictures on wartime filmmaking discussed in the previous chapter, it was essential to show him as a man who respected army discipline and regulations. In fact, his presence is much the same as it is in his melodramas, to provide a solid counterbalance to, in this case, Cagney's flamboyant and often hysterical theatrics.

Brent enjoyed a career at Warners that made him a wealthy and, in his day, famous man. That he has been largely neglected by film history is a reflection of the kind of role he made his own. The men he portrayed required him to be handsome but not forceful, his characterisation was most often secondary to that of the tough dames and volatile heiresses opposite whom he played. If we look outside his roles at Warners to those films that he made for other studios on a loan-out basis, we can see how an alternative career path might have opened up for him in different hands. Although this could not be said for all his non-Warners pictures (in *The Painted Veil*, Brent is particularly wooden opposite Greta Garbo), an examination of his work with Clarence Brown in *The Rains Came* shows how, given full scope to exploit his debonair persona, Brent could produce a much more engaging performance than those for which he is best remembered now.

The Rains Came saw Brown putting his star's on- and off-screen history at the service of a lavish imperial melodrama. Ransome (Brent) is a classic worldly colonial, scion of a wealthy English family, a man who arrived in Ranchipur seven years before the film's 1938 setting to paint the Maharajah's portrait, and has neither finished the portrait nor put himself to any other use in the intervening time. In the eyes of the other British and American residents of the district: 'You're a drunkard and a bounder and a remittance man. They hang about you because your father was an earl.' These are the words of young American, Fern Simon (Brenda Joyce), who is in love with Ransome. His dishonour is only matched by that of Lady Edwina Esketh (Myrna Loy), who turns up in the company of her wealthy and boorish husband. They are, as she puts it, soul mates: 'We've double-crossed everyone in the world, let's not start on each other.' Yet Ransome is a patriot, if a disillusioned one. Lounging on his veranda, he takes pot shots with his catapult at the statue of Queen Victoria that will later be submerged in the symbolic floods that wipe out the old India of the colonial period. Queen Victoria, he muses, is a reminder of the fine brave days, 'when London did its falling to a dance step, not to the threat of tomorrow's bombs, when every American was a millionaire, or about to be one, and people sang in Vienna. There she stands, unconcerned about wars, dictators or appeasement, as serene as ever.'

When the rains come, they bring with them a natural disaster that tears down Ranchipur's oldest buildings and causes an immediate medical crisis. Ransome and Lady Esketh find a use for themselves helping out at the palace and the hospital, offering the latter the opportunity to pursue her desire for Indian doctor, Major Rama Safti (Tyrone Power in blackface). Of course, the restrictions of the Hays Code meant that such a union could not be consummated and a subplot sees Lady Esketh dying a beautiful death that releases Major Safti for duties of state. Meanwhile, Ransome is redeemed by the love of Fern and becomes the heroic citizen life always intended him to be.

Playing opposite Myrna Loy in place of the tough dames of the Warners' lot, Brent is a much more convincing object of desire. Both stars exude a languid indifference to public opinion and society's strictures, suggesting by gesture and word a shared history of infidelities and debauchery. This common past is evoked through a cigarette lighting routine that suggests shared and even present intimacies, with fades to black discreetly leaving the two former lovers alone in the maharajah's palace. Like so many colonial narratives, *The Rains Came* is divided in its loyalties to the enticingly decadent order that Ransome and Lady Esketh personify and the new India of the competent and idealistic Major Safti. Playing to each other, rather than against, Loy and Brent are a much more believable match than the fiction allows, and it is only with difficulty that Tyrone Power and Brenda Joyce, representatives of the new order, insert themselves into the film's dynamic. For once, Brent's size and physique are photographed to suggest physical dominance with a faint suggestion of a military background, making him an appropriate object of desire within the romance of imperialism. Ransome, when his titled ancestry is mentioned, affects a slight raising of his eyebrows that could equally suggest that this is an invention or, more likely, that it means nothing to him, allowing him to distance himself from the crasser aspects of the old colonial order, while retaining his romantic aura.

Fulfilling the requirements of the male romantic lead allowed Brent to carve out a Hollywood career that made of him a wealthy man for life. Throughout this career, Brent expressed a kind of liminality that was specific to the era of the contract player. His off-screen identity was as much a creation as his on-screen roles; his brand of Irishness a concoction designed to give Irish-America the hero Warners, or Brent's agent, felt they would respond to. Perhaps because he played so few Irish roles, or because he could not fit into Irish society when he came 'home', or maybe because he really never managed to convince anyone that he had been a freedom fighter, forced to leave the country with a price on his head, Brent remains largely uncelebrated in his home country. Yet he was, in his time, Ireland's most successful male film star.

NOTES

1 'Review of *The Great Lie*', *The Times*, 2 October 1941, p. 6.
2 T. Schatz, *The Genius of the System* (New York: Metropolitan Books, 1996), p. 138.
3 Ibid., pp. 138–9.
4 Ibid., pp. 218–27; Hal Wallis, Head of Production at Warners, had his own suspicions as to the causes for Wyler's slow work on *Jezebel*. Wyler and Henry Fonda had both been married to the actor, Margaret Sullavan, and Wallis wondered if the need to submit Fonda to at least ten or eleven takes, where four or five might well have done, was not something to do with their common history. *Jezebel* was Warners' response to *Gone With the Wind* (Victor Fleming, USA, 1939), to which Davis' name had been attached in the search for Scarlett O'Hara, although she was never seriously in contention for the part. On the release of *Jezebel*, David O. Selznick instantly wrote to Jack Warner, detailing the points it had in common with *Gone With the Wind*, though Warner refuted them vigorously. See R. Behlmer (ed.), *Inside Warner Bros.* (London: Weidenfeld & Nicolson, 1986), pp. 40–4.
5 E. Anderson, 'Introduction', in J.R. Parish and D.E. Stanke, *The Debonairs* (New Rochelle, New York: Arlington House, 1975), pp. 11–21. p. 21.
6 Schatz, *Genius of the System*, p. 139.
7 N. Roddick, *A New Deal in Entertainment, Warner Brothers in the 1930s* (London: British Film Institute, 1983), p. 66.
8 G. Brent, quoted in Parish and Stanke, *The Debonairs*, p. 24.
9 George Brent Files, Warner Bros. Archive, USC, Box 2824A.
10 *Ireland's Own*, 30 May 1936, p. 13.
11 H. Sharpe, 'Bright Victory', *Photoplay*, 53, 7 (July 1939), pp. 66–7; 87–8, p. 66.
12 Passenger records reproduced on http://www.ellisisland.org (accessed 13 January 2005).
13 V. Trodd, *Clonmacnois and West Offaly* (Banagher, Scéal Publications, 1998).
14 G. Brent in F. Watkins, 'George Brent', *Film Fan Monthly*, 136 (1972), pp. 3–14. p. 5.
15 Parish and Stanke, *The Debonairs*, p. 32.
16 Box 2824A, George Brent Files.
17 G. Brent in Watkins, 'George Brent', p. 6.

18   Box 2824A, George Brent Files.
19   G. Brent in Parish and Stanke, *The Debonairs*, p. 43.
20   G. Brent in Watkins, 'George Brent', p. 3.
21   The film was, as Roddick reminds us, billed as a 'New Deal in Entertainment'. See Roddick, *A New Deal in Entertainment*, p. 65.
22   Memo to Hal Wallis from Casey Robinson, 19 August 1938, *Dark Victory* File, Warner Bros. Archive, USC.
23   Memo from Goulding to Hal Wallis, 22 March 1939, *The Old Maid* file, Warner Bros. Archive, USC.
24   Draft script, *The Old Maid* files.
25   *San Francisco Examiner*, 8 September 1939, *The Old Maid* files.
26   B. Davis, *The Lonely Life* (London: Macdonald, 1962), p. 148. See also, W. Stine, *No Guts, No Glory, Conversations with Bette Davis* (London: Virgin, 1990).
27   Uncredited review, *Dark Victory* file, Warner Bros. Archive, USC.
28   G. Tracey, 'Outside/Inside: James Cagney as ethnic in-between, 1930–1933', *Images* (online journal), http://www.imagesjournal.com/issue01/infocus/cagney2.htm. (accessed 22 December 2004).
29   All correspondence taken from *The Fighting 69th* file, Warners Bros archive, USC. Not everyone was so happy about Brent's casting. The files contain a letter from a regiment member who had just heard that Tracy was not to have the role: 'In my judgement Brent is a slabbering idiot with little manliness to his insipid facial expressions and if you want to spoil the makings of a great picture put him in the lead.' Letter from John C. Cassidy to Jack Warner, 16 September 1939.

3

Maureen O'Sullivan

'Fascinating little savage'
(1911–98; film career: 1930–92)

MAUREEN O'SULLIVAN gained her first Hollywood contract (with Twentieth Century-Fox) on the back of her role as Eileen O'Brien in Frank Borzage's *Song O' My Heart* (USA, 1930). Cast on sight by Borzage for her appearance as a sweet Irish colleen, O'Sullivan had no stage or screen acting experience. This mattered little in a film that was primarily intended as a vehicle for Count John McCormack, nor was it a concern for the studio who, on foot of the success of their Janet Gaynor films, were on the look out for another fresh-faced ingénue. However, neither they nor O'Sullivan were pleased to find that assumptions surrounding the new discovery's national identity had preceded her arrival; once in Los Angeles, this middle-class graduate of an elite girls' public school found that she had been typecast as 'a poverty stricken little Irish girl just kicked out of the bogs, that I had never before had the shawl off my back nor shoes on my feet, that I was a "Mick" and "Shanty Irish" – two expressions that I never heard of until I came to America'.[1]

O'Sullivan and her mother were equally horrified to see grown women walking the streets wearing skirts to their knees: 'Such painted faces! Such carmined lips! Such shockingly short skirts, bare legs, mascaraed eyes, bleached hair! We had never seen anything approaching the like!'[2]

If O'Sullivan was to be the new Gaynor, this was just the latest turn in the recycling of ingénue-types. Janet Gaynor in her turn had been heralded as the new Mary Pickford, and had played Irish roles in two early John Ford films, Lady Sheila O'Hara in *The Shamrock Handicap* (USA, 1926) and Rose Kelly in *The Blue Eagle* (USA, 1926). She was also directed by Frank Borzage in a series of productions in the late 1920s including *Seventh Heaven* (USA, 1927) and *Street Angel* (USA, 1928). Gaynor's appeal lay in an image of sweet innocence and in 1934, she was voted top box-office female star. Innocence might have been a sought-after commodity, but ignorance was not and the studio was unhappy to find that its latest discovery was believed to have come straight off the bogs. When O'Sullivan met and fell in love with John Farrow, they were even less pleased and forbad her be seen with or see a man considerably her elder. After the couple had flouted this edict, Farrow was sent, according to O'Sullivan's recollections, to England to remove him from her orbit.[3]

Meanwhile, Gaynor had temporarily fallen out with the studio in a row over her contract and O'Sullivan replaced her as the Graustarkian princess in *The Princess and the Plumber* (Alexander Korda, USA, 1930), one of many film versions of George Barr McCutcheon's popular romances. Shortly afterwards, O'Sullivan made a triumphant return to Ireland where she was widely feted for her success. On her return to Hollywood, O'Sullivan found that Fox was no longer interested in her; despite some positive reviews – 'The sweet, pure little Princess is played by little Miss O'Sullivan, the Irish girl with the English accent. You will love Maureen, she is so naïve in her role of Princess Louise' – without the popular combination of Gaynor and Charles Farrell, *The Princess and the Plumber* had flopped.[4] Gaynor had returned to the fold and there was no obvious role for O'Sullivan in the studio's future plans.

At this point, in memoirs that were specially written for Irish consumption, O'Sullivan reminds the largely female readership of *Woman's Life* that emigrant success does not come without a struggle, but that this is one that the national spirit had equipped her for: 'now began a desperate and long drawn-out battle between a cold, impersonal entity called Hollywood and an impulsive, determined Irish girl named Maureen O'Sullivan. My "Irish" was up! I was determined that Hollywood should not defeat me!'[5]

In the event, O'Sullivan was rescued by an Irish producer, who provided her with an introduction to MGM. At the time, MGM was identified by its lavish period dramas, many of them, as we shall see below, set in England or drawing on English literary classics. Throughout the 1930s she featured in a slew of productions, both for MGM and on loan to other studios and was cast most consistently as an upper-class young English ingénue. By the time of the release of *The Barretts of Wimpole Street* (Sidney Franklin, USA, 1934), she had made that kind of role her own and was being tipped for stardom. Critics also agreed that she was 'an intelligent, resourceful actress'.[6] It was, however, as Jane Parker in the Tarzan series that O'Sullivan made her name. Starting with *Tarzan the Ape Man* (W.S. Van Dyke, USA, 1932), she played opposite Johnny Weissmuller in six of the films, a career move that at the time was considered by many popular writers on film to be unwise:

> One of the most unfortunate things in her career is that she has been in the Tarzan pictures, produced by M-G-M...These pictures, exciting and interesting though they are, are useless to any actress. There is little she can do, except to try and look as romantic as possible under trying circumstances. A little winsomeness, a great deal of anxiety and a patronising way with the larger mammals is about all this called for. They are definitely not the kind of vehicles Bernhardt would have picked.[7]

The difference was, of course, that O'Sullivan was no Sarah Bernhardt and, in common with the other contract stars and character actors of the day, had little say in the parts she played. In fact, as Jane, O'Sullivan enjoys an agency that her other film roles do not permit her. Freed from the codes of propriety that dictate her behaviour as an upper-class Englishwoman of the kind that she plays in films such as *The Barretts of Wimpole Street* or *A Yank at Oxford* (Jack Conway, USA, 1937), she can shoot a gun, go off on an adventure into the African jungle, and find herself a more manly lover than is on offer 'at home'. She can swing from trees, ride an elephant's trunk, sleep naked (the films imply) and, when the occasion requires, defend white men against the cannibal hordes. In her other appearances, O'Sullivan was inevitably relegated to the part of younger sister (*The Barretts of Wimpole Street*, *Anna Karenina* [Clarence Brown, USA, 1935], *Pride and Prejudice* [Robert Z. Leonard, USA, 1940]) or to the less interesting 'good girl' who is a pale shadow of the vampish 'bad girl' – her fate in *A Yank at Oxford*, a film now better remembered for Vivien Leigh's performance as the seductive Elsa Craddock. In *A Day at the Races* (Sam Wood, USA, 1937), she is simply the stooge for the Marx Brothers.

In the early 1940s O'Sullivan went into retirement, having now had seven children. She acted in occasional films, two (*The Big Clock*, USA, 1948 and *Where Danger Lives*, USA, 1950) directed by her husband, John Farrow, and in the mid-1950s hosted the television series, *Irish Heritage*. In 1961 fellow Irish actor, Pat O'Brien, persuaded her to appear on stage in *Roomful of Roses*. She followed this with a successful move into Broadway theatre, starring in the long-running comedy, *It's Never Too Late*. After Farrow's death in 1963, she continued to appear in theatre, on television and in sporadic films but only returned to the limelight with her role as Norma, mother of the eponymous Hannah, who was played by her real life daughter, Mia Farrow, in Woody Allen's *Hannah and her Sisters* (USA, 1986). Maureen O'Sullivan died in 1998.

I want now to look more closely at a career that was predicated upon multiple layers of identity performance – as Irish colleen, English aristocrat and jungle beauty – all filtered through an exilic consciousness. O'Sullivan's career, to a far greater extent than that of Maureen O'Hara, illustrates the working through of the masquerade that assimilation entails, the process of retaining an old identity while 'passing' successfully under the guise of a new identity. Focusing in particular on the Tarzan cycle of films, I want to argue that MGM saw in O'Sullivan a kind of idealised English-ness that was reflected in her off-screen persona as, ironically, a good Catholic Irish woman. In this manner, they could create a character whose sexuality was mitigated by her innocence and who subsequently could convince as a demure housewife.

Tarzan films and the novels by Edgar Rice Burroughs on which they draw are conventionally analysed for their creation of an ideal of masculinity and for their unreconstructed racism.[8] These are certainly the principal ideological features of the books and the many films that derive from them; yet, it is Jane who articulates, deflects and problematises many of the recurrent themes of this sub-genre, and as such is worthy of more critical attention than she has so far attracted. Jane is the intermediary between the viewer and Tarzan, who, in a reversal of the conventional trope, is presented as her/our object of desire. She enjoys a liminal status as 'civilised savage', part of a game of signification that hints at the taboo attractions of miscegenation only to disavow them. More than that, she is the link between civilisation and the wilderness, and between the old and new worlds of Europe and America.

Maureen O'Sullivan's cycle of 1930s films with MGM coincided with a period that H. Mark Glancy has described as 'When Hollywood Loved Britain' and is covered from a more anecdotal standpoint in Sheridan Morley's *Tales From the Hollywood Raj*.[9] From the 1930s through to the end of the Second World War, the Hollywood studios, of which MGM was foremost, produced a cycle of films with British characters, plots and settings. As Glancy discusses, this is attributable to a number of causes. Many Americans of this period identified themselves with Britain, and specifically England, as a country of origin, a sentiment that accumulated with the rise of Fascism. From a box-office perspective, the films could generally be counted on to make money not just locally in America but in the valuable British market and within the English-speaking territories of the Commonwealth. The introduction of the British quota system in the Cinematograph Films Act of 1927 encouraged the American studios to set up British production bases in order to circumvent quota restrictions and to feed their markets with films that were shot on location and featured 'genuine' British stars. Then again, Hollywood was anxious that British filmmakers should not themselves make these films. Alexander Korda's success in providing a foreigner's view of British culture in productions such as *The Private Life of Henry the Eighth* (GB, 1933) and his flamboyant, Hollywood mogul style indicated that, even if local British producers might not have what it took to challenge Hollywood, others from within that industry might. Many of the American films of the 1930s followed Korda's formula, foregrounding a roguish and decadent aristocracy, the visual spectacle of British historical pageantry, and actors who could produce 'theatrical', understood as upmarket, performances. Hollywood further made sure of cornering the market in 'British' films by offering British actors contracts at rates that were far higher than those on offer at home.

Charles Laughton, as we shall see in Chapter 4, was one of these. Another was Cary Grant. Errol Flynn also fell under this rubric, as did Brian Aherne. The latter two were labelled Irish or British or, in the case of Flynn, Australian as the occasion required. Both played Irish parts (Aherne in *Beloved Enemy* [H.C. Potter, USA, 1936] and Flynn in *Captain Blood* [Michael Curtiz, USA, 1935] and *Gentleman Jim Corbett* [Raoul Walsh, USA, 1942] but were more often cast as British or American. Aherne was also considered for the title role in *Parnell* [John M. Stahl, USA, 1937] before it went to Clark Gable. As Sheridan Morley observes:

> Some of the best-known of the Hollywood British had never been British at all: Errol Flynn, who defeated the Armada and led the *Charge of the Light Brigade*, in fact hailed from Australia, George Sanders was Russian; Laurence Harvey was Lithuanian; Leslie Howard was Hungarian. Yet, somehow they all managed to symbolize something utterly English that Hollywood felt was unavailable locally.[10]

Fewer prominent female actors of the period emerged from British cinema and stage in large part because there were more male than female roles on offer for British actors, of whatever origin. Maureen O'Sullivan was part of a vanguard of 'British' female actors imported to respond to the new political conditions of the moment. Another was English-born Greer Garson, whose heritage was Northern Irish–Scots. Garson was to become 'queen of the lot' at MGM, and strongly identified as the quintessential Englishwoman after her performances in *Goodbye, Mr Chips* (Sam Wood, USA, 1939), *Pride and Prejudice* and *Mrs Miniver* (William Wyler, USA, 1940). Identified in the Hollywood press equally as enjoying the 'sunny disposition of the Irish' or behaving like the perfect English lady, Greer flew the Union Jack outside her home and referred to herself as Irish.[11] Another import was O'Sullivan's former school-mate from her period in the Convent of the Sacred Heart at Roehampton, Vivien Leigh, who in turn made her name in the part of Irish-American Scarlett O'Hara in *Gone With the Wind*.

Acting British meant conforming to a Hollywood expectation of the British character, one that was generally divided between 'upstairs' and 'downstairs' and was most popular when viewed through the filter of the costume drama. Just as non-nationals produced some of the most popular 'British' films, so non-nationals often understood better than their 'authentic' counterparts how to perform national identity. Accent was key to this:

> And if the [Hollywood–British] colony tended to close ranks and stick together, it was at least partly so as to preserve their most valuable professional asset: the English or at the very least British accent. They all had before them the terrible warning of Ida Lupino, who, cast for a leading role in *The Bishop Misbehaves* was replaced on the first day of shooting by Maureen O'Sullivan because Miss Lupino, having been settled in California now for four or five years, was found to be 'no longer sufficiently British'.[12]

In the Irish fan press, O'Sullivan's sophistication and her adherence to family values of the kind notably absent from most Hollywood relationships were highly praised. While being able to act more British than the British, she was also lauded for not playing up to embarrassing and outmoded Irish stereotyping:

> Perhaps what strikes you most about her is the fact that she is so authentically 'one of ourselves'. There are, let me tell you, temptations

in the way of Irish acting-folk abroad. The bejabers-complex is still pretty widespread in foreign parts, and it takes guts to resist it – either on or off the stage. Maureen flattened it at every encounter, with the result that it has learned to leave her severely alone.[13]

Hollywood's 'British' films tended to celebrate aspects of British fearlessness or honour. The Empire was a favoured setting, although Empire films had to tread carefully in order not to offend popular American ideas of democracy. Maureen O'Sullivan's Tarzan cycle arguably belongs to this category, and demonstrates many of the ambiguities felt by its makers over the imperial endeavour. The films also intersect with another popular genre of the 1920s and 1930s, namely the jungle movie or, as Thomas Doherty distinguishes it, 'the racial adventure film'.[14] Now perhaps best remembered for *King Kong* (Merian C. Cooper/Ernest B Schoedsack, USA, 1933), jungle movies relied on a well-tried formula. This included documentary-style backgrounds, the use of live wild animals, a quest narrative that placed white men in peril and brought them face to face with an aberration of nature, usually some kind of apeman or, as in the case of *The Lost World* (Harry O. Hoyt, USA, 1925), a rampaging dinosaur. That encounter forced the adventurers to abandon their rational concept of the world and of evolution's linear progress from ape to human. The exotic locations of the films allowed for the suggestion of titillating sexual aberrations, usually figured through the trope of the imperilled white woman. They also depicted the indigenous population of Africa as relentlessly savage, a displace-ment, arguably, of racial sentiments at home. Both the jungle film and the imperial drama found their narrative origins in popular literature, and their visual style in the travelogue. Many of the most successful of these enjoyed multiple remakes. *The Four Feathers*, A.E.W. Mason's rousing tale of cowardice and redemption in the Sudan campaign of the 1890s, was filmed four times between 1915 and 1939; the first Tarzan film, *Tarzan of the Apes* (Scott Sidney, USA), appeared in 1918 and was remade over and again during the next few decades. Meanwhile, Edgar Rice Burroughs' novels sold in their millions: 'Despite Conrad's searing depiction of evil at the core of the "civilizing" enterprise [in *Heart of Darkness*, 1902] tropical Africa remained in Burroughs's and the public's imagination a great arena for white male adventure, one of the last wild places on earth.'[15]

Fictional as they obviously were, the films fixed an idea of Africa into the imaginary of a generation:

> For over four decades [from the 1930s onwards] these films provided Americans with their major source of information and mis-information about Africa and Africans, and thus for a sizable portion of the population the only real sense of their native land. That this appeal was real, no matter how distorted or genuine the image, was documented by the popularity of Tarzan films among black viewers.[16]

Tarzan films, in common with imperial and other jungle films, asserted white, male supremacy over the threat and disorder of native Black Africa in a manner similar to the Western's treatment of 'Indians' (native Americans). For the black viewer, this led to complex issues of identification: 'In the Antilles, the young Negro identifies himself *de facto* with Tarzan against the Negroes. This is much more difficult for him in a European theater, for the rest of the audience, which is white, automatically identifies him with the savages on the screen.'[17]

The Tarzan films, as do their literary progenitors, owe much to what has been termed the West's 'Prospero Complex', 'which is premised on an East/South portrayed as a Prospero's isle, seen as the site of superimposed lacks calling for Western transformation of primeval matter.'[18] They also, 'embody wondrous stereotypes, myth structures and archetypes of the sort which generally set the intellectual hearts of neo-Freudians, neo-Jungians and neo-Levi-Strausians aflutter'.[19] The films, as we shall see below, display an awareness of popular Freudian and Darwinian theories, playing with some glee on the concept of the taboo and on natural selection.

The most lasting of the Tarzan adaptations was the Weissmuller/O'Sullivan Tarzan cycle, made by MGM between 1932 and 1942. At this point O'Sullivan quit the series, but Weissmuller stayed on to make a further six with RKO under the independent producer, Sol Lesser, who had already made two Tarzan films in the 1930s, the first with Buster Crabbe as Tarzan and the second with Glenn Morris in the role.[20] Crabbe, a swimming champion like Weissmuller, also starred in the hugely successful *King of the Jungle* (H. Bruce Humberstone, Max Marcin, USA, 1933).

The Weissmuller/O'Sullivan Tarzan cycle was initiated in MGM as a direct result of the success of *Trader Horn* (W.S. Van Dyke, USA, 1931). The studio commissioned the key personnel from that film to put together a similar production, this time drawing on the Tarzan stories but without infringing on Burroughs' originals. This was, in fact, a contractual necessity – as MGM had bought the name Tarzan rather than the individual stories from Burroughs.[21] In *Trader Horn*, the trader had come across a 'white goddess' who has been reared by an African tribe; now the Englishman, Colonel Parker, a character not in Burroughs' books, and his daughter were to find a white jungle king on their search for the elephants' graveyard. Unlike *Trader Horn*, the Tarzan films were shot entirely on studio lots and around California but incorporated footage from their progenitor.

Although most readers will be familiar with the catchphrase, 'Me Tarzan, You Jane', erroneously associated with the Weissmuller/O'Sullivan Tarzan series (in fact, when Jane has taught Tarzan [Weissmuller] the rudiments of the naming process, he launches into a round of chest-thumping, hitting firstly himself then her, 'Tarzan, Jane, Tarzan, Jane', until she makes him stop), a quick reminder of the films' content may be useful. The first of the series was *Tarzan the Ape Man*. Englishman James Parker (C. Aubrey Smith) is a white trader in an unnamed African state, a man with one ambition left – to find the elephants' burial ground and remove their ivory tusks for sale. His daughter, Jane, arrives unexpectedly to join him, explaining only:

Figure 3.1 Initiating Tarzan into culture. Maureen O'Sullivan and Johnny Weissmuller in *Tarzan the Ape Man*

'From now on, I'm through with civilisation. I'm going to be a savage, just like you.' Parker, and his friend, the younger Harry Holt (Neil Hamilton) insist to the unbelieving Jane that they hate Africa. Soon after Jane's arrival, a tribe of Africans arrives to trade with Parker and Holt. Settling in around the perimeter of his grounds, they proceed to sing and dance before lining up for Jane's and the camera's lingering perusal. In one of the film's several excursions into the ethnographic documentary mode, the white men explain the Africans' markings to Jane, while she admires the women's jewellery. They in turn stand silently before her as she walks past examining them.

Throughout this and the remainder of the films, the black characters function to connote either commercialism or savagery. Other than Riano (Ivory Williams) or Saidi (Nathan Curry), in *Tarzan and his Mate* (Cedric Gibbons, Jack Conway, USA, 1934), they are not named and are quite disposable, being routinely eaten by crocodiles or picked off by other hostile tribes. Although Jane instantly exclaims how much she loves Africa and how completely at home she feels there, her identification takes place at the level of scenery and wildlife; the continent's inhabitants are, within this discourse, symbols of nature's menace. When the Africans are not outsiders attacking the white group, they are the bearers who out of fear refuse to continue on with the journey to locate the elephants' graveyard and have to be whipped into obedience, if not shot.

It is during one such mêlée that Tarzan turns up and carries Jane off to his home in the treetops. After a good deal of screaming, Jane begins to see the attractiveness of the man she has just been calling a brute, but further understanding is abandoned with the arrival of Parker, Holt and their bearers. Jane goes back to her father who warns her that:

> He's not like us.
> He's white.
> Those people living a life like that – they have no emotions.
> They're not human.

Soon, Jane is back with Tarzan after the ape fetches her to nurse the injury he sustained rescuing the trapped elephant. They proceed towards an idyllic relationship, nurtured through a return to childlike play and linguistic regression. As Tarzan's instructor in language, Jane initiates him into the world of culture; at the same time she revels in leaving that world behind, parodying it in linguistic games that Tarzan cannot comprehend. In an extended set piece, repeated with little variation in the series, Tarzan cements his identification with the white group by rescuing them from a tribe of crazed black 'dwarfs' who hold their captives in a compound and, working themselves into a frenzy of music and chanting, drop them into a pit to be eaten by an orang-utan. The film closes with Parker finding the graveyard but dying in the attempt and Holt leaving Jane with Tarzan, she promising that they will ensure Holt's safe passage back to plunder the ivory.

The remaining films in the series proceed along somewhat similar lines. In *Tarzan and his Mate*, Harry Holt returns with his friend Martin Arlington (Paul Cavanagh) to raid the elephants' graveyard and to rescue Jane. Both men are killed in another violent confrontation with a native tribe. *Tarzan Escapes* sees Tarzan and Jane being kidnapped by the bounty-hunter, Captain Fry (John Buckler) but freeing themselves and Jane's cousins, Rita (Benita Hume) and Eric Parker (Bill Henry), who have come to tell Jane that she has inherited a fortune. In the course of *Tarzan Finds a Son!* (Richard Thorpe, USA, 1939), the series reprises a theme of the books in having a plane crash in the jungle killing all its passengers, bar the rightful heir to the Greystoke fortune, a baby whom Tarzan and Jane rescue and bring up as their own, christening him 'Boy' (Johnny Sheffield). *Tarzan's Secret Treasure*, discussed in the first chapter of the book, sees the family under threat again and by *Tarzan's New York Adventure* (Richard Thorpe, USA, 1942), they have left their jungle home to rescue the kidnapped Boy from evil American profiteers.

As the synopsis of *Tarzan the Ape Man* suggests, it and the subsequent films achieve narrative coherence by virtue of a series of strategic elisions. The first film dispensed with explaining what a white man who communicated through echoing whoops was doing in the African jungle. Viewers were obviously expected to have an existing familiarity with the Edgar Rice Burroughs novels even though they had undergone considerable transformation. If Tarzan's presence in the jungle is unexplained, Jane's was only a little clearer. She is evidently in flight from home and now seeks a country to which she can really belong. Why is she through with civilization? Ivor Novello, hired as scriptwriter on the project, was clear on this: 'She has been living a very sophisticated life in England and has grown very tired of it, that's the reason she's packed up everything and has arrived there – as much to get back to simplicity as anything else.'[22] That Jane should be British was also important, as the same script conference records:

Novello: Why she couldn't have come from America, I don't know. Suppose he had an American wife? Suppose...

Hyman: I think you can be so much more charming with her if she's British.

Novello: There's nothing so silly as an American girl saying conventional English things. It makes her sound affected, where an English girl is perfectly natural saying them.[23]

English, maybe world civilisation, is under threat and Jane must undertake a voyage to a place where she can find a new authenticity. Indeed, arguably, Africa is now the (re)birthplace of white ascendancy with Tarzan reconfigured as the new Adam, possessor of the perfect white male body, at once desirable and desiring. Jane's sophistication, symbolised by a pair of tight, lace-up boots, is meaningless and she too must revert to a primitive innocence if she is to consort with Tarzan.

Picking up on a line uttered by Jane towards the end of *Tarzan the Ape Man*, 'There's something sad about retracing', Richard McGhee has analysed the films in terms of their mediation between reality and fantasy. Jane, he argues, is the key figure in this movement from the world of restraint and bourgeois manners, from reality, to the freedom of Tarzan's romantic, primitive environment:

She is our link with the inarticulate, mysterious, potent, and intimidating Tarzan; she is our doorway into the sublime disorder of Tarzan's wilderness world. As an audience (particularly of males) looking on from the world of reality out of which Jane Parker has come, we must see Jane as a figure of our sexual fantasies perverted and twisted by allegiances to conscious, bourgeois reality.[24]

This motif is rendered somewhat clearer in *Tarzan and his Mate*. By now undoubtedly conscious of the elements that had contributed to the commercial success of *Tarzan the Ape Man* ($919,000 profit on its domestic and foreign release), its producers made much of the sexual appeal of a nearly naked white woman in the jungle ('This scene [where Jane and Tarzan wake up] must be played close enough so that we can get away with the suggestion of Jane's nudity.')[25] O'Sullivan's clothing was arranged so as to conceal as little as possible and, in the original version, she was doubled swimming naked underwater.

It is an irony that the part played by an Irish actor (even if doubled) was to become one of the early victims of the new Hollywood morality, itself attributable to pressures from the heavily Irish-American influenced Catholic Church and the Legion of Decency (the latter formed in 1934). Also in 1934, the Production Code Administration (PCA) was founded with Joe Breen installed as president. From this point on, no script could go into production without prior PCA approval and no film released without a PCA seal. The swimming scene inevitably ran foul of Breen who convened a jury to adjudicate on it. The panel recommended that it be made plain at the start of the scene that Jane wears clothes and that the diving scene be shot so as any nudity would not be evident. According to Rudy Behlmer in his detailed accounts of the making of the films:

> From all evidence, *three* versions of the sequence eventually went out to separate territories during the film's initial release. One with Jane clothed in her jungle loincloth outfit, one with her topless, and one in the nude. The Production Code (Hays Code) Office saw and approved the clothed edition but found out later that the variant versions were in circulation – depending upon the different rules and restrictions among certain state and city censors and the noncensorable areas. Clearly this was a code violation. Eventually the studio eliminated the scene in its entirety and had it edited out of the negative.[26]

Discussing this case, Thomas Doherty has suggested that MGM inserted the scene in the knowledge that it would cause instant offence and thus distract the censors from 'the many scenes of Weismuller [*sic*] and O'Sullivan prancing about in their revealing jungle togs'.[27]

It is Jane's liminal status as nearly naked 'savage' that most excites the film's curiosity in sentiments that are articulated only to be later dealt with punitively. The mouthpiece for this curiosity is Martin Arlington. Already marked as promiscuous after a glimpsed encounter with a married Frenchwoman (another exotic fantasy), the louche Englishman is fascinated by Holt's continued love for Jane. To travel to the elephants' graveyard, they must once again cross the Mutia Escarpment which, as Holt tells Arlington, divides the Africa they know from the one no white man has been to. 'Taboo!' Arlington responds knowingly and with enthusiasm.

Armed with his generation's second-hand Freudian theories, Arlington understands that this is the space in which he can act out the fantasies that must remain repressed in white, 'civilised' culture. After they have journeyed into the heart of Africa, the men and their party come upon Jane and Tarzan. Arlington is thrilled: 'She's priceless, a woman who's learnt the abandon of the savage, yet she'd be at home in Mayfair.' Lacing his Freudian perceptions with the other master narrative of these films, Arlington further points out to Holt: 'This is raw nature, old man, survival of the fittest.' Holt is less confident: 'Well, Martin, the fittest around here is Tarzan and he won't let her go.' At this, the two men glance towards the tent where Jane is trying on the silks and gowns Holt has ordered from England to entice her home. The shot is carefully lit to reveal O'Sullivan in silhouette, almost nude. Once dressed, she joins them and they put on the gramophone. Now completely given over to his fantasy, Arlington clasps Jane, gasping: 'You're a fascinating little savage', and kisses her.

Figure 3.2 'A woman who's learnt the abandon of the savage'.
Maureen O'Sullivan in *Tarzan and his Mate*

Jane's flirtatious curiosity is piqued by this attention but, of course, Tarzan will have none of this, descending to sweep his 'mate' off, for what the film makes clear is satisfying sex in the treetops. Arlington is duly punished (death at the hands of the attacking African tribe of cannibals) for his dual transgression, sexual and sacred, for his designs on Jane and on the elephants' graveyard. Yet, the words remain behind him, a key to the appeal of O'Sullivan's persona in the series, particularly before it fell prey to the rigours of the Hays Code. Jane offers the fantasy of the sexually uninhibited 'native', and the sanction of her white skin, an ideal of womanhood of which she is apparently quite innocent. This is surely that process of recognition and disavowal that Homi Bhabha refers to when he asks: 'What is this theory of encapsulation or fixation which moves between the recognition of cultural and racial difference and its disavowal, by affixing the unfamiliar to something established, in a form that is repetitious and vacillates between delight and fear?'[28] Although Bhabha here is describing more generally the stereotyping of people of colour, this film, more than any other in the series, articulates the fantasy of sex with the native displaced onto the body of the white woman. That O'Sullivan's very pale Irish skin photographed so luminously leaves no room for doubt as to this whiteness.

The film can only get away with coming this close to giving voice to such a fantasy by having O'Sullivan play Jane as innocent of her allure. At the same time, she is quite evidently sexually fulfilled and exudes a kind of post-coital smugness alongside her more English public school girlishness. It is the latter, a resolute guilelessness that binds together O'Sullivan's performance across the Tarzan cycle and ties it in to her other 'British' films. Even a year on from her arrival in Tarzan's kingdom, Jane continues to speak to Tarzan in a manner that goes over his head. The latter is designated as pre-verbal and when we are reunited with the couple in *Tarzan and His Mate* has only added a scattering of words and phrases to his vocabulary. 'He did not really need to speak,' Morton reminds us, 'since he was there to be seen, not heard.'[29] Jane, by contrast, chatters constantly, in a flow of ironic non-sequitors. Greeted by Tarzan in their tree-house in the morning, she wonders out loud: 'So you've been out shopping early. Or did you spend the night at the club?' Her words remain those of the Mayfair ingénue, a reassurance of her continuing whiteness, yet their playful delivery is also a disavowal of that world and its values, its fragility symbolised by the easily torn clothes Holt has imported from its best fashion houses. Jane's initial journey, while ostensibly in search of the elephants' graveyard, was a voyage back in time and place, an abandonment of Western civilisation and a return to the origins of humanity. It is literally a rite of passage, during which she must stop flirting with her father, as she does on arrival, and find herself an appropriate mate.[30] In this new Eden, she discovers her Adam, who as most viewers would have been aware of, was a physically superior but apparently plebeian and primitive American, and not the English lord of Burroughs' fiction. Indeed, the film series effects a double reversal of Burroughs' original premise. In his first novel of what was to become a long-running series, Burroughs takes the conventionally 'enlightened' view of British imperialism:

> The natives of the British Colony complained that many of their young men were enticed away through the medium of fair and glowing promises, but that few if any ever returned to their families.
>
> The Englishmen in Africa went even further; saying that these poor blacks were held in virtual slavery, since when their terms of enlistment expired their ignorance was imposed upon by their white officers, and they were told that they had yet several years to serve.
>
> And so the Colonial Office appointed John Clayton to a new post in British West Africa, but his confidential instructions centered on a thorough investigation of the unfair treatment of black British subjects by the officers of a friendly European power.[31]

The films, on the other hand, consistently portray the English upper classes as motivated solely by fantasies of plunder and financial gain; only the few working-class members of the group or, as in Barry Fitzgerald's case, the Irish O'Doul, who have nothing to gain from these expeditions, are seen in a sympathetic light. Part of Jane's education in the jungle is to adopt Tarzan's suspicion of white men, while acting as the liaison point between them and him. Jane's love for Tarzan implies a rejection of the corrupt and hierarchically structured society of the Old World and an acceptance of a new order organised around an ideal of primitive (American) virility. This is again a reversal of Burroughs' original fiction, where Jane is the American and Tarzan the full-blooded English lord, empowered by his lineage. In the prototype, Tarzan abandons his jungle home to rescue Jane from forced marriage to the man to whom her father is indebted. In the films, Jane remains the unifying force between England and America but now the contrast is between an enfeebled and corrupt old world and a virile new order.

By portraying Jane as largely unchanged by jungle life, O'Sullivan is able to reassure the viewer that she has not 'gone native'. Given Hollywood and the Hays Code's deep-seated fear of miscegenation, this was crucial if Jane were to remain 'a figure of our sexual fantasies'. But she is also a 'fascinating little savage', because, if she were in Mayfair or in a film set in Mayfair, she would not walk around nearly naked, or pop off to bed with her lover whenever he beckoned, as she does in *Tarzan and His Mate*. Africa, like the Orient or Latin America, 'is posited as the locus of eroticism by a puritanical society, and a film industry, hemmed in by a moralistic code'.[32]

By the making of *Tarzan Escapes*, the restrictions of the Hays Code found Jane dressed in a modest shift. As Rudy Behlmer has detailed, this was the second version of the film to be shot. The first, directed by James C. McKay, had been abandoned by the studio on a number of grounds, including a plotline that involved a flirtation between Jane's sister, Rita, and Tarzan.[33] In the released version Jane and Tarzan now live in a tree-house equipped with all the conveniences of modern-day life: 'Tarzan made it and I designed the kitchen myself. Hot and cold.' They are utterly devoted to each other, the performances so exaggerated that it is tempting to read the relationship as a parody of the conventional bourgeois marriage.

Tarzan Escapes tones down Jane's sexuality considerably and redirects the emphasis towards the pleasures of family life, soon to be enhanced by the arrival of 'Boy'. In doing so, it could be argued to make a greater play for the engagement of the female viewer. For the first time, Jane is shown to enjoy a relationship with another woman, her sister, who articulates the attractions of Tarzan in terms that are not restricted to an admiration of his physique: 'You've got the grandest possession that any woman can have – peace and comradeship and perfect communion with a man whose whole strength is devoted to making your life beautiful.' Where the white Englishmen see in Tarzan only threat or, indirectly, financial capital, the Englishwomen realise that he is a man of sensitivity and strength and, thus, quite superior to what is on offer 'back home'. For the viewer who might have previously wondered how a well-bred Englishwoman could bear to live in a tree-house surrounded by uncomfortably tactile apes, there is now the reassurance that Jane's life in the jungle is a recognisable variant of their own, complete with an adoring man (the series occasionally refers to Tarzan as Jane's husband but otherwise skirts around their non-marital status).

Play and role-play are at the heart of the Tarzan films and evinced through O'Sullivan's performance of identity. She plays at being a homemaker, just as she plays at being British. At the same time, she is the principal spectator for Tarzan's displays of virility. Reading the films in this manner may run the risk of applying a mode of Derridean deconstruction to performances that may not have been consciously conceived of in such a self-conscious manner. Yet, O'Sullivan in interview clearly understood that role-playing was embedded in her characterisation, if for slightly different reasons. A syndicated article (taken from studio-generated publicity) in *The Screen* commented: 'Being Tarzan's mate on the screen, Maureen O'Sullivan naturally can't be the "clinging vine" type. But that doesn't prevent her from being utterly feminine just the same.' O'Sullivan is then quoted as saying: 'If a woman were really a clinging vine at heart, it seems to me she'd be rather uninteresting to men. But some of us probably adopt the pose. The real clinging vine, I think is only created by man's imagination.'[34]

As it worked out, Jane's integrity and independence, along with her erotic appeal, were gradually eliminated from the series. The final three films in the O'Sullivan–Weissmuller series relegate the female role to that of homemaker, and it is she who in each case threatens the family's happiness by undermining Tarzan's authority, leaving her to beg his forgiveness at the films' endings. By now, studio publicity had ensured that the public be fully aware of O'Sullivan's contented marriage and her new motherhood. As Larry May reminds us, the ideal wartime woman kept her home together, while contributing, as best she could, to the economy. Gone was the flapper, in came the woman who 'saw her work as a means to support her man fighting abroad, yet she focused her identity on providing in the home the freedom and personal fulfilment that were being lost in the larger public realm'.[35]

Gone too, in the post-war period, was the ingénue and even had O'Sullivan preferred career to motherhood, she would have needed to adapt her persona to a new type of role. Instead, she remained an icon of Irish Catholic motherhood; in 1947, after the release of *The Big Clock*, she received the annual St. Patrick's Day presentation from the *Catholic Film and Radio Review*, awarded to 'an actor and actress of Irish lineage, eminent in the profession, who have in their public and private lives manifested a devotion to Irish ideals as set forth in the Constitution of Eire'.[36] In fact, as I hope to have demonstrated, her legacy was a little more exotic than that.

NOTES

1   M. O'Sullivan, 'My Life in Hollywood', *Woman's Life*, 9 January 1937, pp. 5–6, p.6.
2   Ibid.
3   M. O'Sullivan, 'Maureen and John Farrow are separated by studio order!', *Woman's Life*, 6 February 1937, pp. 3–4.
4   L.O. Parsons, '"Princess and Plumber" merry film at Loew's', *Los Angeles Examiner*, 19 December 1930 (Maureen O'Sullivan file, AMPAS).
5   M. O'Sullivan, 'When I lost my job!' *Woman's Life*, 13 February, 1937, pp. 3–4. p. 4.
6   Review of *The Flame Within, Daily Variety*, 2 May 1935 (Maureen O'Sullivan file, AMPAS).
7   J.K. Newnham, 'Where's Maureen?', *Film Weekly*, 10 April 1937, p. 13.
8   See T. Doherty, *Pre-Code Hollywood, Sex, Immorality, and Insurrection in American Cinema, 1930–1934* (New York: Columbia University Press, 1999); J.F. Kasson, *Houdini, Tarzan and the Perfect Man* (New York: Hill & Wang, 2001); W. Morton, 'Tracking the Sign of Tarzan', in P. Kirkham and J. Thumin (eds), *You Tarzan, Masculinity, Movies and Men* (London: Lawrence & Wishart, 1993), pp. 106–25; and R. Dyer, *White* (London and New York: Routledge, 1997), pp. 145–83.
9   H.M. Glancy, *When Hollywood Loved Britain* (Manchester and New York; Manchester University Press, 1999). Glancy's book is subtitled *The Hollywood 'British' Film, 1939–45*. In fact his filmography includes films from 1929 to the 1950s. The phenomenon he describes, of Hollywood making British-themes and set films, is usually taken to run from the early 1930s to the end of the Second World War. S. Morley, *Tales From the Hollywood Raj* (London: Weidenfeld & Nicholson, 1983).
10 Morley, *Tales From the Hollywood Raj*, p. 6.
11 M. Troyan, *A Rose for Mrs. Miniver* (Kentucky: The University of Kentucky Press, 1999).
12 Morley, *Tales From the Hollywood Raj*, p. 139.
13 *The Screen* (August 1948), p. 2.
14 Doherty, *Pre-Code Hollywood*.
15 Kasson, *Houdini, Tarzan and the Perfect Man*, p. 184.
16 D. Cheatwood, 'The Tarzan Films: An Analysis of Determinants of Maintenance and Change in Conventions', in J. Staiger (ed.), *The Studio System* (New Brunswick, NJ: Rutgers University Press, 1995, first published 1982), pp. 163–83, p. 163.
17 F. Fanon, *Black Skins White Masks* (translated by Charles Lam Markmann) (London: Pluto Press, 1986), pp. 152–3n.
18 E. Shohat, 'Gender and culture of empire: toward a feminist ethnography of the cinema', in M. Bernstein and G. Studlar (eds), *Visions of the East* (London and New York: I.B. Tauris, 1997), pp. 19–66, p. 21.
19 Cheatwood, 'The Tarzan Films', p. 163.
20 G. Essoe, *Tarzan of the Movies* (Syracuse, NJ: Citadel Press, 1979).
21 R. Behlmer, 'Tarzan: Hollywood's greatest jungle hero', *American Cinematographer*, 68, 1 (January 1987), pp. 39–48, p. 39.
22 Story Conference on *Tarzan of the Apes*, 21 October, 1931, MGM Collection, USC.
23 Ibid., Bernie Hyman was supervisor (line producer) for MGM.
24 R. McGhee, '"There's something sad about retracing": Jane Parker in the "Tarzan" films of the thirties', *Kansas Quarterly*, 16, 3 (1984), pp. 101–23, p. 103.

25 Figures quoted in Glancy, *When Hollywood Loved Britain*, p. 70; script notes as above.
26 Behlmer, 'Tarzan: Hollywood's Greatest Jungle Hero', p. 47.
27 Doherty, *Pre-Code Hollywood,* p. 261.
28 H.K. Bhabha, 'The Other Question: The Stereotype and Colonial Discourse', in *The Sexual Subject: A* Screen *Reader in Sexuality* (London and New York: Routledge, 1992; first published 1983), pp. 312–31, p. 319.
29 Morton, 'Tracking the Sign of Tarzan', p. 116.
30 McGhee, '"There's Something Sad About Retracing"', p. 107.
31 E.R. Burroughs, *Tarzan of the Apes* (New York, Dover Publications 1997; first published 1914), p. 2.
32 Shohat, 'Gender and Culture of Empire', p. 48.
33 R. Behlmer, 'Tarzan and M-G-M: the rest of the story', *American Cinematographer*, 68, 2 (February 1987), pp. 34–44.
34 *The Screen* (May 1942) p. 19.
35 May, 'Making the American Consensus, p. 89.
36 *Paramount News*, 7 April 1947, Maureen O'Sullivan File, USC.

4

Maureen O'Hara

Pirate queen, feminist icon?
(1920 – ; film career: 1938–97)

For most moviegoers, the name Maureen O'Hara
is indelibly associated with sharp images of lush
Technicolor swashbucklers starring the fiery, redheaded, Irish-born actress. While a leading lady
who excels so nobly at this athletic genre may be
tremendously popular (as indeed Maureen
O'Hara has been), it is well-nigh impossible for
such a screen type to become a superstar.
J. Parish, The RKO Gals[1]

MAUREEN O'HARA'S screen career is shot through with contradictions. Her popular reputation, as James Parish reminds us
in the quotation above, rested on a series of roles in a genre that until
recently had fallen into obsolescence (the successful commercial
release of *Mask of Zorro* [Martin Campbell, USA, 1998], *The Man
in the Iron Mask* [Randall Wallace, GB, 1998] and *Pirates of the
Caribbean* [Gore Verbinski, USA, 2003], all starring high-profile
Hollywood actors, suggests that the swashbuckler may have
returned, if not to mass-market appeal, then at least to popular
consciousness). Although it might seem that the swashbuckler offers
useful opportunities for critical attention, particularly from the
perspective of feminist film studies, it remains remarkably under-
researched. Out of an oeuvre that numbers more than sixty films for
cinema and television, two of O'Hara's roles, in *Dance, Girl, Dance*
(Dorothy Arzner, USA, 1940) and *The Quiet Man*, have provided
feminist theorists with fruitful ground for discussion; yet neither her
persona nor her performance have to date generated the critical
interest awarded to other strong-willed female stars of her era. For
many critics and film historians, O'Hara's career is inseparable from
those of John Ford and John Wayne, where it often seemed that she
was little more than a foil for a series of narratives devoted to

exploring a damaged masculinity. Even in her late-life comeback in *Only the Lonely* (Chris Columbus, USA, 1991), O'Hara's dramatic function is to provide the impediment to her son, Danny's (John Candy), proper oedipal development.

Promoted by Hollywood as a feisty Irish colleen and characterised by Ford in his films alternately as a Southern belle and as an Irish peasant girl with a scolding tongue, O'Hara came from a middle-class, educated urban background that instilled in her from birth a sense of her own worth and groomed her for a career on the Abbey stage. She was, and remains, outspoken. Her memoirs, *'Tis Herself*, insist on her opposition to studio manipulation and exploitation.[2] In one instance, she refused to be termed British when applying for American citizenship, leading ultimately to Irish immigrants being officially classified as Irish and to a commendation from Eamon de Valera. In another, she brought the notoriously scurrilous *Confidential* magazine to court over a report that she had been engaging in obscene behaviour in a cinema, succeeded in winning her case and having the magazine closed down. Yet, in these memoirs she also details a history of abusive relationships; first wedding under pressure a man, George Hanley Brown, whom she barely knew, simply because he pressurised her into it; then, after her divorce, marrying Will Price, a chronic alcoholic and womaniser who struck her when she was pregnant with her only child, Bronwyn, and whose sexual leanings were ambiguous. Married to Price for over ten years, she also had a relationship that John Ford ended, and a relationship with Ford that, she suggests, was founded on his fantasies of her. Once she had scotched these, he sent her lewd letters and stymied her ambitions with other directors, as well as snooping around her home and interfering with other family matters, including her own brother Jimmy's fledgling acting career. That an individual with such strength of character should have tolerated all this seems, as reviews of her book have indicated, startling to contemporaries. Yet, it is perhaps better understood against a background of a studio system that, as we have seen in the case of George Brent, enjoyed complete control over its contract artists, and within a patriarchal society that fetishised the strong female while simultaneously working to undermine her.

Many of these contradictions are diegetically re-enacted throughout O'Hara's screen career, one that often reads like an endless reworking of *The Taming of the Shrew*. The actor is always at her most convincing when playing parts that require her to resist

the dominant male order, and at her least when succumbing to the
love of the good man who will reconcile her to that order. Events
outside the frame again leech into these narratives; dubbed 'frozen
champagne' by the studios for her on-camera love-making scenes,
her reluctance to yield to the sexual attractions of her would-be
suitors is thrown in her face in plots from Westerns to swashbucklers. Her patrician attitudes marked her out as a new Katherine
Hepburn (she reprised Hepburn's part in *A Bill of Divorcement*
[John Farrow, USA, 1940]), something that, as James Naremore's
analysis of Hepburn suggests, placed her at odds with the populist
ethos of the studio era.[3] O'Hara was, however, not American enough
for the parts that made Hepburn's reputation, or probably, it must
be said, a versatile enough performer. Nor could she enjoy the strong
vamp roles that other European actors among her contemporaries
were assigned in Hollywood. Like Maureen O'Sullivan before her,
O'Hara was frequently cast as a high-class foreigner, occasionally as
a high-class Irish woman.

So, just what was the basis of O'Hara's screen popularity and does
she lend herself to feminist recuperation? Part of the answer to the
first half of that question does little to help us with the second.
Maureen O'Hara was popular quite simply because she was
beautiful. She came into her own with the post-war explosion of
Technicolor, a process that showed off her vivid red hair and flashing
eyes to their best. As the queen of the swashbuckler, she wore a
succession of costumes that vied with each other for flamboyant
effect. The swirling gown she parades for her entrance in *The Black
Swan* (Henry King, USA, 1942) is complemented by a florid red rose
that occupies much of her bosom. In *Sinbad the Sailor* (Richard
Wallace, USA, 1945), her gold brocade two-piece allows for
titillating midriff exposure and her motivation for finding the secret
of Deribar in the same film is to make, in her character's words,
'Sheeba look like a frump'. Although often incongruous in the
Western, this embrace of spectacle was part of the appeal of the
fantasy genre and one that enabled it to reach out beyond the
conventional male audience for action cinema to the female viewer,
feeding the eye with exotic furnishings and utterly redundant
artefacts, from massive vases to satin drapes, scatter cushions and
filigreed balconies. Not only was this O'Hara's natural environment,
she was to be seen in the company of equally exotic men, who were
as much part of the spectacle as the baroque chandeliers. Jeffrey
Richards' quotation from Columbia Studios' publicity for *Rogues of*

Sherwood Forest (Gordon Douglas, USA, 1950) could, as he suggests, be applied to the genre as a whole:

> There are two good reasons why swashbuckling stories score. They are masculine filmgoers and feminine filmgoers! Men (or should it be boys of all ages) admire athletic prowess, the heroic quest and the rescue of the damsel in distress. Girls, too applaud these things, particularly if the hero is good looking – and they like the contrast between his fighting and romantic moods. Another reason girls enjoy watching such gallantry is because the hero's rugged torso is well-displayed, and many an uninhibited young lady has written to Columbia Pictures asking for a photograph of John Derek in *Rogues of Sherwood Forest* wearing skintight pants.[4]

In fact, O'Hara was as likely to rescue as to be rescued, only at the end of the narrative, as I shall be discussing in more detail below, being reined in by the requirements of convention. Her roles required of her a high degree of mobility, and attendant publicity emphasised that she carried out her own stunts herself. As she did in many of her films, O'Hara forced the camera to follow her, refusing to be pinned down.

With taglines such as 'he stormed a veiled beauty's boudoir... and made her love it!', it is difficult to make a case for O'Hara as feminist icon, yet there is that fleeting resistance, an ambivalence towards her male ravishers that suggests that all may not be as it seems.[5] It is from within this space, this caesura in the action, I will be arguing, that O'Hara extended her appeal beyond the putative male voyeur, master in the rape fantasy, to a more equivocal viewer. Alternatively, and primarily in the swashbucklers, there is the promise that marriage will not be the end of her character's adventures. When she melts into Prince Hassan's (Paul Christian) arms in the finale of *Bagdad* [sic] (Charles Lamont, USA, 1949), is she opting for a lifetime of security and domestic bliss? Surely she will live out her days gallivanting around the desert with a man who shares her pleasures, just as she will enjoy a life of piracy with her lover, Jamie Waring (Tyrone Power), after the credits have rolled in *The Black Swan*.

There is a consistency in O'Hara's roles, from *Jamaica Inn* (Alfred Hitchcock, GB, 1939) to her final films, a display of character that evoked differing responses from the largely male posse of directors with whom she worked. John Ford may usually be credited with creating O'Hara's image, yet this mode of characterisation was in place from the beginning of her career, suggesting that the cultivation of the O'Hara persona was not strictly an auteurist intervention but drew on an interplay between popular cultural expectations, the actor's own interpretation of her roles and the manipulation of both of these by a succession of directors and producers. O'Hara's strength of character was bound up with a discourse on Irish femininity that informed many of her parts, sometimes overtly, often through attendant studio publicity; it was reinforced by that visual signifier of Irishness, feistiness and exoticism – her red hair.[6] This as we shall see was an inheritance that was as problematic as it was useful, particularly when taken in conjunction with Hollywood's own ambiguities over class, race and gender. By looking more closely at certain of O'Hara's key films, we can see how her screen identity was circumscribed by her national identity.

Maureen O'Hara's first starring role, as Mary Yellan in *Jamaica Inn*, established much of the persona, and many of the contradictions, that were to accompany her screen career. By all accounts a throwaway production, Hitchcock's final British film seems to have suffered from a surfeit of *auteurs*. Initiated by Charles Laughton under the banner of his and Eric Pommer's Mayflower Films and adapted from Daphne du Maurier's original story by Sidney Gilliat and Joan Harrison, with additional dialogue by J.B. Priestley, the finished product lurched from regency melodrama to gothic terror acted out against a background of creaky, expressionist-influenced studio sets.[7] The adaptation plays fast and loose with the original, retaining a few key figures, some events and the overall gothic mood. In order not to offend the middle-brow audiences for whom this film was intended, Pengallan's occupation in *Jamaica Inn* had been altered from parson, as it is in the novel, to squire. Laughton apparently found it hard to adjust to this change and initially would not go before the cameras so that the film had to be shot around him. Eventually he found his way into the part but long after Hitchcock had lost interest in the project.[8]

It was Laughton who cast O'Hara as Mary, the recently orphaned young Irish woman (in the novel she is English), who has come to live in the Jamaica Inn with Joss Merlyn (Leslie Banks) and his wife, her Aunt Patience (Marie Ney). Laughton was also responsible for changing his protégée's surname from FitzSimons to O'Hara and is depicted by O'Hara in her autobiography as a benevolent father figure. In this and in their second film together, *The Hunchback of Notre Dame* (William Dieterle, USA, 1939), this benevolence is tinged with a grotesquerie that insinuates its way through Laughton's performance and is expressed in a kind of leering sexual longing. Laughton's biographer, Simon Callow, also interprets their relationship as filial, as he does Laughton's friendship with Maureen O'Sullivan. Yet, in *This Land is Mine* (Jean Renoir, USA, 1943), Laughton again played a repressed personality, here the village schoolteacher, hopelessly in love with a colleague, played by O'Hara (with Una O'Connor as his smothering mother); this curious mentor/protégée relationship was also to mark O'Hara's work with John Ford, a liaison conducted, however, on more sinister terms.

Laughton is the centrepiece of the film and his role recalls his portrayal of Henry VIII in the earlier *The Private Life of Henry VIII*. In this instance, however, his lip-twitching, eye-rolling gesticulations locate his Squire Pengallan within an older acting style, what Roberta Pearson defines as the 'histrionic code'. This is 'reflexive, referring always to the theatrical event rather than to the outside world... Audiences and critics condemned as inadequate those who did not demonstrably act: the pleasure derived not from participating in an illusion but from witnessing a virtuoso performance.'[9] Laughton, of course, had at his disposal newer tools – the mobile camera and the close-up – that emphasised that performance. Tight facial close-ups are widely dispersed through the film, momentarily freezing the action to produce something akin to a rogues' gallery of portraits.

The other performances in the film belong by and large to Pearson's 'verisimilar code', the more conventional realist style of acting that was now associated with mainstream cinema.[10] Maureen O'Hara plays Mary Yellan in this style, displaying here a lissomness of movement that accompanied her through her screen career and militated against the camera's drive to constrain her. We can see this right from her first appearance in *Jamaica Inn*. An introductory sequence establishes Laughton's position and character, with Pengallan holding forth on the theme of beauty to his assembled dinner guests. The squire's toast to beauty is accompanied by his fetishistic handling of a porcelain figurine. Beauty, he ruminates, is dead and only lives on in his horse, his 'exquisite Nancy', which is duly led into the dining hall by a manservant. The action cuts to the coach and horses riding through the moor at night, bearing a full cargo of passengers. The first shot of O'Hara is of her face framed by dark curls, a bonnet and the cinema screen. Her expression is of childlike wholesomeness and innocence, her skin gleaming white against the dark, gothic background of the exterior set and the interior of the coach. This very tight shot is held for a couple of seconds, encouraging the audience's gaze to linger on and hold O'Hara/Mary Yellan within the frame. The shot is repeated when Squire Pengallan first sees Mary Yellan after she has appeared in the hall of the manor. On the announcement of her arrival, Pengallan wagers Ringwood (A. Bromley Davenport) that she will be ugly. Hearing the squire's voice, she turns and again her face fills the screen.

On seeing the young woman, Pengallan exclaims: 'My dear, you're a beauty!' and tosses a purse of coins to Ringwood. He then slowly circles her, unwrapping her cloak as he moves while quoting the poetry of Byron. This scene is only outdone by a later one where Pengallan, now completely deranged, binds and gags Mary before carrying her off to the ship in which he will escape to St Malo.

Figure 4.1 Apparently trapped in the frame. Maureen O'Hara in *Jamaica Inn*

On each of these three occasions, where O'Hara is apparently trapped in the frame, she seems a perfect exemplar of Laura Mulvey's classic analysis of the objectification of the female within mainstream narrative cinema.[11] Moreover, although not an icy blonde, she conforms to a Hitchcockian type, a strong woman who is the target of the director's, as Mulvey argues, sadistic voyeurism. On each of these three occasions, also, O'Hara as Mary Yellan breaks the hold of the frame, rupturing that moment of intense contemplation to assert her own will. She lashes out (verbally) at the coach driver for not stopping at Jamaica Inn; in her first encounter with Pengallan, she demands a horse to take her to her aunt's home and, finally, on board ship, knowing that he is insane, she prevents the military from shooting the squire.

O'Hara's role in *Jamaica Inn* alternates between moments of narrative dominance and disadvantage. After the scene in the squire's manor, Mary and Pengallan ride together to Jamaica Inn, where Mary will rescue Trehearne (Robert Newton), a secret agent disguised as a bandit, from death by hanging, be rescued in turn by him after she allows their escape boat to become unmoored during a spat, save Joss and Patience from the police, be captured (again), save a ship from wrecking, be kidnapped by Pengallan, witness the deaths of Joss, Patience and finally Pengallan's plunge to his own end, before, it is suggested, being romantically paired with Trehearne at the narrative's end. This less than convincing denouement is completely overshadowed by the hysterical energies of the previous scenes with Laughton.

Over and again, O'Hara holds and returns the gaze, refusing to be controlled by the male who presumes to own her or the camera that attempts to objectify her.[12] She carries off her role of helpless orphan with a hauteur that defies conventional representations of young Irish women, particularly on the British screen. The dangers of allowing desiring Irish women to penetrate the British imaginary are spelled out quite differently in later films such as *Daughter of Darkness* (Lance Comfort, GB, 1948). Here Siobhan McKenna plays Irish peasant, Emmy Baudine, as a kind of banshee who kills or maims those who pursue her sexually. Another instance of the Irish gothic invading the English pastoral is hinted at in Deborah Kerr's portrayal of Bridie Quilty in *I See A Dark Stranger* (Frank Launder, GB, 1946) although the film soon settles into explaining Bridie's subversiveness as that of a misguided but otherwise charming country girl who is rescued from an embryonic career as Nazi spy by Trevor Howard's Lieutenant David Baynes. Both productions bring their central female character from the Irish countryside to rural England. In Comfort's film this encounter culminates in a denouement that sees a crazed Emmy dementedly playing the church organ as the night-time storm rages around her while in Launder's, Bridie is redeemed by and re-educated in patriotism by Baynes. Both are British films with an investment in triangulating Irishness, femininity and hysteria. In *Jamaica Inn*, by contrast, it is the pillar of the British establishment, Squire Pengallan, who embodies the Gothic's suspicion of the rational. Laughton's descent into madness is also an abandonment of his masculinity, already signalled as problematic via his fetishisation of the porcelain figurine. O'Hara's repudiation of the role of hysteric, on the other hand, and her obvious assurance foreshadow many of her later roles.

For audiences familiar with the nuances of Irish accent, O'Hara was clearly no simple Irish peasant and her voice is a marker of her own comfortably-off, middle-class background. Only in *The Quiet Man* and later in *The Long Gray Line* (John Ford, USA, 1954) did she adopt the kind of stage-Irish rural accent that was part of the screen's inheritance from the Abbey actors and of a wider cultural stereotyping of Irish identity.

The critical success of *Jamaica Inn* encouraged Laughton and Pommer to decamp to America, taking their protégée with them. The Hollywood of 1939 into which O'Hara arrived was one that was certainly accustomed to seeing women playing dominant roles, such as those commandeered by Bette Davis at Warner Bros. It was a cinema, as we have seen, on the cusp of change, newly committed to a politics of ethnic assimilation and wartime inclusiveness. From now on, women were to dedicate themselves equally to the national cause and to home life.

Only after the war did O'Hara manage to secure the kind of strong parts for which she was most evidently suited, yet, as I suggested above, she has never quite been accepted into the pantheon of female stars – Joan Crawford, Rita Hayworth, Bette Davis – who symbolise a proto-feminist resistance to the patriarchal structure of Hollywood narratives. Like the heroines of the *film noir* and melodrama, O'Hara's roles beg to be analysed for their strengths rather than their weaknesses, for the force of her resistance to the dominant order, rather than for her eventual capitulation to it. That this has not happened may be ascribed in part to critical neglect of the swashbuckler, the genre in which O'Hara shone. It also certainly is a consequence of the whiff of conservatism that O'Hara's persona trailed behind her. Her public refusal to drink or, as Parish puts it, 'pose for sexy cheesecake' and her rather glacial beauty all hinted at a refusal to embrace the supposedly democratic values of Hollywood and beyond it, America.[13]

O'Hara's patrician demeanour may have carried the day in *Jamaica Inn*, but throughout her Hollywood career it evoked two overriding responses. Both are evident in *Dance, Girl, Dance*, where O'Hara is invited to embrace an earthier ethnicity and to succumb to a man whom she realises is her 'better'. The latter may often (*Rio Grande* [John Ford, USA, 1950], *The Rare Breed* [Andrew McLaglen, USA, 1965]) come from a less privileged social background so that union with him also represents the rejection of her own upper-class inhibitions. A closer look at *Dance, Girl, Dance*, will allow us to see some of these forces at play and how they intersect with existing feminist readings of Arzner's film. We need first to recognise that *Dance, Girl, Dance*, important as it is to feminist film history, was a minor release in the totality of O'Hara's screen career and a loss-maker for its studio. As the *New York Times* warned its readers, '"Dance, Girl, Dance" is just a cliché-ridden, garbled repetition of the story of the aches and pains in a dancer's rise to fame and fortune, it isn't art.'[14] A reworking of the RKO backstage musical/woman's film produced by Eric Pommer, it was already cast before Dorothy Arzner was appointed director. She came in to replace Roy Del Ruth who had fallen out with Pommer over the direction of the film. Demanding that every sequence Del Ruth had filmed be reshot, Arzner 'moved it away from Del Ruth's love-triangle focus and approached the story as a deep exploration of strong-willed, independent women'.[15] The extent of Arzner's influence on the film is questioned by Pommer's biographer, Ursula Hardt, who reminds us both of O'Hara's assertion that 'I owe my whole career to Mr. Pommer', and that Pommer, like many producers of his day, exerted considerable creative control over his films.[16]

The key sequence for most writers on the film is the one in which O'Hara as Judy faces down the spectators who have been jeering her on-stage performance. As part of her double act with Bubbles (Lucille Ball), Judy has to perform a stilted ballet number in front of an audience who cheerfully boos her and demands the return of the burlesque artiste, Bubbles.[17] Flouncing to the front of the stage, Judy addresses the spectators directly, challenging their voyeurism: 'I know you want me to tear my clothes off so you can look your fifty cents worth. Fifty cents for the privilege of staring at a girl the way your wives won't let you. What do you suppose we think of you up here with your silly smirks your mothers would be ashamed of?'

As Karyn Kay and Gerald Peary put it: 'This utterly remarkable and abnormal speech is not only a phenomenon coming forth from Judy, but without parallel in the whole history of cinema.'[18] The speech is indeed remarkable and abnormal, partly because it is so unexpected. Up until this point the film has focused on the rivalry and friendship between Judy, the classical ballerina, and Bubbles, the gold-digging burlesque queen. This is indeed the driving force, as O'Hara has remarked, of the narrative although the film also retains the shadow of its original structure, its love-triangle intrigue. That formula – two women competing for career opportunities and a lover against a showbiz background – was a Hollywood staple, to be milked for all its misogynistic potential in Joseph Mankiewicz's *All About Eve* (USA, 1950).

Although *Dance, Girl, Dance* is a key text in feminist film criticism, little if no attention has been paid to the significance of O'Hara's casting in the lead role of Judy. We may assume that this was Pommer's decision and that it was motivated by her recent appearances in *Jamaica Inn* and *The Hunchback of Notre Dame*, both of which he also produced. The film was made at a time when O'Hara, along with Pommer, were themselves discovering Hollywood's antipathy to 'classy' acting and producing, when its storywriter, Austrian exile, Vicki Baum, widely regarded as a reliable and successful author of literary potboilers, was struggling to have her 'serious' writing recognised and when its director was fighting for her space in Hollywood's male-dominated environment.[19] A further biographical detail certainly adds a layer of authenticity to O'Hara's performance – shortly before this collaboration with Pommer, she found herself sold to RKO by him and Laughton as Mayflower Films was insolvent. RKO in turn part-sold her on to Twentieth Century-Fox to alleviate their financial difficulties, thus enabling Ford to cast her in *How Green Was My Valley* (John Ford, USA, 1941). One of the themes of *Dance, Girl, Dance* is an exploration of a woman's career ambitions in an environment – showbiz – where men call the shots.

O'Hara's personality, the film makes it clear, is explained by two factors– she is classy and she is Irish. These elements are brought to our attention from the opening of the film. For a start, there is a notable contrast between O'Hara's and Ball's accents, the former has a deeper, more measured, slightly plummy voice, the latter has a brassy New York accent and spits out her words. They also deliver contrasting performances – Judy is reserved; Ball expresses herself through winks and pouts, as well as a Monroe-like wiggle of her hips. O'Hara is dark, Ball blonde. In their first encounter, Jimmy (Louis Hayward), the millionaire whom she and Bubbles will fall out over, picks up on Judy's difference:

'You've got a funny face, I mean, this is a funny place for your face.'
'Seemed a grand enough place when we landed it.'
'Irish?'
'Once removed.'
'You know, you look like a star...'

Shortly afterwards, the troupe is performing a Caribbean dance to an impresario. In Bubbles' absence, Judy is lead dancer and moves with that slightly abstracted, inward-looking smile that marks her public performances as well as her private ballet practice. The impresario is not convinced. She is, he pronounces, 'too classy'. Suddenly Bubbles arrives and repeats the dance movement, inflecting it with a voluptuousness that is achieved through a series of knowing winks to the viewer and includes slapping herself on the rump as she bends forward. The man is instantly won over.

Within the film's discourse, being Irish is one thing, classy another and Judy's brand of Irishness is unacceptable. As Judith Mayne, in her auteurist study of Arzner describes it, '"class" for Arzner's heroines is always simultaneously a function of social class and sexuality'.[20] Close to the finale, the protagonists (Judy, Bubbles and the ballet company owner, Steve [Ralph Bellamy] who has been watching Judy's performance at Bailey Brothers' Show) wind up at the night court after Judy has physically laid into Bubbles for stealing Jimmy. The judge's line of questioning consists of asking Judy: 'Now about this temper of yours. You are Irish, aren't you?' 'Well,' Judy replies, 'I have a habit of simmering your honour, but I usually keep myself from boiling over.' However, it is just by boiling over that Judy is signalled as having fully achieved her potential – by accessing a more earthy and temperamental Irishness, she is no longer encumbered by being classy. This further paves the way for her speech from the dock, in which she reunites Jimmy with his estranged wife, Elinor (Virginia Field), and in so doing clears the way for a reopening of her friendship with Bubbles. The film concludes with two jarring sequences. As Judy leaves the courtroom insisting on going to prison rather than have her fine paid for her, an African-American couple, Abraham Lincoln Johnson and Martha

Lincoln Johnson (neither actor is credited) are led in. As an absolutely unmotivated moment, it raises a number of suggestions. Have they been engaged in the kind of domestic row that might also describe Judy and Bubbles' fight and, so, are Judy and Bubbles the true couple of the film? Can we connect the stereotype of the impulsive black couple with the impulsive Irish woman and her working-class 'partner'? And finally, the film ends with a gratingly artificial love scene, and one much discussed within feminist film criticism, between Judy and Steve.[21] Abandoning her independence, Judy falls into Steve's arms as he admonishes her: 'Now, listen to me you silly child... You've had your own way long enough.' Apparently agreeing that he is quite right, Judy allows herself to be clasped by him but, as the camera pulls away from the couple, we see her look not into his eyes but away from him, almost into the lens' sightlines, as if imploring the viewer for help.

As Bergstrom acknowledges, counter-readings of *Dance, Girl, Dance* (and here we may include Mayne's subsequent re-reading of Arzner's work as 'closet lesbian') may well clash with dominant, mainstream reception of that work.[22] Certainly O'Hara does not suggest for a moment in her biography that the film bears any lesbian subtext. This should not, however, deter the writer from venturing alternative viewing positions and I hope here to have augmented these by reinscribing star biography and ethnicity into the critical analysis of *Dance, Girl, Dance*. By abandoning her classiness in favour of a more spontaneous ethnicity, is Judy not cementing her bond with Bubbles? She may well marry the unwaveringly patriarchal Steve, but can she not also continue to have fun with her old friend?

Dance, Girl, Dance offers a hint of the kind of roles that O'Hara's fame rests on. Although she moved between numerous genres, she was, as we have already mentioned, at her most popular when playing the pirate queen or similar swashbuckling parts.[23] As the female lead in a series of Westerns, O'Hara is disappointing. Cast, we may adduce, more for the colour she brings to an otherwise somewhat monochrome background, few directors allowed her the opportunity to flash her eyes and challenge all comers. Occasionally, as in *The Redhead from Wyoming* (Lee Sholem, USA, 1953) some attempt is made to characterise O'Hara as an active participant in the narrative. In Sholem's film she plays Kate Maxwell, a salon keeper who is also an adept horsewoman and cattle rustler. However, the actor is evidently unhappy in a role that requires her to be sexually alluring and morally ambiguous; she is just too decorous to be another Marlene Dietrich (in the almost contemporaneous *Rancho Notorious* [Fritz Lang, USA, 1952]) and overall the films seem to be an opportunistic attempt to transfer O'Hara's swashbuckling persona to the Western.

Maureen O'Hara's fame as pirate queen was established in her first outing with Tyrone Power, *The Black Swan*. She followed this with similar roles in *The Spanish Main* (Frank Borzage, USA, 1945), *Sinbad the Sailor, Bagdad, Tripoli* (Will Price, USA, 1950), *At Sword's Point* (Lewis Allen, USA, 1952), *Flame of Araby* (Charles Lamont, USA, 1952) and *Against All Flags* (George Sherman, USA, 1952). Any analysis of these films must first acknowledge that they reify every sin of Orientalism in the book. They exhibit a will to control and create representations of a manifestly different world that exists, as Said has lucidly argued, in an uneven power relationship with Western, particularly American–European culture.[24] They assume that this world cannot represent itself and they reinforce accumulating stereotypes of the 'mysterious Orient'. They create an imaginative geography of regions that do not exist in real time but in some kind of perpetual present in the past; they infantilise and exoticise native characters, regarding them with equal measures of fear and desire. That they are evidently fantasies should not entirely excuse them.

O'Hara's first films were released contiguously with Universal Studios' cycle of John Hall/Maria Montez films from 1942–5, although O'Hara's screen persona contrasts with that of Maria Montez in a number of ways, primarily as a consequence of her greater agency and physicality. O'Hara, of course, was also unmistakeably white, unlike Montez who was Spanish. Throughout her career, O'Hara played a range of roles that required her to pass as 'other'. In *The Hunchback of Notre Dame*, she was Esmeralda the gypsy, in *They Met in Argentina* (Leslie Goodwins, Jack Hively, USA, 1941), she was half-Irish, half-Argentinian Lolita O'Shea; in the swashbucklers, she regularly played non-Caucasian parts, including Contessa Francesca in *The Spanish Main*, Shireen in *Sinbad the Sailor*, Princess Marjan in *Bagdad* and Princess Tanya in *Flame of Araby*. As these titles indicate, O'Hara was most often cast as an upper-class character or member of the royalty.

We cannot know exactly why this should have occurred, but we may surmise that there were a number of related grounds for this practice. The first was fear of miscegenation, which we have seen influenced the casting of Maureen O'Sullivan in the Tarzan films. At a deeper, symbolic level, the Production Code drew on a history of representation that portrayed the East as feminine territory, ripe for invasion/rape by the conquering male power. Further, the costuming of oriental women, whether veiled or scantily clad, with their promise of nakedness/cover, threatened to lure on the adventurer in the man. The practice of casting a white actor as the oriental female allowed for an element of disavowal to enter this potent ethnic collision, with viewers invited to (mis) recognise the exotic princess' origins.

In her article, 'Out-Salomeing Salome', Gaylyn Studlar discusses the appeal to a female spectatorship of Orientalism in films of the 1920s. Acknowledging that consumerism was a significant motivating force behind Hollywood's inter-war cycle of orientalist fantasies, she proposes that dance functioned as a specific opportunity for the expression of modernity and mobility and in a manner that appealed directly to the New Woman of the day. 'In dance', she argues, 'those qualities of the New Woman often at odds with cultural norms of traditional femininity became attached to sensual ritualized movement and to the spectacle of orientalized identities associated with ambiguous feminine power.'[25] Dance, she notes, was culturally sanctioned as an appropriate female activity and as such, 'stood as an ideal symbolic merger between traditional middle-class female gentility and contemporary ideals of feminine freedom from bodily and imaginative restraints'.[26] Dance also hinted at a transgression of social and gender constraints that found its apotheosis in the figure of the vamp, the Salome of the article's title, onto whom the anxieties of the period could be conveniently displaced.

Moving forward in time to the O'Hara swashbucklers, we may see many of the same issues at play, this time militated by references to O'Hara's Irish-Catholic background: 'She is her own Hays office. She balked at taking a bath in a tub for a movie scene because "my folks in Dublin would think I had turned out all bad". She has kept a strict promise to her mother never to pose for leg art. She is strict about the negligees she wears for the movies.'[27]

Articles accompanying the release of *Sinbad The Sailor* danced a tightrope between titillation and moral rectitude; the *Hollywood Citizen News* turned to RKO's technical advisor on the production, Dr Paul Singh from Punjab Province, India, to advise their female readers on the lessons they might learn from the film's style, one which reminded them of the 1945 'diaper drape':

'Women should never, never walk around completely undressed in front of their husbands,' Dr. Singh declared. 'That's the quickest way in the world to lose him. He'll look for somebody who keeps part of her figure in mystery.'

He eyed luscious Maureen O'Hara, whose curves were poured into a lowcut gold brocade bra and clinging silk pantaloons. As the princess in 'Sinbad', which takes place in 800 A.D., she wasn't wearing much.

'But enough,' Dr. Singh added hastily, 'Just enough to be tantalizing. Much more so than a woman who parades around completely undressed.'[28]

Joseph Breen was less convinced. After reading a report in the *Herald Express* (of 4 February 1946) that reported that 'Maureen O'Hara's wardrobe for *Sinbad the Sailor* will make her costume in *The Spanish Main* seem Puritanical', he swiftly wrote to RKO. 'You will recall the difficulty we had with the costumes of this same lady in your production, *The Spanish Main*. I hope that our experience with that picture will not be repeated.'[29]

I would like to argue that Maureen O'Hara traversed the binaries of West/East, active/passive, masculine/feminine in a manner that was ultimately containable within a discourse committed to upholding those very binaries. In film after film, she participated in a masquerade of gender and ethnic identities that opened up a space for female as much as male viewing pleasure. Moreover, she was romantically paired with exotic lovers who were more often feminised than masterly and whose revolt against the patriarchal despot she shared. Think of the teaming of O'Hara with Tyrone Power in *The Black Swan*; both (she as the daughter of Lord Denby [George Zucco], deposed governor of Jamaica; he as the tool of Captain Morgan's [Laird Cregar] political manoeuvrings) are rebels in a system of power that offers them either staid conformity or reckless adventuring. Here, the female viewer is invited not just to wonder at the costumes, the sumptuousness of the mise-en-scène and the naked male torsos but to partake vicariously in the heroine's display of athletic prowess. O'Hara does not just dance (and sing), she rides horseback, initiates kidnappings, fences and slaps men who displease her in the face. In *The Black Swan*, she appears to swoon under Waring's insistent attentions, only to clock him over the head with a stone when he leans forward to kiss her. Verging on the dominatrix, she is inevitably brought to heel by the film's ending and subjected to a token punishment for her transgressions, before being rewarded with a man with whom she can ride off to greater adventures. In *Bagdad*, O'Hara's Princess Marjan arrives in the palace of the Pasha Ali Nadim (Vincent Price) to avenge her father's death at the hands of the Black Robes, led, she believes, by Prince Hassan (Paul Christian). The latter displays a languid, cosmopolitan masculinity and speaks in an accent that the English-educated Princess mistakes for French but is revealed to be Viennese. In an almost indecipherable plot, Princess Marjan, accompanied by her loyal servant, Mohammed Jad (Jeff Corey), discovers that the Pasha is in league with her father's assassins and gallops off after the Black Robes. Disguised as a gypsy, she attempts to put a spoke in the Pasha's plan for domination of the Arab world. Before she can pull this off, she is unmasked and her accomplices brutally tortured in front of her eyes. Only the last moment intervention of Hassan saves her from a lingering death at the stake and provides for their happy union. *At Sword's Point* saw her masquerade briefly as male; the script makes it clear that much of the audience's pleasure will be invested in O'Hara's costumes:

> Claire, daughter of Athos, a beautiful young woman, fresh, alive and quite skillful [*sic*] with the rapier. She is dressed in a form-fitting fencing outfit, which shows off her form as a woman. Now with a final parry and thrust directed with magical dexterity and a wrist of steel for all its slimness, she holds the point of her sword against the instructor's heart.[30]

Figure 4.2 The pleasures of cross-dressing. Maureen O'Hara in
At Sword's Point

Rescuing Maureen O'Hara for feminism is, as has already been noted, problematic, particularly when her popular fame is derived from a genre known within the studios as 'tits and sand' films. Yet that should not dissuade us from taking a positive approach to these roles; certainly the films challenge the assumption in, say, Yvonne Tasker's scholarship that the female action hero did not exist before the rise of 1970s feminism.[31] From her earliest star appearance, O'Hara challenged the active/male, passive/female binary, one that following Mulvey is inscribed in psychoanalytically based feminist criticism of the 1970s and 1980s.[32] The defeatist conclusions of these theorists – that woman is either absent or punished by the mechanics of classic narrative looking practices, and that the female viewer, where imaginable, can only be theorised via a masochist insertion into the text or through cross-gender identification – has since given way to a strand of recuperative historicism that seeks out female-friendly practitioners within Hollywood's history and has spent time on attempting to reconstruct, through publicity and fan journalism, such films' address to, and reception by, women spectators.

The latter process must remain aware that the Hollywood studio system was as patriarchal as the society in which it operated and that recuperation has to be balanced with recognition of that system's limitations. O'Hara's dominatrix-like qualities evidently appealed to the unreconstructed male in the audience; she is presented as a spectacle to be consumed by the masculinised eye and a commodity to be owned at the films' endings. Yet her strength of character and freedom of movement, her control of the films' narratives certainly offered many pleasures to the female or feminine spectator. Again, the knowledge that this exotic princess was really 'one of our own', a white woman who was also a wife and mother and who 'by some curious chemistry of the screen, remains delightfully within arm's reach' allowed for a fantasy of self and other, for a vicarious participation in the heroine's escapades that were marked from the outset as safely unreal.[33]

Turning to Maureen O'Hara's films with John Ford, we can see how that director exploited O'Hara's on- and off-screen reputation for challenging social restrictions, in the process insisting that her rebellion take place from within the domestic space. In film after film, Ford asserts that O'Hara's place is within the home and that it is from this environment that she draws her strength: 'I'll be queen in my own kitchen!' she pronounces in *How Green Was My Valley*, and that remains her stance and her favoured pose – hands on her hips, shoulders back, challenging the male who threatens her territorial supremacy – in their subsequent films. O'Hara appeared in five films for Ford: *How Green Was My Valley, Rio Grande, The Quiet Man, The Long Gray Line* and *The Wings of Eagles* (USA, 1957). In all but the first of these, O'Hara plays Irish characters and there is much in *How Green* that recalls the classic Irish emigration narrative, including the casting of Sara Allgood as the suffering, good-hearted mother, a familiar role for her and one she plays with a distinct Irish accent, despite her character being Welsh. Ford famously did not explain his films or acknowledge their subtexts but his status as auteur has sanctioned critical readings of his works that draw on biographical detail to interpret fictional narratives. Much of this writing concerns Ford's off-screen relationship with his best-known leads, John Wayne and Maureen O'Hara, and dwells on Ford's manipulative treatment of these two actors.[34] Regularly used actors were his 'family', with Ford as the all-knowing, all-controlling *pater familias*. O'Hara in her autobiography enumerates a litany of occasions when Ford trespassed on her privacy, paid her back for perceived slights by blocking her own or her family's career opportunities while also writing her cloying love letters. She also claims that she found him *in flagrante* with an unnamed man when visiting his studio offices. Her roles in his films reflect this apparent concupiscence, establishing her as a free spirit and object of desire before suggesting that today's beauty is tomorrow's shrew.

The Quiet Man is the consummate Ford–Wayne–O'Hara film and contains the essence of all O'Hara's roles with Ford. It is also the most widely discussed of Ford's 'Irish' films and is central, as we have seen in Chapter 1, to the academic analysis of Ireland on screen. Most controversial for its characterisation of Mary-Kate Danaher (O'Hara) as the 'feisty colleen' who abandons her fire at the story's end to settle down with the quiet man of the title, and for the scene when Sean Thornton (John Wayne) drags her home across the fields from the train, to be handed, in the words of its donor, 'a good stick to beat the lovely lady', it is the second of O'Hara's roles to gain critical praise for its gender representation. Janey Place argues that Mary-Kate's insistence on getting her hands on her dowry before she will consummate her marriage with Thornton is an assertion of her 'independence and her need for identity' and that by destroying the money after Sean has fought her brother for it, she establishes her own equality within the marriage.[35] Brandon French praises Ford's liberated sexual politics, noting that Thornton does not rape Mary-Kate as did Rhett Butler Scarlett O'Hara but that they meet as adults and equals. Their relationship, she argues, 'anticipated the sixties by eschewing war in favor of love and by showing that liberation must be a goal of both sexes if they wish to live together in true harmony'.[36] Most critics read the dragging sequence as stage-managed by Mary-Kate with the connivance of Sean Thornton.

Much of the discussion summarised above takes place at the level of textual analysis and through the prism of narrative. We can add depth to it by paying attention to Maureen O'Hara's performance of Mary-Kate, bearing in mind the history of performance and casting referred to throughout this chapter. O'Hara states that she worked on the film's script over several years with John Ford, and that her character was named Mary-Kate not, as is generally assumed, after the two women Ford loved most in his life, herself and Katherine Hepburn, but after her alone, and that her nemesis in the film, her brother Red Will, was named after her own errant husband, Will Price.[37] *The Quiet Man* integrates into its characterisation of Mary-Kate elements of O'Hara's presence in Ford's films and in other works where, as we have seen, her strength of character was most frequently articulated through her mobility – be it dancing, horseback riding or sword fighting. This expressive mobility is evident throughout *The Quiet Man*, where O'Hara is seldom glimpsed in repose. At mealtime, she flounces around her family kitchen dishing out potatoes and scolding her brother and the other men, all of whom are seated at a lower level to her. She almost dances around Wayne, who looks particularly solid, and she flits around her own house, when they move into it, refusing the conventional pose of the Irish woman seated at the hearth. As ever, this allows her to assert her dominance over the camera, and by extension the narrative. There is something overtly performative about Mary-Kate here, a way of moving that almost seems choreographed, and offers a further layering of the 'constructedness' of Ford's vision of Ireland that is also evident in Barry Fitzgerald's Michaeleen Óg Flynn. A further indicator of the theatricality of Ford's film is O'Hara's accent. The director himself draws our attention to *The Quiet Man*'s staginess when the actors pose before the camera at the end. Long before that, however, we are alerted to this trope by O'Hara's adoption of a stage-Irish accent for her role. Having played Mary Yellan with naturalistic middle-class Dublin tones, O'Hara now endows Mary-Kate Danaher with a concocted rural intonation that is indigenous to nowhere other than the stage. Evidently pleased with the effect, director and star reprise this performative Irishness in *The Long Gray Line* where O'Hara plays Mary O'Donnell as an extension of her Mary-Kate Danaher persona.

Maureen O'Hara's abandonment of naturalism for performativity allowed her to position herself within that history of a staged ethnicity already discussed in relation to Barry Fitzgerald and in the 'Introduction'. What her acting lost in authenticity, particularly for audiences 'at home', it gained in cultural currency. At the same time, this ethnicity is narrativised in a manner that distinguishes it from the more anarchic norms of early ethnic vaudeville; and with that narrativisation comes a greater threat of patriarchal control; hence, Ford's positioning of O'Hara within domestic situations, and his star's resistance to that positioning.

At the centre of the film is O'Hara's relationship with Wayne, one that allows for an unexpectedly erotic charge. Longtime friends off-screen, their performance in *The Quiet Man* is filled with longing. Again, as before, O'Hara holds and plays to Wayne's gaze; as early as the first occasion that Sean Thornton sees the flame-haired colleen herding her sheep and exclaims 'Is that real. She couldn't be!', O'Hara turns and looks back and upwards at him; at once refusing to be positioned as object, but also hinting at what will be the film's defining motif, a readiness to submit to him. Slapping Wayne in the face when he dares to kiss her in the windswept cottage, O'Hara is once more the pirate queen, taunting the viewer and Thornton with her dominatrix-like allure. Their relationship continues to be defined by a level of physicality and pleasure in pain that is highly provocative. The conventions of Irish rural society that keep the couple apart, the issue of Mary-Kate's dowry, are narrative devices as much as ideological flashpoints, a tease to delay the final moment of consummation. Arguably, this occurs long before the film's ending – in the graveyard sequence. Escaping the village with its subtle policing of social morality, Mary-Kate and Sean Thornton take refuge from the storm in a setting defined by its Gothic mise-en-scène; the darkening skies give away to a thunderstorm, Thornton clasps Mary-Kate and Ford drenches Wayne's white shirt so that it clings to his body. He and she kiss passionately and this time, when she pulls back from him, she does not slap his face, but throws herself once more against him, before finally they fall back in post-coital release. Dominance and submission are the game these lovers play, right to the film's ending when Mary-Kate apparently willingly allows herself to be 'manfully' summoned by a drunken Thornton to attend to his dinner. Frozen champagne no more, this is the film that encourages O'Hara to express the pleasures as well as the contradictions of power and powerlessness.

By 1991 and her return to the screen after twenty years absence in *Only the Lonely*, O'Hara's Irishness and her screen history define her diegetic character. Columbus has stated that he wrote the part with O'Hara in mind, imagining what her life might have been like if Mary-Kate Danaher had had one son and gone to live in Chicago.[38] By the time the film opens, her husband has died and O'Hara as Rose Muldoon remains the domineering, strong-willed character of her youth, keeping her son, Danny (John Candy) in a state of suspended childhood, despite his being a substantially built Chicago cop. Further intertextual referencing is provided by the casting of Anthony Quinn, O'Hara's co-star in many of her swashbucklers, as Rose's suitor, Nick Acropolis. Rose's outlook on American life is offensively racist and deeply paranoid; her concept of motherhood that of domestic martyr. The film's trajectory involves her arrival at a point of understanding that enables her to recognise that she ruined her late husband's life and is now in danger of destroying Danny's.

One of the chief pleasures of *Only The Lonely* is this ironic referencing of O'Hara's career; it also defines Irish-American identity in the 1990s in terms of a generational conflict that is predicated on a recidivist femininity versus a more 'integrated' and liberal masculinity. O'Hara's Rose harks back to the castrating mother figures of the classic cycle of Irish-American gangster films, notably Cody Jarrett's (James Cagney) Ma (Margaret Wycherly) in *White Heat* (Raoul Walsh, USA, 1949). The figure of the desiring and desirable ethnic female is replaced by Ally Sheedy's Theresa Luna, swiftly dismissed by Rose as a 'wop' and, worse, a Sicilian. As the girlfriend who brings about the ultimate confrontation between Danny and Rose, her ethnicity is viewed as being of less consequence than Rose's, and her own internal conflict is ascribed to occupational stress (she makes up dead bodies at her father's morgue). In the end, Rose and Nick Acropolis are allowed to sail off into the sunset on an airline bound for Florida, and a life, we can imagine, of mutual, strong-willed opposition.

Within the parameters of its own knowing and ironic play with ethnicity, *Only The Lonely* consigns the fiery Irish colleen and pirate queen of the past to the storehouse of fading cultural stereotypes with more than a touch of longing. As we shall see in Chapter 5, O'Hara's success in Hollywood was, for aspiring female stars, more the exception that the norm. No Irish woman actor since has enjoyed the status and the reputation she did, hence the dominance of the male star in this study. Certainly, as *Only The Lonely* recognised, that particular ethnic character part has not survived into present-day Hollywood. Nor, too, has the popularity of the extreme whiteness that O'Hara shared with Maureen O'Sullivan, and that their casting often rested on. Now the dictates of beauty favour darker skins (ideally mixed-race). Arguably, they also favour more compliant women. The fantasy of the pirate queen has had its day.

NOTES

1   J. Parish, *The RKO Gals* (London: Ian Allan, 1974), p. 643.
2   M. O'Hara (with John Nicoletti), *'Tis Herself* (London, New York, Sydney, Toronto and Dublin: Simon & Schuster, 2004).
3   Naremore, *Acting in the Cinema*, pp. 174–92.
4   J. Richards, *The Swordsmen of the Screen* (London: Routledge & Kegan Paul, 1977), pp. 39–40.
5   From *Sinbad the Sailor*, quoted in Parish, *The RKO Gals*, p. 660.
6   For an interesting discussion of the racialisation of the red-haired woman, see Amanda Third, '"Does the rug match the carpet?": Race, Gender and the Redheaded Woman', in D. Negra, *The Irish In Us*, Duke University Press, forthcoming.
7   P. McGilligan, *Alfred Hitchcock: A Life in Darkness and Light* (London: Wiley, 2003), pp. 222–3.
8   S. Callow, *Charles Laughton, A Difficult Actor* (London: Methuen, 1987), pp. 129–30.
9   R. Pearson, *Eloquent Gestures*, p 21.
10 Ibid., p. 20.
11 L. Mulvey, 'Visual pleasure and narrative cinema', *Screen*, 16, 3 (Autumn, 1975), pp. 6–18.
12 See again Mulvey, 'Visual pleasure'.
13 Parish, *The RKO Gals*, p. 653.
14 *Dance, Girl, Dance* (review), *New York Times*, 11 October 1940, p. 25.
15 O'Hara, *'Tis Herself*, p. 51.
16 U. Hardt, *From Caligari to California* (Oxford, Providence, RI: Berghahn Books, 1996), p. 1.
17 Lucille Ball may well have modelled her post-1945 persona on O'Hara in contrast to whom she considered herself inferior. My thanks to James MacKillop for mentioning this to me.
18 K. Kay and G. Peary, 'Dorothy Arzner's *Dance, Girl, Dance*', *Velvet Light Trap*, 10 (Autumn, 1973), pp. 26–31, p. 31.
19 Baum also wrote the novel on which another O'Hara film, *A Woman's Secret* (Nicholas Ray, USA, 1949) was based. Baum's early work in German often foregrounded modern, liberated heroines.
20 J. Mayne, *Directed by Dorothy Arzner* (Bloomington & Indianapolis, IN:

Indiana University Press, 1994), p. 142.

21 See J. Bergstrom, 'Rereading the Work of Dorothy Arzner', in C. Penley (ed.), *Feminism and Film Theory* (London and New York: BFI Publishing, Routledge, 1988), pp. 80–8; P. Cook, 'Approaching the Work of Dorothy Arzner' in Penley, *Feminism*, pp. 46–56.

22 Bergstrom, 'Rereading'.

23 Too popular, it seems, for Richard Rodgers who personally vetoed her from being cast as lead in *The King and I* (Walter Lang, USA, 1956), pronouncing that he would have: 'No Pirate Queens!'. Again thanks to James MacKillop for that information.

24 E.W. Said, *Orientalism* (London, New York, Victoria, Toronto and Auckland: Penguin. 1995; reprinted with a new Afterword).

25 G. Studlar, '"Out-Salomeing Salome": Dance, the new woman, and fan magazine orientalism', in M. Bernstein and G. Studlar (eds), *Visions of the East* (London and New York: I.B. Tauris, 1997), pp. 99–129, p. 106.

26 Ibid., p. 113.

27 Production notes for *The Black Swan* (Maureen O'Hara file, AMPAS).

28 V. MacPherson, 'Tip from a harem expert: be tantalizing, ladies!', *Hollywood Citizen News*, 26 March 1946 (Maureen O'Hara File, AMPAS).

29 RKO Production Files, Box P154, UCLA.

30 Final Script, *Sons of the Musketeers* (later retitled *At Sword's Point*), RKO script files Box 1085, UCLA.

31 Y. Tasker, *Spectacular Bodies: Gender, Genre and the Action Cinema* (London and New York: Routledge, 1993).

32 M.A. Doane, 'Film and the masquerade: theorising the female spectator' in G. Mast, M. Cohen and L. Braudy (eds), *Film Theory and Criticism* (Oxford: Oxford University Press, 1992; first published 1982), pp. 758–72; K. Silverman, 'Masochism and Subjectivity', *Framework* 12 (1979), pp. 2–9; G. Studlar, 'Masochism and the perverse pleasures of the cinema', in Mast, Cohen and Braudy, *Film Theory and Criticism*, pp. 773–90.

33 Qtd. in Richards, *Swordsmen*, p. 38.

34 T. Gallagher, *John Ford: the Man and his Films* (London and Berkeley, CA: University of California Press, 1986); McBride, *Searching for John Ford*.

35 J.A. Place, *The Non-Western Films of John Ford* (Secaucus: Citadel Press, 1979), pp. 198–200.

36 B. French, *On the Verge of Revolt* (New York: Frederick Ungar, 1978), p. 22.

37 O'Hara, *'Tis Herself*, p. 153.

38 *Maureen O'Hara*, Biography Channel documentary, 2000.

5

Constance Smith

Ireland's forgotten star
(1928?–2003; film career: 1947?–58)

IN *Man in the Attic* (Hugo Fregonese, USA, 1953), an adaptation of *The Lodger* by Mary Belloc Lowndes, Lily Bonner (Constance Smith) is preparing to go on stage for the opening night of her first show when a woman appears at her dressing room door.[1] The visitor is the former showgirl, Annie Rowley (Lilian Bond), whose room this used to be. Bonner welcomes her in and Rowley enters slightly hesitantly, saying that she has heard that they are expecting royalty tonight. She pauses in front of a poster of herself, just beneath a caption that reads 'La Belle Anne', her pose mirroring that of the image on the wall. 'I had it all once,' she tells Bonner, 'royalty, champagne, flowers. I remember my opening night and how excited I was.' She turns to look towards the dressing table: 'I looked in this very mirror. I wish I knew then what I know now. I came up overnight. Overnight I was forgotten. It won't be that way with you.' 'Who knows?' Lily Bonner responds. 'No, it won't,' Rowley assures her, 'I went on looks alone. You have talent and all the rest.' When Bonner turns around again, Annie Rowley has gone, shortly afterwards to become another victim of Jack the Ripper, the eponymous man in the attic.

It is hard to avoid describing Constance Smith's life and career in words other than those of the melodrama or the backstage musical, or seeing in scenes such as these a reflection on her own rise to fame, and a premonition of her fall from grace. If Smith's film career sits uncomfortably within an academic discourse on stardom, it has been included here partly because it is another version of the emigration narrative, and unlike the others described in these chapters, or the majority of their fictional counterparts, one that ended neither in assimilation nor the triumph of fame. I have included it, too, because it seemed regrettable that Constance Smith should have been so completely forgotten, given that she was once, if briefly, a Hollywood star.

Figure 5.1 'It won't be that way with you'. Constance Smith in
Man in the Attic

Constance Smith was born in Limerick, probably in 1928.[2]
Accounts of her early life vary but it seems that she moved to Dublin
within a year of her birth. Her mother, Mary, was from Limerick and
her father from Dublin. He had served with the British army in the
First World War and was working on the construction of
Ardnacrusha Power Station at the time of Constance's birth. This
was completed in 1929 and the family relocated to Mount Pleasant
Buildings in Ranelagh. One of Dublin's chronically rundown slums,
Mount Pleasant Buildings have since been demolished. As one of the
area's former residents remembers it, there were the 'three-rooms',
the 'two-rooms' and the 'one-rooms'. The Smiths lived in the latter,
which were 'like cells':

> The rooms were about eight by eight [feet]. They had no dresser,
> maybe an orange box. They used to cook with shavings they used to
> get out of Murphy's, the sawmills, in Rathmines. None of them had a
> job. There were a load of ex-soldiers, British and Irish. When the men
> died, if they were in the British army, the coffin would come out
> covered by a Union Jack. There was one bedroom, and a living room
> and a scullery, and a range, and a toilet and a wash hand basin.
>   Underneath the wash hand basin, there was a bin. The medical
> officer said it wasn't hygienic. So he got a bin out in the hall and the

women used to sit out there suckling their babies, laughing and joking and the bluebottles buzzing around.

Anyone who was in the army had the advantage of the army greatcoat. The fleas and the hoppers, they were terrible. There was no hot water. It was dire, dire poverty. The babies used to die at birth and they were buried secretly. They couldn't afford the coffins.[3]

The Smiths had four other children, Christy, Sylvester, Brenda and Brian. After the death of her husband, Mary Smith gave birth again, possibly to twins or triplets. The boys played pitch and toss on the streets and scrapped with each other, and in the middle of the flats there was a ball alley and a space where they played football. Here too political meetings were held during election times. Song sheets cost a penny and:

We used to sit around on the stairs, singing 'She was the Miller's Daughter Fair'. There was no radio, no entertainment. Mr Fitzpatrick had a radio. On Grand National Day he'd open the window and we'd all lean on the windowsill, or for the football. Then when he'd get annoyed, 'That's enough!' he'd say and close down the window. If you put your head out the window, the slop would come down! The women took it in turns to wash down the stairs, the smell of Jeyes' Fluid. The women fighting – one woman leaning out the windows – 'There you go from morning to night, with your mouth. Where are you going to tonight? You're man mad.' And the children listening to them. And the fights – they'd be pulling each other's hair. That was the way we were brought up; that was our entertainment.[4]

The St Vincent de Paul, the Salvation Army and the Legion of Mary all came round the flats; and the work of Dr Lynn, who converted a derelict building in Rathmines into St Ultans Infants' Hospital, went some way towards alleviating the miserable conditions of the tenement dwellers.[5]

Mount Pleasant Flats provide the fictionalised setting for Lee Dunne's *Goodbye to the Hill*, a coming-of-age novel set in the 1940s.[6] It, unlike many of his other novels, was not banned, although the film version, *Paddy* (Daniel Haller, Ireland, 1969) was. Dunne's book draws on his own memories of growing up in Ranelagh, but they lack the warmth that many of the flats' former residents still feel for the people who lived there. Her contemporaries remember Constance Smith, who was by all accounts strikingly beautiful, with pride. Like the other children in the flats, she attended St Louis

Convent primary school in Rathmines: 'Bare boards and baskets; you put your wet coat into a basket; dry inkwells, no pens, no books, a blackboard, a pointer and a cane. "Anois cad é sin? An feicim tu an focal sin?" And we were all laughing. They were teaching you Irish when you didn't even know English.'[7]

At that time, there was a chip shop under the bridge in Charleston Road in Ranelagh and Constance Smith worked there. More importantly, she took a job in one of the big houses in the area and it was they, apparently, who suggested to her that she enter a competition that had been launched in the February 1945 issue of *The Screen*, an Irish-published film fan magazine.[8] Readers were invited to submit a photograph of themselves to a Film Star Doubles contest; each month, *The Screen* promised to publish two winning photographs and at the end of the competition, at the '*The Screen* Ball', a leading film star would meet the entrants and select an overall winner.

In January 1946, the ball took place, and was presided over by Anna Neagle and her husband, Herbert Wilcox. The Abbey actor, Ria Mooney, led the judging and many prominent Dublin dignitaries, including the Lord Mayor, attended. As the guests danced to Billy Dingle's orchestra, Elba Films recorded the events of the evening, to be screened later in cinemas under the title of *The Mirror of Ireland*. Prizes, many of them sponsored by the major film producers, were awarded in numerous categories. The culmination of the evening was the announcement of the overall winners in the Men's and Ladies' Sections. Entered as Hedy Lamarr, Constance Smith took First Prize.

'Several film scouts were present during the evening,' *The Screen* reported, 'and made selections of types in which they were interested.'[9] Soon afterwards, Smith was able to announce that she had been approached by the Rank Organisation to screen test at their Denham Studios. In April 1946, she signed a seven-year contract with Rank.

As early as September 1947, Smith's story was already regarded as a classic tale of the triumph of talent: 'The truth about the making of a star is really stranger than fiction,' John Boulting remarked. 'One of these days the real story can be told – the story of trials and tribulations that must be endured by those who have the courage and ability to really "go places" in films – and that will be the story of a successful Irish film aspirant!'[10] Smith's first role, as a maid in *Captain Boycott* (Frank Launder, GB, 1947), wound up on the cutting room floor. Her second, as the cabaret singer in *Brighton Rock* (John Boulting, GB, 1947), was more substantial. At the same time, she and John Boulting became engaged.

Smith's contract with Rank included grooming at the Rank Charm School. One of the British film industry's notoriously unsuccessful ventures, it has been described thus:

> A sort of mixture between Lee Strasberg's Actors studio and a London finishing school for young ladies, a place where you learned posture by balancing books on your head, where you trained for the film cameras by fighting a thousand fencing duels (fencing helps your poise and keeps you from blinking, useful skills for the screen), the 'Charm School' – the phrase was coined by an American journalist – represented Rank's bold attempt to mass-produce 'stars', an attempt which was conspicuously unsuccessful.[11]

As Macnab further points out, Rank's umbrella production companies were not under obligation to hire the members of the school and the starlets were most often employed opening garden fairs and bazaars.[12] Smith herself played in no Rank films though she gained small parts in a number of independent productions, including *The Perfect Woman* (Bernard Knowles, GB, 1949), *Blackmailed* (Marc Allegrét, GB, 1950) *Room to Let* (Godfrey Grayson, GB, 1950) and *Never Say Die* (Vivian Milroy, GB, 1950). According to a studio biography circulated in 1951 to accompany the release of *The 13th Letter* (Otto Preminger, USA, 1951) in which Smith played Cora Laurent, she was eventually fired by Rank when she objected to criticisms of her Irish accent.[13] Smith herself explained that Rank wanted her to change her name to Tamara because she looked Italian but, to counter the British public's distrust of foreigners, she was also to be Tamara Hickey.[14]

After the break with Rank, Smith tested for a number of films, including *Top O' The Morning*, before finally gaining the part of the maid in *The Mudlark* (Jean Negulesco, GB/USA, 1950), for which she was to be paid £20 per day for five weeks.[15] The story of an encounter between a young street urchin, Wheeler (Andrew Ray), and Queen Victoria (Irene Dunne), Negulesco's film is a light comedy whose primary purpose is to demonstrate that the British monarchy can be more populist than they imagine. A subplot involves an Irish butler, Slattery (Ronan O'Casey), whose anti-Royalist mutterings lead him and Wheeler to becoming implicated in an Irish plot against the monarch. Only Disraeli (Alec Guinness) can persuade parliament that there is no such plot, which he duly does. Constance Smith plays the Irish maid, Kate Noonan, who helps to conceal Wheeler after she has come across him hiding under the dining table. Although only a minor part, Smith photographed well and gives the impression on screen of the kind of freshness that Hollywood looked for in its Irish female roles. Darryl Zanuck, head of production at Twentieth Century-Fox, was taken by her performance and ordered that additional screen tests be made of her. These led to a rush of excitement from Hollywood and a seven-year contract with Fox. Studio publicity made much of their unexpected find, now proclaimed to be Ireland's latest and most exciting contribution to the Hollywood screen. Constance achieved star billing for *The 13th Letter,* shot in Canada on the way to Hollywood and on arrival in Los Angeles screen-tested for *The House in the Square* (Roy Ward Baker, USA, 1951). Cast opposite Tyrone Power, she returned to London for additional shooting. There she met and married Bryan Forbes, a rising actor and best known now as actor/director/writer and memoirist. Local memory has it that shortly after their marriage, she returned to Mount Pleasant Buildings with her new husband only to be humiliated by her mother who threw in her face that she thought she was too good for them all now.

In *Notes for A Life,* Forbes recalls a marriage made on a rebound (from John Boulting in Smith's case) and with little chance of success. While in London, the couple opened the papers one morning to find that Smith had been replaced by Ann Blyth in *The House in the Square*:

> It was difficult for outsiders to appreciate the extent of the blow to Connie. The role opposite Tyrone Power was considered to be the plum of the year and carried with it all the statutory prerequisites of a film star [. . .] When the blow fell she was totally unequipped to deal with the aftermath. The old-style Hollywood system allowed of no mercy. She was immediately reduced to the status of a Hindu road sweeper, all privileges were withdrawn overnight, and the army of sycophants and glad-handers avoided us like the plague. The publicity machine shifted into top gear for Miss Blyth. All Connie's scenes were quickly reshot at a cost of some £100,000, and the incident written off in the balance sheets.[16]

Roy Ward Baker later described the debacle as an exercise in hubris on the part of Zanuck. The mogul had made up his mind that Constance should have the starring role in this film and demanded that Ward Baker screen-test her. This he reluctantly did, arranging an elaborate test for Constance, complete with Tyrone Power and several of the other actors. It turned out badly, but Zanuck continued to insist that his discovery be cast. Ward Baker and Tyrone Power commenced shooting the film, all the time expressing their reservations about the wisdom of casting a completely inexperienced actor in a difficult role. Everything went well until the time came to shoot Constance's scenes and their progress slowed almost to a halt:

> None of this was her fault. It was unfair and a grave mistake to put such demands on her and it did her no favours at all [. . .] With all the patience and encouragement in the world, after six weeks of shooting, we were getting nowhere. No doubt she felt that she was surrounded by implacable enemies. At one point she told me that the next time she saw Zanuck she'd have me fired off the picture. The way I felt about it, I wouldn't have cared. I was working hard to make her look as good as I could. It was not in anybody's interest to sabotage her performance: all our names would be on the credits for better or worse. If it were a success she would get her share of the applause.
>
> Eventually everybody had to accept defeat. Ann Blyth arrived from Hollywood to take the part and we started shooting again, re-taking Connie's scenes.[17]

Still under contract to Fox, Constance returned to Hollywood and her career picked up again. Forbes followed. 'Her husband is a nice-looking young English actor, Brian Forbes, who is well up in his profession in England,' one magazine informed its readers. 'You may hear of him in pictures eventually, but right now Connie is the Hollywood attraction.'[18] By late 1951, Smith was, however, pregnant and Fox 'did not take kindly to the news [. . .]. So they loaned her $3,000 to obtain an abortion a few days before Christmas, thus irrevocably dooming a marriage that was already faltering.'[19] Their relationship did not survive; however, those who remember her later years in London suggest that Forbes offered his former wife help when she was in prison. She too, apparently, always spoke well of her first husband.

Now routinely compared with Maureen O'Hara, Smith starred in a succession of films, *The Lure of the Wilderness* (Jean Negulesco, USA, 1952), *Red Skies of Montana* (Joseph M. Newman, USA, 1952) and *The Treasure of the Golden Condor* (Delmer Daves, USA, 1953). Like O'Hara, she was positioned as a rebel whose spirited opposition to studio manipulation was a marker of her individuality: 'Miss Smith is a natural, that is to say, an Irish, rebel. More power to her, and Up the Republic!'[20] In 1953, she played a young Irish immigrant come to New York to track down her husband in *Taxi* (Gregory Patoff, USA, opposite Dan Dailey) and, in the same year, she was the star of *Man in the Attic*. As we have already seen, the film is a version of the Ripper story and the second in which Smith played, the first being *Room to Let*. In the earlier film, she is Molly Musgrave, daughter of the wheelchair-bound Mrs Musgrave (Christine Silver), who lets a room to Dr Fell (a thoroughly sinister performance from British actor, Valentine Dyall). Now, she is a showgirl, and niece of Helen (Frances Bavier) and William Harley (Rhys Williams), in whose house Slade (Jack Palance) is lodging. Smith's Lily Bonner is confident and gregarious, and the change in Smith's performance of an identical part in just three years is an indication of her increased acting experience. She carries herself with the certainty of a star, flashing her eyes and playing up to Slade when they meet. Her scenes in the nightclub, where she sings and dances the can-can, suggest a performer who enjoys the attention she commands. The rebelliousness that so engaged the Hollywood columnists is etched into these screen appearances, so that when her character announces to Slade that she doesn't want to be a slave, her words carry the force of conviction. Jack Palance is reported to have suggested that Smith be billed 'The Dublin Dietrich', and the press speculated that the actor had potential as a live performer: 'There's a pretty good possibility that Connie just might be a sensational nitery [*sic*] star. Her face and figure, together with an easy vocal style, are the kind of assets a gal needs – not to mention a pair of the nicest gams to ever leave the Old Sod.'[21]

Given that she had recently parted company with Twentieth Century-Fox, Smith may have been casting her eye around for future career options. In 1954, she signed with Bob Goldstein, a casting director for Universal Pictures. He had established a co-production organisation in Britain to broker arrangements between British production companies and American actors and finance; the actors involved were not first-rank stars but were well enough known to guarantee audiences in the United States. One of these was Constance Smith, another was blacklisted actor, Larry Parks. Both travelled to London where they shot *Tiger by the Tail* (John Gilling, GB, 1955) for Tempean Films. A routine thriller, with a distinct transatlantic feel, Smith was cast as the reliable English secretary, Jane Claymore, who aids and abets journalist, John Desmond (Parks), when he finds himself caught up in an international counterfeiting ring. With a now perfect English accent, even in this undemanding role, Smith still manages to suggest energy and sexuality behind her 'plain Jane' persona.[22] Smith apparently did not hit it off with Parks but fared better with Arthur Kennedy, with whom she starred in another Tempean Films production, *Impulse* (Charles de Lautour, GB, 1955).[23] As the double-crossing, seductive Lila, Smith was better cast than in *Tiger*, and her screen presence is forceful.

The Tempean films were B features and, without the Fox contract, Constance was unable to gain access to higher profile roles. Undoubtedly, she was also temperamental and assertive; later she insisted that she was a victim of casting couch politics. By 1955, her Hollywood career was languishing and she decamped for Italy, where she made four films: *Un po' di Cielo/A Little Bit of Blue Sky* (Girogio Moser, Italy, 1955), *Giovanni Dalle Bande Nere/Violent Patriot* (Luigi Grieco, Italy, 1956), *Addio, per sempre!* (Mario Costa, Italy, 1958) and *La Congiura dei Borgia/Conspiracy of the Borgias* (Antonio Racioppi, Italy, 1958). There, in December 1956, she also remarried; her new husband was photographer Araldo Crollolanza, whose father was a former Fascist senator. According to press reports, the groom's parents refused to accept Constance and did not attend the wedding ceremony. Her new father-in-law refused to see her and disinherited his son.

In Italy, Constance was promoted as the new Grace Kelly and it was rumoured that she came from the Irish landed gentry, her parts reflecting this myth. In, for instance, *Giovanni Dalle Bande Nere*, she is cast as Lady Emma Caldana, a member of the sixteenth-century Italian aristocracy who falls in love with Giovanni de Medici, the violent patriot of the translated title. Smith was required to do little in this low-budget, formulaic historical romance other than flash her startling eyes at Vittorio Gassman who plays the hero. Directed by Sergio Grieco (aka Terence Hathaway), who specialised in low-budget co-productions of genre films, *Giovanni Dalle Bande Nere* played the drive-in circuit on release and was later distributed on vhs.

In 1958 the Irish actor was again in the news, this time because she had taken an overdose of sleeping tablets and was being treated in a hospital in Rome. According to some newspaper reports, her husband was in jail in Milan, other journalists insisted that Araldo di Crollolanza was rushing to Rome to see his wife. This was not the last time that she was reported to have overdosed, and Constance's life was marked by frequent, unspecified visits to hospital. Many of these, we can assume, were to treat her mental health and her growing alcohol-related problems. Her marriage to Crollolanza did not last long, and at the end of the 1950s Constance Smith left Italy to return to Britain. There, in the summer of 1959, possibly at a reception at the National Film Theatre, she met Paul Rotha, the eminent British documentary filmmaker and author of numerous books and articles on film, most notably, *The Film Till Now*.[24] The two became lovers, united in part by a common sense of being outsiders. The British documentary film movement was comfortably middle-class and Oxbridge-educated. Rotha's father was a pharmacist who, in order to make extra money for his family (he had four children), also wrote novels and biographies under the family name of Thompson (Paul adopted the name of Rotha to sound less English). The family was middle-class but had little money. Born in 1907, Rotha started taking notes on the films he had attended when he was six or seven and later used these to write *The Film Till Now*. At seventeen, he entered the Slade School of Art. At the time he was most interested in graphic design and German Expressionism, and won the International Theatre Design Award at the Paris Exhibition in 1925. He became an art critic and only in 1928 joined the film industry, working as an assistant property man at Elstree Studios. Later he became an assistant designer to Alfred Hitchcock but was fired for writing an attack on the British film industry in the *London Film Weekly*. When he first was employed in film, Rotha mixed with many of the German technicians who populated Britain's film studios, both as émigrés and making dual-language productions. Rotha developed a preference for the company of foreigners, perhaps because he felt himself to be excluded by education and income from the mainstream of the British documentary movement.

John Grierson invited Rotha to join the film unit of the Empire Marketing Board and in 1932 he made his first documentary, *Contact*. Rotha's most highly regarded films belong to the pre-war period, when he made documentaries such as *The Face of Britain* (1935) and *Health for the Nation*, commissioned by the Ministry of Health in 1938. Rotha never joined a political party:

> He was too independent a man to do so. He was, first and foremost a critic of society as it then was: the quintessential English radical in the mould of Orwell or William Cobbett – a true non-conformist, enemy of all Establishments, Left, Right or Centre, and of compromise. It

was the struggle against unemployment, poverty and inequality, and later fascism, that was, and remained, important to him.[25]

In his writings, he was dismissive of Hollywood and believed that more people should be exposed to and educated through the kind of filmmaking practices to which he subscribed.

In 1951, Rotha moved into fiction filmmaking, directing and co-producing *No Resting Place* (GB). The film is set among the Irish travelling community and explores one family's encounter with the Irish police following an accidental killing. *No Resting Place* was shot on location in Ireland and Rotha retained his Irish contacts, staying in touch with members of the Irish Film Society; indeed it was through them that he was introduced to the producers of *Cradle of Genius*, the documentary that reunited Barry Fitzgerald with Sean O'Casey. From 1953–5, he was head of the BBC's documentary film unit. His productions were marked by detailed preparation and a desire for control that irked many of those who worked with him.

Rotha's career in Britain was notable for numerous changes of employment that almost certainly reflect issues of personality as much as the precarious nature of professional documentary filmmaking (in fact, the British documentary movement was fraught with dissent). Although she had not had a major film part for several years when they met, Smith still enjoyed a reputation as an actor of note. According to Robert Kruger, for many of his cinefile contemporaries she was, 'the intelligent man's Elizabeth Taylor'.[26] In 1959 Rotha was offered the opportunity to make a documentary on Adolph Hitler, *Das Leben von Adolph Hitler/The Life of Adolph Hitler* (W. Germany, 1961). Rotha could not speak German and worked closely on the making of the film with his editor and associate, Robert Kruger. The purpose of the documentary was to provide the younger generation of Germans with some level of understanding as to who Hitler was, and of their parents' wartime experiences. Walter Koppel, the producer, was a concentration camp survivor and wanted to use the biographical form to engage audiences. Two years later, Kruger and Rotha worked together on *De Overval* (*The Silent Raid*, 1962) about the Dutch wartime resistance. A controversial choice, Rotha was not welcomed by the local Dutch film industry but the film, once completed, was a critical and popular success.

Constance went to Germany with Rotha and subsequently to Holland. In Germany they travelled around the country as Rotha visited archives and interviewed potential contributors to the documentary. Together they met people who had known Hitler, including his former butler, as well as camp survivors. In these early years of their relationship, the couple enjoyed shared beliefs and ideas. Both were committed anti-fascists and socialists, they were strongly anti-authoritarian and atheistic; Constance subscribed too to Rotha's outspoken anti-imperialism. Both loved jazz and Constance was fond of art and painted; both often talked about the films they planned to make together. In conversation, Constance frequently referred to her childhood of poverty, which now she resented, particularly the fact that her father had been in the British army. Like Rotha, Constance did not suffer fools gladly and, in her dark clothes and black glasses, placed the image of the film star between herself and the wider world. Once you got past that façade, as Robert Kruger remembers it, she could be good company and, despite their enormous differences, of age, experience and background, Rotha and she were initially very happy together.

In December 1960, as *Cradle of Genius* was opening in New York, the couple made a widely reported trip to Limerick, where Constance visited the house of her birth in Wolfe Tone Street. While Constance signed autographs and chatted to her family's former neighbours, Rotha told reporters that the purpose of their trip was to carry out background research for a book, entitled *A Weed in the Ground*, that he was going to write on Constance's life. He was also planning to make a film of *Jumbo's Wife*, from a story by Frank O'Connor, to star Constance and Cyril Cusack.[27] When this fell through, he contacted Bryan MacMahon, hoping to film his Traveller play, *The Honey Spike* (first performed in 1961) and going as far as to contact Peter O'Toole with an offer of a starring role should the finance come through. Constance was to take the female lead.[28]

Constance and Rotha had another thing in common – both were heavy drinkers; they loved ordering champagne and lavish dinners that they then did not eat. Back in their hotel rooms in Germany, fights started and, on one occasion, Rotha had to delay a planned research trip to Poland so damaged was his face; eventually he travelled, as he notes in his diary, 'battered but game'.[29] An orderly man, with his polished shoes and his neat writing, in the untidy, spontaneous, self-educated Irish woman he had also found his opposite.

After completing *De Overval*, Constance and Rotha returned to England. They continued living together, and in December 1961 Rotha was found knifed in his fourth-floor flat in London; the assailant, the newspapers reported, was Irish-born actress, Miss Constance Smith. She, in turn, had tried to commit suicide by slashing her wrists. This widely reported event was accompanied by demands from the victim that his wife and former secretary, Margot, who was in Stoke Mandeville hospital and critically ill with a rare blood disease, should not know what had happened. Despite being seriously wounded, Rotha recovered, and in January 1962 Constance went to trial. During the hearing, both her defence counsel, Michael Sharrard, and the media made much of the tragic price the film star was paying for her beauty. Detailing Constance's deprived childhood and her rush to fame, Sharrard appealed to the court to take into account the star's ill-preparedness for the career in which she had found herself. This was, he said, 'a story of a poor girl who was squeezed into a situation of sophistication and fame when emotionally quite unable to cope with it'.[30] On top of this, the recent trip to Germany had exposed Constance to horrors she had never imagined and on their return to London she had become a recluse in the London flat she shared with her lover. A trivial argument had set the two at each other and, losing her control temporarily, Constance went for Rotha with the knife.

Little impressed by this litany of horror, the magistrate, Alderman Sir Ralph Perring, gave Constance a three-month sentence, remarking on the inappropriateness of the private and somewhat sordid details of the defendant's life to the business of the court. Rotha saw her to the entrance of Holloway prison, insisting that this changed nothing between them. Nor did it, it seemed; when she was released, Constance was met at the gates of the prison by Rotha. In the interim, his wife had died and the press speculated that the two might marry. Instead they outraged Rotha's peers by selling their story to the *Sunday Pictorial*, who ran a banner headline with a quotation from the couple: 'We Will Never Marry, Our Love is Too Exciting for Wedlock'. In fact, Rotha and Constance had met with Fred Redman and Harry Ashbrooke of the *Daily Mirror* and *Sunday Pictorial* and agreed to the story for the *Pictorial* on the basis that a second follow-up story would be published in which Constance would describe her experiences in Holloway. To their combined chagrin, the papers reneged on the arrangement.[31]

So began a cycle of stabbings, drug overdoses and periods in psychiatric hospitals. In 1968, in Manchester, Constance again stabbed Rotha in the back with a steak knife, this time apparently because he made disparaging remarks about her family. On this occasion, she was put on three years probation with the proviso that she was not to see Rotha during this time. Once again, they came back together and in May 1974, they married. In 1975, after another stabbing, Constance was back in Holloway. Despite suffering from the endless chatter of her prison companions, Constance seems to have found an unexpected measure of personal freedom in jail. Here she could paint and here she made plans for a future that did not include Rotha: 'I just wish to spread my wings, see some films and walk in freedom without the hand of Rotha pulling me back.'[32] He too agreed that a separation would be in both their interests. However, after an interim period in a hostel, she returned to him and they continued in what seems to have been a relationship bound by moments of genuine and mutual love, but also drink, physical abuse and financial hardship. In the anti-Irish years of the 1970s, Constance took to going into pubs and insulting the English, which resulted in her being told to get back to Ireland.[33] Students requesting interviews with Rotha were advised that they could visit on the grounds that they pay £50 and bring with them for refreshment 'a bottle of good Scotch for myself and a bottle of Vodka for my wife'.[34]

In 1978 the couple were evicted from a cottage in Oxfordshire and Rotha's books were seized by the bailiffs. Only thanks to a last minute intercession by the Royal Literary Fund were they returned to him but he remained utterly impoverished; on top of this he had to pay hefty bills for Constance's medical treatment. Despite a succession of honorary awards, Rotha was increasingly on his own with Constance and their much loved Labrador, and felt that he had been abandoned by those who knew him when he was at the peak of his career. Only a few people – Robert Kruger and fellow documentarist, John Taylor, among them – now kept in touch. Constance did seek work during this period and in the early 1970s was employed as a cleaner in a Wiltshire hospital for £6 per week. At the time a number of her old films were showing on television; the patients and other staff saw them and, according to Rotha, made her life there impossible, wondering what a film star was doing cleaning the wards.[35] In July 1979 as a brief line in Rotha's correspondence, 'My wild Irish wife has finally left me, gone God knows where' indicates, Constance walked out of their shared lives.[36]

In the 1980s Constance was found destitute, she was frostbitten and had lost two or three toes. She was taken into a psychiatric hospital in London and then placed in a hostel for recovering patients. Her and Rotha's most enduring friends tried to help her but found themselves more often than not rebuffed or regarded from an icy distance. Those who used to work with her became accustomed to seeing her sitting drinking in London's Soho Square, just around the corner from Wardour Street, at the heart of the British film industry. From time to time, she recovered enough to look for cleaning and childcare positions. Peter Cotes, theatre director and stepbrother of the Boulting brothers, and an old friend of Rotha's who had accompanied him to the 1962 trial, was one of those who kept in touch with Constance. In 1984, the Irish actor Patrick Brock met Cotes at a film union event, held in honour of Paul Rotha, who had died that year. Brock too had known Constance and had been friendly for a while with her and Rotha. He asked Cotes after the Irish actor, and was told that she was in Lewisham Hospital, having been picked up off the street. Cotes and his wife (the actor, Joan Miller) had visited her and had found her, Cotes said, unrecognisable. Brock went straight round to Lewisham the next day, only to be told that Constance had checked herself out of the hospital.[37] Still, she had not yet vanished finally; John Taylor, Peter Cotes and Joan Miller remained in touch with her for another year or so, as did Robert Kruger and his wife, Joan, the latter couple only losing touch when they left London.

This is not a story with a happy ending, or at the moment an ending at all. Those people who knew Constance assumed that she could not live much longer in the manner that she did; yet it seems that she only died in 2003, according to one internet source, of natural causes in Islington, London.[38]

NOTES

1 *The Lodger* was first published in 1912. It was used as the basis for a number of films, most notably Alfred Hitchcock's 1927 silent version; this was re-made in 1932, also in Britain, as a talking picture under the direction of Maurice Elvey with Ivor Novello reprising his role as the Ripper. The first American adaptation appeared in 1944, directed by John Brahm, with Laird Cregar, George Sanders and Merle Oberon. Like *Man in the Attic*, it was scripted by Barré Lyndon. The first four versions were all called *The Lodger*. The Ripper narrative was also the subject of another of Constance Smith's British films, *Room to Let*, a Hammer Films production, directed in 1950 by Godfrey Grayson.

2 No record of her birth exists in the Registry of Births, Deaths and Marriages. Almost certainly, she was born in February 1928.

3 Patrick Grimes, interview with the author, London, 21 June 2004.

4 Ibid.

5   See M. Ruane, 'Kathleen Lynn', in M. Cullen and M. Luddy (eds), *Female Activists: Irish Women and Change 1900–1960* (Dublin: Woodfield Press, 2001), pp. 61–88.

6   L. Dunne, *Goodbye to the Hill* (Dublin: Wolfhound Press, 1986; originally published, London: Hutchinson, 1965).

7   Grimes, interview.

8   Other accounts state that she was selling ice-creams at Maccari's [*sic*] on O'Connell Street, Dublin and wore Signora Maria Maccari's ball gown to the contest. See, J. Nicholson, 'She's Italy's Irish Rebel', *Picture Post*, 15 October 1955, pp. 39–40, p. 40.

9   'The Screen Ball', *The Screen*, 5, 3 (March 1946), p. 1.

10 '"Truth about Irish actress stranger than fiction", says Director', *The Screen* (September 1947), p. 23.

11 G. Macnab, *J. Arthur Rank and the British Film Industry* (London and New York: Routledge, 1993), pp. 141–2.

12 Ibid., pp. 143–4.

13 Constance Smith microfiche, BFI Library.

14 Nicholson, 'She's Italy's Irish Rebel'.

15 Fox legal collection, Box FX LR – 742; UCLA archives.

16 B. Forbes, *Notes for a Life* (London: Everest Books, 1977), p. 207.

17 R. Ward Baker, *The Director's Cut* (London: Reynolds & Hearn, 2000), p. 60.

18 L. Berg, 'Beautiful Pie-Face', *LA Times* (*This Week* magazine), 16 March 1952. Constance Smith file, Margaret Herrick Library, AMPAS.

19 B. Forbes, *A Divided Life* (London: Heinemann, 1992), p. 287.

20 Berg, 'Beautiful Pie-Face'.

21 H. McClay, 'Connie to try nitery act', *LA Daily News*, 28 December 1953, Constance Smith File, AMPAS.

22 I am grateful to Declan McLoughlin of the Limerick Film Archive for lending me a copy of this and several of Constance Smith's films and for supplying me with details of local and other press coverage of her life and career.

23 See entry on Robert S. Baker in B. McFarlane, *An Autobiography of British Cinema* (London: Methuen, 1997), pp. 41–8. As well as producing *Tiger By the Tail* and *Impulse*, Baker and his regular collaborator, Monty Berman, produced *Professor Tim* (Henry Cass, Ireland, 1957), *Sally's Irish Rogue* (George Pollock, Ireland, 1958), *Home is the Hero* (J. Fielder Cook, Ireland, 1959) and *Boyd's Shop* (Henry Cass, Ireland, 1960) with the Abbey actors.

24 P. Rotha, *The Film Till Now* (London: Jonathan Cape, 1930).

25 R. Kruger, 'Paul Rotha and the documentary film', in D. Petrie and R. Kruger (eds), *A Paul Rotha Reader* (Exeter: University of Exeter Press, 1999), pp. 16–44, p. 27.

26 Interview with the author, St Ives, Cornwall, November 2004. I am very grateful to Robert Kruger for sharing his memories of his travels with Rotha and Constance with me and I have drawn extensively on this interview for information on their relationship. Robert Kruger and Joan Kruger tried to keep in touch with Constance after her relationship with Rotha, visiting her in hospital and in the various hostels that gave her refuge after she became derelict.

27 'Noted film actress visits her native city', *Limerick Chronicle*, 29 December 1960, p. 1. My thanks to Declan McLoughlin of the Limerick Film Archive for drawing my attention to this report.

28 Letter from Paul Rotha to Peter O'Toole, 25 October 1967, Paul Rotha Papers, Special Collections, UCLA.

29 P. Rotha, diary entry, 27 July 1960, reproduced with kind permission of

Robert Kruger.

30 A. Latcham, 'Star who couldn't cope with fame', *Daily Express*, 12 January 1962, pp. 4–5, p. 4.

31 Letter from Paul Rotha to Hugh Cudlipp, 9 July 1962, Paul Rotha Papers. The collection also contains a rough opening draft of the article written by Constance Smith.

32 Letter to Robert Kruger from Holloway prison, 20 November 1975, reproduced with kind permission of Robert Kruger.

33 Letter from Paul Rotha to Gloria (second name unknown), 24 June 1975, Paul Rotha Papers.

34 Letter from Paul Rotha to Mr Joel Zukor, Paul Rotha Papers.

35 Letter from Paul Rotha to Carl Foreman, 16 February 1972, Paul Rotha Papers.

36 Letter to Arthur (second name unknown), 11 July 1979, Paul Rotha Papers.

37 P. Brock, 'These I Have Known', *Classic Images*, 216 (June 1993), pp. 40–1, 44. Brock was better known as Cecil Brock and had a long career as an actor in Ireland and Britain.

38 Internet Movie Database (IMDb) (accessed 18 September 2003).

6

Richard Harris

Touching the gods
(1933–2002; film career: 1958–2002)

Reviewing the opening performance in London of Brendan Behan's *The Quare Fellow*, Kenneth Tynan wrote that:

> The English hoard words like misers, the Irish spend them like sailors and in Brendan Behan's tremendous new play language is out on a spree, ribald, dauntless and spoiling for a fight. In a sense of course this is scarcely amazing. It is Ireland's sacred duty to send over every few years a playwright who will save the English theatre from inarticulate dumbness. And Irish dialogue almost invariably sparkles.[1]

When the play moved to the Comedy Theatre in the West End, Richard Harris joined the cast, replacing Eric Ogle in the minor role of Mickser.[2] *The Quare Fellow* marked Behan's breakthrough in Britain, where his drunken interview with Malcolm Muggeridge on BBC's 'Panorama' programme confirmed his reputation as anti-Establishment hero. Harris' rise to fame was not so immediate and, following the small role in Behan's play, he continued appearing with Joan Littlewood's Theatre Workshop, interspersing his theatre performances with television parts (in *The Iron Harp*, Granada Television, 1957) and slowly working his way into cinema – as the Irish-speaking lover in *Alive and Kicking* (Cyril Frankel, GB, 1958) and the IRA man, Terence O'Brien, in *Shake Hands with the Devil* (Michael Anderson, GB, 1959). Although the latter was shot in Ireland's newly opened Ardmore Studios, there was still little or no Irish film industry outside of the Abbey films. Harris was one of a number of Irish actors, including Joe Lynch and Donal Donnelly, who saw in England opportunities that were not on offer at home. Where Harris' career distinguishes itself from those of the film actors discussed so far is in the fact that his breakthrough came via the London stage, after initial training at the London Academy of Music and Dramatic Art. Harris, like Behan, played up to the expectation that the Irish should embody, and through their art, liberate all that was repressed in the middle-class British psyche. Alongside his life-long friend, Peter O'Toole, the Limerick actor rampaged to great effect, guaranteeing for himself, just as Colin Farrell was subsequently to do, part-thrilled, part-horrified press coverage of his persona and performances.

When Barry Fitzgerald took his boozy, pugnacious characters to London, he remained an oddity, unable to find a place within the theatrical establishment. Nor did he ever embrace a lifestyle comparable to that of the characters he portrayed. By the 1950s British theatre, like British cinema, was generally considered to be in the doldrums and Harris arrived in London just as a rising generation of writers, directors, performers and critics, loosely gathered together under the 'Angry Young Man' rubric, was commencing its assault on both forms.[3] No longer was the hard-drinking, subversive Irishman the object of the amused, middle-class gaze, now he was ripe for appropriation by the New Wave. Reviewing J.P. Donleavy's *The Ginger Man* (1959), in which Harris took the lead part of Sebastian Dangerfield, the reviewer for *The Times* spelled out the connections:

> Mr J.P. Donleavy's adaptation of his own novel, *The Ginger Man*, at the Fortune Theatre works out curiously like an Irish version of *Look Back in Anger*. The wildly talkative hero is a guilty rather than an angry young man. His sense of guilt comes about because he is quite unable to (as he would put it contemptuously) put his shoulder to the wheel. He lives in an alcoholic dream of big houses, spacious gardens, fair women, and a formidable legal reputation, but as a law student he cannot read his books and is apt to cheat at exams.[4]

Critiqued, with justification, for its fetishisation of male subjectivity, the Movement, or New Wave, opened up career opportunities for a new generation of actors from regional and working-class backgrounds and demanded of them that they develop a performance style that could respond to the kind of plays, such as John Osborne's *Look Back in Anger* (1956) and Behan's *The Hostage* (1958), that were now being produced. Although he made his name with *The Ginger Man*, Harris' formative training came with the Theatre Workshop, itself central to the development of a new British performance style. Influenced by Vsevolod Meyerhold, by Rudolf Laban's system of body language notation, and by the sixteenth-century Italian Commedia dell'Arte with its radical troupe of travelling players, Joan Littlewood's disciples were rigorously trained in the art of movement, encouraged to strip themselves of their accumulated layers of social conditioning, to absorb themselves in the background to the play they were performing and to improvise. Joan Littlewood had met the Jewish Laban, who had been sacked by Göring from his directorship of the Berlin State Opera, when he was living in Manchester as a wartime refugee and invited him to a Theatre Workshop performance. From then on he and she kept in touch; in her memoirs Littlewood explains the importance of Laban's teachings for her own practice:

> Laban's movement scales are very satisfying to perform. You touch each point in space which can be reached without elevation or propulsion. They are encapsulated in the icosahedron [a twenty-sided shape] [...] After a session with Laban you began to look at the world with different eyes, as if it had changed its colours or its shapes, or you could see neutrons and protons instead of mass. You watched for the slightest gesture which would give away a secret. After a while, with some degree of accuracy, you could tell what people did for a living or analyse their state of mind as they passed you on the street.
>
> Whether in dance or any form of theatre, to create a character you must first divest yourself of your own characteristics, become a new being, live in a different time and place. With Laban it became possible.[5]

Unlike the Actors' Studio under Lee Strasberg, the Workshop did not cater for film stars. Whereas Michael Caine was swiftly written off as unsuitable, Litttlewood was well-disposed towards Harris whom she renamed 'Mickser'. Although he was not with them for long, Harris took part in a number of Workshop productions including Lionel Bart's musical, *Fings Ain't What They Used to Be* (1959), and there is much in his seminal interpretation of the role of Frank Machin in *This Sporting Life* (Lindsay Anderson, GB, 1963) that suggests that he learned from his time with Littlewood. For many critics, Harris was the new Brando but when the two played together in *Mutiny on the Bounty* (Lewis Milestone, USA, 1962), there was little to suggest a shared style or persona. A notoriously fraught production, during which the original director, Carol Reed, was replaced by Milestone, its making was punctuated by interventions from its star who constantly demanded rewrites. Harris and Brando fell out early in the making of the film and joint scenes had to be filmed with a stand-in.[6] At this stage of his career, Harris' performance style was considerably less mannered than

Brando's; subsequently this was to change but distinct differences remained.

James Naremore has invited us to question Brando's relationship with the Method, arguing that it is more useful to see him as, 'symptomatic of the period that produced Montgomery Clift, James Dean, Elvis Presley, and Marilyn Monroe – all of them brooding, ostensibly inarticulate types who suggested a scandalous sexuality and who signalled American entertainment's drift toward adolescent audiences in the decades after the war'.[7] Under Lee Strasberg, the Actors' Studio, according to Naremore, fostered a type of perform-ance that insisted on the '"private moment", [on] "freedom", "naturalness", "organic" – the keywords of romantic individual-ism', all this at the expense of avant-garde and deconstructive theatre.[8] Brando is, therefore, better understood for his image than for any unifying acting style; his distinctiveness lay in three principal tenets: he appeared in naturalistic settings, acted out 'existential paradigms' and deviated from the norms of classic rhetoric, most notably with his mumbling mode of delivery.[9]

Naremore draws frequent parallels between Brando's perform-ances and those of the actors in the 'Angry Young Man' films; similarly, Andrew Higson has detected in Harris' Frank Machin the influence of the Method.[10] Ultimately, it seems fair to suggest that both movements erupted out of the same cultural crisis and one that is linked to a reappraisal of masculinity. Rejecting his appropriation by the revolutionaries of the British film and literary world, Harris insisted that: 'In England, I was typed as an angry young man once because I drank, and I came out very strongly that I am the opposite. I'm not angry with anyone. This is my life and I've got to lead it to the full.'[11] They may have shared an existential philosophy but Harris' acting style in *This Sporting Life* is certainly less intensely narcissistic than Brando's in his equivalent parts.

The story of a miner (Machin) turned professional rugby player, *This Sporting Life* is relayed through a series of flashbacks, catching up with itself before its ending. The film opens with Frank breaking his front teeth on the field and moves through a series of halluci-natory recollections as the dentist plies him with gas in order to treat his mouth. Machin is lodging with the widow, Mrs Hammond (Rachel Roberts), whose reserve he is determined to break down; gradually she seems to warm to him and they begin to have sex together. Machin presses her to take things further yet seems unable to understand that she feels bought by him and that her position in her impoverished neighbourhood is being compromised. At the same time, Machin is under pressure to respond to the attentions of his rugby boss' wife, the socially aspirational Mrs Weaver (Vanda Godsell). We see Frank's attitude towards Mrs Hammond become increasingly possessive until the film's final moments, when she succumbs to a brain haemorrhage; as she dies, Machin discovers his own tenderness towards her.

This Sporting Life is a film bookended by pain and dominated by Frank's battles with himself and those around him. In common with other of the British New Wave films, as John Hill has argued, it is not particularly sensitive to Mrs Hammond's perspective, implying that she is emotionally, if not sexually, frigid.[12] She may indeed have 'a seriousness, an emotional weight, altogether lacking in the pathetically trivial roles women had to play in most 1950s British films', as Robert Murphy has countered, but her function in the film is primarily to add greater emotional intensity to Machin's voyage towards self-realisation.[13] Hill has critiqued the New Wave directors for their preoccupation with individualism at the expense of an exploration of social issues and, again, there is no doubt that the mise-en-scène functions more as aesthetic backdrop deployed to heighten the film's sense of claustrophobia than to illuminate Machin's class issues.[14] Anderson himself made no claims about the film's ideological mission, writing that:

> *This Sporting Life* is not a film about sport. Nor is it to be categorised as a 'North Country working-class story' [...] It is a film about a man. A man of extraordinary power and aggressiveness, both tempera-mental and physical, but at the same time with a great innate sensitiveness and a need for love of which he is at first hardly aware. And this temperament is reflected in a very strange and complicated relationship with a woman – from this aspect you could call the film a love story. And this whole conflict and relationship is [*sic*] seen against a particular social setting. All these things play their part in the picture.[15]

The film's production was beset by disputes between Harris and Anderson, who according to Gavin Lambert was infatuated by his star, a factor exploited by Harris.[16] Certainly, a strong homo-erotic undercurrent runs through *This Sporting Life*; Weaver (Alan Badel) slides his hand onto Frank's knee in the taxi home after he has signed up with the city rugby team, Mrs Hammond questions the rugby scout, Johnson's (William Hartnell) intentions towards Machin, and the film's happiest moments are reserved for loving shots of the men cavorting naked in the changing rooms after matches. Harris' own performance is a virtuoso portrayal of a man whose only means of expressing his own hurt is to see it mirrored in other people.

Harris' Machin is edgy and restless, he chews gum constantly and paces around indoor spaces as if they cannot accommodate his body's energy. His physical gestures are expressions of psychic unease; in one of the flashbacks, he asks Johnson if he can get him a trial for the club. As the older man hesitates, Machin senses a rebuff coming and quickly backs off, swinging himself around a pole in mock carelessness, although Johnson now agrees to pass on his request. A repeated motif sees Harris hang by his hands off the curtain rail in Mrs Hammond's kitchen, the gesture emphasising his physique but also suggesting the boyishness that hampers him from developing a mature sexuality. Finally, after the widow's death, Machin walks around her house as if he can still find traces of her in the rooms; for the last time he swings off the curtain rail but now his face crumples and he falls forward; swaying, holding his head in his hands, he crouches on the ground, distraught, in foetal position.

If he is vulnerable, Machin is also brutal both on the field and off it. In the scrum, he deliberately has a man sent off after setting him

Figure 6.1 Troubled, rebellious masculinity. Richard Harris in
This Sporting Life

up to take the blame for an illegal tackle that Machin himself has made. More shockingly, he slaps Mrs Hammond's face twice, once in the churchyard and once after she refuses him sex. In no sense is this a portrayal of a man with whom the audience is intended to sympathise or who could be labelled with the romantic loner tag of a Brando or Dean character. Then again, in the film's celebrated scene where Machin smashes the spider on the hospital wall after Mrs Hammond's death, that brutality, it is suggested, is only the expression of Machin's repressed emotional state. If the film's final moments come closest to the representation of an inner moment, overall Harris' performance is less naturalistic than theatrical, drawing attention to the actor as performer. The effect is not so much Brechtian distancing as biographical layering (heightened, for audiences attuned to nuances of accent, by Harris' easily detectable Limerick tones).

The *Monthly Film Bulletin* reviewer commented that the film's few shortcomings 'are the virtually insignificant price Anderson has had to pay for a personal and artistic conflict within himself which provides the film with its remarkable tension. One suspects that writer [David Storey], director and actor were fortunate enough to share much the same sort of inner tension.' These conflicts are 'the inability to express with patience and gentleness his [Machin's] need to be loved; to reconcile the feminine side of man's, any man's, make-up with his own overridingly masculine and physical temperament'.[17] Such a response elevates the film's themes from the local to the universal, from a depiction of Northern working-class inhibitions to a more generalised concern with the shifting paradigms of masculinity; further it links the performance with the performer, perceptively establishing a template for Harris' subsequent work.

Even in his less noteworthy films (of which, given the actor's profligacy, there were many), Harris' performances are marked by an often agonised and partial acknowledgement of his internal conflicts; veering between brute physicality and rueful introspection, his roles most consistently placed him in the crucible where a recalcitrant masculinity (frequently linked with militarism) collided with a longing for understanding. Asked about his acting technique in 1965, Harries replied that:

> The secret of acting from my own point of view, I think that everybody living in the streets, every human being who breathes God's air, lives in what I call a secret world. Nobody else has any access to

it at all, not wife or family or friends. Within this world, things happen to you. This is where your real self exists, or fantasy exists, where you really play out a part of your life. The first thing I look for in a part I'm playing is not the obvious, not the lines, but the secret world of the man that nobody else is aware of. And I play off it [...]

Basically, I'm sort of an interior actor, through interior objectives and motivations. But a lot of points that one has to make as an actor are made, of course, externally. I've got a sort of histrionic and flamboyant thing which I can do very easily [...] when I actually start to work, I throw away all the work I've previously done which I hope by then has kind of imbedded itself in my subconscious anyway, and then I work instinctively through my crotch.[18]

This physicality distinguishes Harris' performance in *This Sporting Life* from the tradition of restraint and understatement that is often associated with British acting. This, according to Bruce Babington, is marked by: 'self-conscious virtuosity, impersonatory skills, wit and irony'.[19] It is also generally considered to differentiate British from American actors and it is in this context that Laurence Olivier's advice to Dustin Hoffman during the making of *Marathon Man* (John Schlesinger, USA, 1976) to: 'Try acting, dear boy', is most frequently cited.[20] Yet, understatement is not the only guiding principle in the British performance tradition. As we have already seen in Chapter 4, Charles Laughton's acting in films such as *The Private Life of Henry VIII* and *Jamaica Inn* was declamatory and highly histrionic. This theatricalisation of screen acting is a recurrent feature of British cinema and derives from its dual ambition of distinguishing itself from Hollywood and exploiting its indigenous theatre heritage. Harris' style was not as excessive as Laughton's and was influenced by the new kind of acting that the British New Wave demanded. Throughout his screen career, and most evidently towards its end, Harris tended towards a theatrical screen style and, arguably, it was this, with its combined overtones of 'classy' British theatre and of Irish oratory, that recommended him to Hollywood. At the same time, his looks, not so much traditionally handsome as characterful, and his persona, of troubled, rebellious masculinity, chimed with the requirements of a new set of screen roles.

After *This Sporting Life*, Harris, always short of money, notoriously appeared in one mediocre production after the other, bottoming out, in many people's opinions, with *Tarzan, the Ape Man* (John Derek, USA, 1981) in which he played Jane's (Bo Derek) father. The bulk of his work in the interim years was in Hollywood cinema, much of it in action/adventure films. Amidst the dross there are, however, some worthwhile performances that merit closer attention.

Harris' Hollywood career began with the part of Captain Benjamin Tyreen in *Major Dundee* (Sam Peckinpah, USA, 1964). Described by the eponymous Major (Charlton Heston) as 'a would-be cavalier, Irish potato farmer with a plumed hat fighting for a white-columned plantation house you never had and never will', Harris is a man divided by his loyalties, on the one hand to his own Confederate companions, and on the other to the Yankee Dundee, whom he has agreed to accompany on his hunt to rescue three kidnapped children from the 'Indians', in return for his own life and those of his men. Harris' Tyreen shows the Irish stereotype, particularly that of Brent's Wild Bill Donovan, in transition. Still a dashing Irish rebel, his romance is about to be eclipsed by a new, more pragmatic America, symbolised by the stiff Dundee. Knowing that his honour has been compromised and that his dreams of betterment, of that plantation house, are over, Tyreen leads his men into brave but fatal combat with the French troops and the film concludes with his death.

In Martin Ritt's *The Molly Maguires* (USA, 1969), we see the further diminishing of the Irishman as romantic rebel. Ritt, who had been blacklisted by the House Un-American Activities Committee (HUAC), taught at the Actors' Studio and his films are marked by strong acting performances and politicised themes. Both are in evidence in *The Molly Maguires*, with Sean Connery, then taking a respite from playing James Bond, acting against type as the leader of the eponymous Irish protest group. He and Harris are miners who form a bond of mutual respect despite Kehoe's (Connery) initial (and correct) suspicions that McParlan, whom he knows as McKenna, may be an informer. In fact, he is an undercover detective, employed by the Pinkerton agency to uncover the leadership of the Mollies and trap them into being caught by the police. Where Kehoe is taciturn and unwaveringly committed to achieving better working conditions for the men, McParlan is a fly-by-night personality, both in his guise as a killer on the run and in his true occupation as a detective. Although the film establishes early on that Harris is on the side of the law, and therefore the Irish-Protestant owners of the mine, and that he must betray his own kind, from this point onwards it encourages the viewer to question whether he can sustain this act of duplicity.

Although Ritt's film seems deliberately to evoke *This Sporting Life* in its opening moments, with Harris arriving at the home of Mary

Raines (Samantha Eggar) and her father (Brendan Thomas Dillon) to a cold welcome from the dour young woman, its central relationship is between Kehoe and McParlan. Under Ritt's guidance, Harris reins in his histrionic gestures, producing a performance that is taut and considered. He is, as Kehoe says, 'a reasonable man', one who can see that violence for its own sake, always a risk with the leader of the Molly Maguires, may be counterproductive. Until the film's closing moments, Harris never lets his emotions control him but is guided by his ambition. Only in his final encounter with Kehoe, as the latter waits to be hanged, does his ability to rationalise his motives fail. Explaining how he tried to prevent Kehoe from falling into the police trap, McParlan accuses the miner of bringing about his own downfall; the prisoner rounds on him, saying that McParlan is looking to be punished to free him from his conscience: 'You'll never be free. There's no punishment this side of hell that will free you for what you did.' At this, Harris lunges at Connery, releasing the energy that he has withheld so far and, we understand, at last letting us see the 'real' McParlan.

As a film, *The Molly Maguires* is remarkable for James Wong Howe's muted cinematography but hampered by its slow pace. Ritt's refusal to create in Kehoe an unambiguous hero, combined with Connery's own downbeat acting, add this to the list of what Andrew Spicer has identified as '*auteur*-director' productions that used Connery's Bond persona to explore the myth of the hero, inevitably at the expense of box-office success.[21] By keeping Harris' physicality in check until the film's ending, it tempts the viewer to believe that violence is not the best weapon in the miners' struggle against the injustices of their employment conditions, before finally exploding the myth that he is 'a reasonable man'. Mentally broken, just as Kehoe will be physically broken, McParlan offers no viable counter-position to that of Kehoe's own doomed resistance. The conclusion is that capitalism is immovable and the Irish commitment to a compromised religion (the priest offers no support to violent resistance) will forever keep them at the bottom of the employment heap. Other than that, the film offers few insights into the historical or political background to the formation of the Molly Maguires and its focus on the relationship between Kehoe and McParlan has the regrettable consequence of sidelining a more relevant discussion of the part played by the mine owners in exploiting labour. Arguing that the narrative of the Molly Maguires has consistently been 'shaped by contemporary events rather than simply portraying past reality', Kevin Kenny has seen the film as Ritt's own expression of disgust at the whistleblowers associated with HUAC.[22]

If Harris' casting in the 1960s and the early 1970s suggested an auteurist desire to deconstruct the myth of the Irish rebel, one of his more successful roles of this period was as an English lord captured by Sioux in Elliot Silverstein's *A Man Called Horse* (USA, 1970). In this revisionist Western, Harris plays the pampered Lord John Morgan who is taken captive and brutally tortured. The native Americans tie him to a stake and then ritually parade him around a bonfire where children ride him like a horse and women taunt him sexually. His ultimate physical punishment comes during the Sun Vow ritual where his chest is pierced and he is hoist upwards on grapples, to be hung by a rope until his vow, 'to prove my courage, to withstand all tests of pain', has been realised. In this intensely masochistic part, Harris seems to be inviting on himself (it is his decision, in the end, to stay with the Sioux) retribution for the history of white settlement. Although much was made of the film's authenticity, and of its ambition to develop an authentic native American perspective, in the end it is most effective in its voyeuristic examination of a tortured male subjectivity and has more to say about the 1970s than the 1820s. Harris' descent from a parodic depiction of upper-class English verbosity to an almost wordless position of cowered humiliation is a retreat from the verbal to the pre-verbal, his rebirth into the symbolic order signalled via his acceptance by the tribe and by his crucial role in its final defence. The film's closing moments identify the new Morgan as a man of the wilderness, one who has finally put civilisation behind him, a reading that underlines the deeply conservative vein running through the re-conceptualisation of masculinity during this period.

The success of *A Man Called Horse* resulted in two sequels. The first, *The Return of a Man Called Horse* (Irvin Kershner, USA, 1976), is a more coherent but also more conventional film, in which Morgan abandons his stately home to return to the tribe. They have been almost eradicated by white settlers and are hiding out in the mountains. Morgan galvanises them into resistance through offering himself to the Great Spirit. This entails another extended self-torture ritual, with Harris once again being hung from the skin of his chest until he commences to hallucinate, believing that he is travelling to the centre of the universe to find his spirit. The ritual lasts for four nights until he is reborn and finds the elusive 'something' he has been looking for. He then leads the tribe's attack on the fort, teaching them how to make rudimentary hand grenades from gunpowder and hollowed wood, and is crucial to their victory.

The film, like so many of Harris' productions, fetishises the actor's physique and the exposure of his body to pain. For the American media, it was the combination of physical superiority and emotional vulnerability that made Harris such a star. This had been compounded with the release of the single, *MacArthur Park*, in 1967, even if most critics were less than enthusiastic about the lyrics or the performance. Most of all, the press delighted in Harris' wild, Irish persona, which seemed, just as it had been previously in Britain, to be a tonic for a jaded society:

> He is a Limerick Irishman, so two thirds of his energy is vocal, but the physical side of him alone is exhausting enough. [...] Harris is one of the few ribald, boisterous souls left in the movie profession. He favourably recalls the best of Errol Flynn, also an Irishman, and like him is given to extraordinary debauches – in theory if not always in reality. [...] The wild colonial boy, the tinderbox of emotions, the troublemaker with flailing fists is busy throwing kisses at the world. The world around him may respond. If he does not burn himself out like a Roman candle – and he does have an amazing sense of survival – he, with his gift of laughter and his madness, could become the greatest light that Irish theatrics has ever tossed on the screen.[23]

Harris' name was associated with as many unrealised as completed productions, including the title role in a film about Michael Collins to be made by Kevin McClory. He also directed one film, *Bloomfield* (aka *The Hero*, GB/Israel, 1971), in which he played an ageing Israeli soccer star. Nicknamed 'O'Brando' by the media, he was reputed to be meticulous on set, if uncontrollable off it. Many of the completed films saw the Irish actor playing English parts, a contradiction given his vociferous anti-Englishness, that neither he nor the press seemed to notice. As King Arthur in *Camelot* (Joshua Logan, USA, 1967), he and Guinevere (Vanessa Redgrave) interpret their roles as studies in Swinging Sixties counter cultural frippery. Harris' successful transfer of the musical to the stage and his foresight in 1981 in purchasing the rights were his saving, earning him a personal gross of $8million.[24] Undoubtedly, both film and stage musical benefited from the American public's association of Camelot with John F. Kennedy's entourage, but Harris, who replaced Richard Burton when the latter fell ill, enjoyed a largely positive critical response to his performance. From that point onwards, and following his decision to stop drinking, Harris was able to select the film projects that interested him. His return to grace came with his 1990 London stage success in Pirandello's *Henry IV* and his role as the Bull McCabe in *The Field* (Jim Sheridan, GB, 1990), followed by *Unforgiven* (Clint Eastwood, USA, 1992), *Gladiator* (Ridley Scott, USA, 2000) and the first two *Harry Potter* films, during which time he acquired the kind of gravitas that was denied Brando.

I have analysed *The Field* elsewhere; what is interesting about his role in this and in subsequent films is the questions it raises about changing expectations of screen acting.[25] Harris' Bull McCabe is the King Lear of the west of Ireland, a figure whose tragedy is of equal dimensions to his tyranny, and who dwarfs his co-players as he rants and rages through a narrative of land dispossession and the encroachment of modernity. That the Bull is an anachronism, a man whose values are rooted in the past, is given added weight by Harris' depiction of him. His declamatory style, that 'histrionic and flamboyant thing', recall a performance style now firmly superseded by naturalism. Nor was it what the film's director, Jim Sheridan, had in mind when he initially cast Ray McAnally in the part. McAnally's unexpected death opened the door for Harris to lobby the producers mercilessly in anticipation of a role that promised him a return to critical grace. He was rewarded with an Academy Award nomination, his first since *This Sporting Life*; yet for some critics, his performance in Sheridan's film was over-wrought and outmoded. For others, it was a reminder of the craft and presence of the great screen actor. Harris, in turn, launched his own attack on a generation of performers such as Ian McKellen and Derek Jacobi whom he declared to be living passionless lives and to be passionless on stage. Only Mark Rylance and Daniel Day-Lewis passed muster.[26] Increasingly, Harris came to be viewed in the media as the last of a kind, a throwback to a time of excess and danger. That Harris, now a millionaire, lived in the Savoy when in London, kept a regular home in the Bahamas and frequented Dromoland Castle in Ireland was reported in the many interviews that accompanied his career comeback. An allied discourse linked his refusal to express any regret for his 'wild years' to his national identity, even if he did not himself make the connection, thus a typical interview in the *Daily Telegraph* was titled 'Why I play the wild rover', even though in the text, Harris did not refer to his Irishness or use that phrase.[27] His loquacity – the same interviewer reports that he held forth for seven hours without pause – was repeatedly cited as evidence of Irish fluency and when Michael Caine branded him, Peter O'Toole and Richard Burton as that 'trio of unreliable drunks', the press were enthralled. Harris' response was all they could have hoped for:

> Connoisseurs of language may savour Mr Harris's analysis of heavy drinking: 'Of course we imbibed. We dared to cross the threshold from sophisticated, drawing-room, strangulated drollery to the wilderness where we not only faced the lion's roar but smelled the breath of their bad habits; a voyage most great actors embarked on where, on occasion, they might touch the Gods to ignite their craft.'[28]

Harris' late-life roles feed off his reputation, most effectively setting him up as a legendary figure forced to face the waning of his powers. This is achieved most graphically in *Unforgiven* when he faces off against Little Bill Daggett (Gene Hackman). Eastwood's film is filled with references to the classic and post-classic Western, the genre in which he made his name. The casting of Harris as English Bob, a man who rides into town accompanied by his biographer, W.W. Beauchamp (Saul Rubinek), bears echoes of *A Man Called Horse* and its sequels, in which, as we have seen, the white man emerges as a hero, whose status is written into the myth of the West. Harris plays English Bob as a showman, declaiming to a carriage of Americans that their country needs a monarchy. His own myth is being recorded by Beauchamp in the book *The Duke of Death*, which Little Bill insists on referring to as *The Duck of Death*. With English Bob's superiority established, it is startling when he is so swiftly knocked to the ground by Little Bill and then kicked until he is bleeding and almost comatose. Later, in the police cell, Little Bill demolishes English Bob's reputation, assuring Beauchamp that it rests on an incident when Bob shot an unarmed man. Little Bill steals Beauchamp from his enemy before setting him on his way, the latter having recovered enough to throw a barrage of parting insults at the sheriff, this time in an accent that suggests more the Cockney than the titled gentleman of his introductory tones. In *Gladiator*, Harris is Marcus Aurelius, a ruler who must confront the consequences of his years of battle and now desires that his son, Commodus (Joaquin Phoenix) end the corruption in Rome and re-establish it as a republic. Commodus' response is to suffocate the old man, thus setting in train the events that see Maximus (Russell Crowe) becoming an outcast and a gladiator.

With an indigenous Irish cinema now developing, Harris appeared in two projects, one, *This is the Sea* (Mary McGuckian, Ireland, USA/GB, 1997), that required little of him other than playing an elderly family patriarch, Old Man Jacobs. The other, *Trojan Eddie* (Gillies MacKinnon, GB/Ireland 1996), takes on another aspect of Harris' reputation, casting him as John Power, the head of a traveller clan, who falls in love with the much younger Kathleen (Aislin McGuckín). As the wedding guests gather to toast the couple, a singer (Dolores Keane) breaks into the song, 'Love Makes A Fool of You'. Very soon, we learn that this is indeed the case as Kathleen runs off with Dermot (Stuart Townsend), leaving Power to vent his anger in classic Hollywood style by sweeping a row of pint glasses off the bar counter and cursing those who tell him to take it easy. Yet it is Power who ultimately triumphs; when Dermot loses interest in Kathleen and the money they were supposed to have run off with ends up in the hands of the eponymous Trojan Eddie (Stephen Rea), Kathleen comes back to her husband. The film ends with the couple going arm in arm into the foyer of a cinema, she now heavily pregnant; young boys laugh at them but they walk on. As they enter the auditorium, the screen is playing a series of kitschy ads for Irish products, one of which features Trojan Eddie, now a big-time small goods auctioneer. In this space, the ageing, legendary actor is transformed into just another cinema-goer, facing a new screen culture, one that, as we shall see in Chapter 7, had little time for conventional theatricality.

Figure 6.2 Just another cinemagoer. Richard Harris and Aislin McGuckín in *Trojan Eddie*

Until very shortly before his death, in October 2002, from Hodgkin's Disease, Harris continued working, making his final appearances as the wizard, Dumbledore, in *Harry Potter and the Sorcerer's Stone* (Chris Columbus, USA, 2001) and *Harry Potter and the Chamber of Secrets* (Chris Columbus, USA, 2002). His death was widely mourned, with tributes being led by the Irish Taoiseach (Prime Minister), Bertie Ahern.

NOTES

1 Quoted in U. O'Connor, *Brendan Behan* (London: Hamish Hamilton, 1970), p. 183. *The Quare Fellow* opened at the Theatre Royal, Stratford on 24 May 1956.
2 M.F. Callan, *Richard Harris* (London: Robson Books, 2003), pp. 66–7.
3 For a biographical account of the Angry Young Men, see H. Carpenter, *The Angry Young Men* (London: Allen Lane, 2002). Whether it was a movement or a moment remains disputed; descriptions of the Movement, kitchen-sink realism and the British New Wave are usually taken to cover much the same personalities and texts. This is discussed in detail in S. Lacey, *British Realist Theatre* (London and New York: Routledge, 1995).
4 'Irish Look Back in Anger, *The Ginger Man* at the Fortune', *The Times*, 16 September 1959, p. 14. On its Dublin performance, the play was closed down after its first night when its director, Philip Wiseman, refused to agree to cuts proposed by Louis Elliman, the impresario and owner of the Gaiety Theatre. For a description of this debacle, see J.P. Donleavy, *What They Did in Dublin with* The Ginger Man, *A Play* (London: MacGibbon & Kee, 1961).
5 J. Littlewood, *Joan's Book* (London: Methuen, 1994), pp. 772–3.
6 See Callan, *Richard Harris*, p. 112.
7 Naremore, *Acting in the Cinema*, p. 195.
8 Ibid., p. 200.
9 Ibid., pp. 200–2.
10 A Higson, 'Acting Taped', *Screen*, 26, 5 (September-October 1985), pp. 2–25, p. 3.
11 Interview with Richard Harris, *Cinema*, 4, 5 (April 1965), pp. 19–21, p. 20.
12 J. Hill, *Sex, Class and Realism* (London: British Film Institute, 1986).
13 R. Murphy, *Sixties British Cinema* (London: British Film Institute, 1992), p. 33.
14 Hill, *Sex, Class and Realism*, p. 136. See also Jeffrey Hill, 'Sport Stripped Bare', *Men and Masculinities*, 7, 4 (April 2005), pp. 405–23.
15 L. Anderson, *Never Apologise*, ed. P. Ryan (London: Plexus, 2004), pp. 92–3.
16 G. Lambert, *Mainly About Lindsay Anderson: a Memoir* (London: Faber, 2000), pp. 92–102.
17 P.J.D. 'This Sporting Life' (review), *Monthly Film Bulletin*, 30, 350 (March 1963), pp. 34–5, p. 35.
18 Interview, *Cinema*, pp. 19, 20.
19 B. Babington, 'Introduction', in B. Babington (ed.), *British Stars and Stardom* (Manchester and New York: Manchester University Press, 2001), pp. 1–28, p. 12.
20 According to Hoffman:

My first marriage was breaking up, Studio 54 was all in vogue and the excuse not to sleep for a week for your art so you could party big time. Love, sex, drugs, rock 'n' roll – I did that for my art and showed up to shoot on location. I had the rawness of voice, it looked like the character hadn't slept, it was the greatest preparation I've ever done...then I go to LA for the rest of the shooting and I tell Olivier about this story, and we're both laughing about it and that's when he said, 'Why don't you try acting, dear boy?'

Interview clip available at: http://www.bbc.co.uk/films/hollywood_greats/dustin_hoffman.shtml (consulted 24 May 2005).

21 A. Spicer, 'Sean Connery: loosening his Bonds', in Babington (ed.), *British Stars and Stardom*, pp. 218–30, p. 223.
22 K. Kenny, 'The Molly Maguires in popular culture', *Journal of American Ethnic History* 14, 4 (Summer 1995), pp. 27–46, p. 41. See also, K. Kenny, *Making Sense of the Molly Maguires* (Oxford and New York: Oxford University Press, 1998).
23 J. Borgzinner, 'Limerick Lad in Arthur's Court', *Life*, 22 September 1967 (Richard Harris file, AMPAS).
24 Callan, *Richard Harris*, p. 264.
25 R. Barton, *Jim Sheridan: Framing the Nation* (Dublin: Liffey Press, 2002), pp. 39–61.
26 Quoted in J. Harlow, 'Passion Players', *Sunday Times* (Section 1), 5 November 1995, p. 14.
27 B. D'Silva, 'Why I play the wild rover', *Daily Telegraph*, 18 March 1997, p. 9.
28 'Actors at war', *Evening Standard*, 7 August 1995, p. 9 (author not credited).

7

Stephen Rea

Politics and the actor
(1949?–; film career: 1978–)

A S WE HAVE SEEN in this book, strong links exist between the Irish theatre and Irish screen acting. On a more fundamental level, being 'theatrical' is supposed to be intrinsic to the Irish psyche; the cunning clowns and wily rogues of the Anglo-Irish tradition were predicated on an assumption that dissembling was a natural characteristic of the indigenous Irish, a cultural typology that was in its turn appropriated and re-negotiated to turn the tables on its early perpetrators. Part of this theatricality was an eloquence that bordered on wordiness, the use of a vigorous form of the English language that was often contrasted with its older, more tired expressions. In the early 1970s, as Christopher Morash has written, 'the Irish theatre had seemed to lag behind the world around it'; however, 'by the early 1980s, it had moved beyond an increasingly tired set of conflicts [located in the culture of traditional Ireland], which it was now able to look back upon with irony, anger, sometimes even compassion and forgiveness'.[1] Similarly, in the 1970s Irish cinema at last emerged from the shadow of outside filmmaking to develop an indigenous set of practices, initially drawing on the tradition of the avant-garde but, in the latter part of the 1980s, moving towards an aesthetic of realism that, at its best, it deployed to interrogate and subvert Irish culture and history.[2] Both media were focused on re-orienting themselves from the primacy of the script and the spoken word towards an exploration of gesture, movement, décor, disjointed speech and silence. In both instances, this meant a new focus on the actor as an active collaborator in the production and, during this period, a number of actors moved freely between stage and screen. From Belfast, although now settled in Dublin, Stephen Rea has been at the centre of this new energy within Irish cultural production. As one of the founders of the Field Day Theatre Company and as the star of a number of Neil Jordan's films,

Rea has long been an articulate and politically engaged presence within both media; he has also become an internationally recognised performer, largely thanks to his work with Jordan.

Rea began his acting career at the Abbey Theatre. However, he left after a short period:

> it reflected the world that existed in Ireland at the time. It wasn't there to provoke that world; it wasn't even reflecting a world that existed any longer; it was a world of the distant past and there were no radical theatre people there. I think the company was very strong and very depressed. You had some wonderful actors who had no focus or function. There was no intellectual rigour any longer.[3]

He then moved to London where he played at the Royal Court and National Theatres, as well as taking a small part in the soap opera, 'Crossroads'. One of his roles at the Royal Court was in Brian Friel's *The Freedom of the City* (1973). In 1979 Rea approached Brian Friel with a proposal to tour his next play around Ireland. Friel, like Rea, was from Northern Ireland and shared a desire to produce work that would reach a wider audience than the Abbey theatre-goer. They agreed to open *Translations* in Derry and then tour it to venues that would not normally be on the repertory circuit. The impulse behind the project was, 'both populist, in that Friel and Rea were reaching out to new audiences of people who did not usually have the opportunity to attend professional theatre, and parochial in a positive sense'.[4] In particular, the decision to open the play in Derry's Guildhall was widely recognised as symbolic of Rea and Friel's desire to speak to the country's disenfranchised communities – literally in this case since Derry's nationalist population had long been the victims of Unionist gerrymandering. The choice of *Translations*, which concerns the encounter in the 1830s between the English soldiers from the Ordnance Survey responsible for renaming Irish place names and the small community of Ballybeg, for this opening night was also important:

> Looking out of the Guildhall's windows during rehearsals, the cast could see the hills of the Inishowen peninsula where the play is set, across the border in the Irish Republic. Moreover, when staging a play so concerned with place names, there could be few better choices than Derry – or, as the unionist community call it, Londonderry. 'Derry', from the Irish *doire* (meaning 'place of the oaks') was the original name, until in 1613 the city was granted to a consortium of London

companies, who changed the name to Londonderry. However, in 1973, electoral reforms gave the city's Catholic population a majority on the City Council, and in 1978 – just as Friel was beginning to sift through the ideas that would become Translations – they rechristened themselves *Derry* City Council. Refusing to recognise the change, the British government still called the city *Londonderry*, as did most unionists. And yet, while London/Derry's name remained contentious, local unionist and nationalist politicians had worked out a power-sharing arrangement on the Council, and it was a unionist Lord Mayor, Marlene Jefferson, who helped to make it possible for *Translations* to be staged in the Guildhall.[5]

In this first production Stephen Rea took the part of Owen, the son of the Irish-speaking schoolmaster, Hugh. After the production moved to England, he switched to playing Manus, Owen's brother. Hugh was played by Ray McAnally, one of the older but most respected of the actors involved in the theatre and film revival of the 1980s. Although McAnally had enjoyed a long career with the Abbey and on the London stage, as well as in Irish and British films, at this point he was on the cusp of a late-life flowering that saw him take the parts of Bloom in Neil Jordan's debut, *Angel* (Ireland, 1982), Cardinal Altamirano in Roland Joffé's *The Mission* (GB, 1986) and Mr Brown in Jim Sheridan's *My Left Foot* (GB, 1989). Born in Buncrana in County Donegal his accent was unforced, as were the young Liam Neeson's, in the role of Doalty, and Rea's as Owen.

In 1981 Friel and Rea decided that the moment had come to expand and formalise Field Day as a theatre group and invited four other individuals to join them. These were Seamus Deane, Seamus Heaney, David Hammond and Tom Paulin. All of them, bar Hammond who was a former teacher turned broadcaster, musicologist and folklorist, were poets and all were educators; all, again excepting Hammond, were from Northern Ireland but were now living elsewhere and thus shared the common experience of displacement. Three, including Rea, were Protestant, three Catholic. The company was later joined by Tom Kilroy. As Marilynn Richtarik has written, 'most of the directors did not like to think of themselves as committed to Field Day indefinitely, so an aura of impermanence suffused the undertaking. Overall Field Day's theatre work was characterized by an ad hoc, improvisatory mode of operation.'[6] Certainly, although the company never formulated a concrete manifesto, Field Day was a highly politicised enterprise, and one of the outcomes of its desire to re-imagine the political events of the day without becoming embroiled in their specifics was the concept of a 'Fifth Province', an idea that Richard Kearney has further explored:

> This province, this place, this centre is not a political or geographical position, it is more like a disposition. This place, I submit, is not a fixed point or centralized power. It is not the source of some 'unitary and indivisible sovereignty'. If anything, it may be re-envisaged today as a network of relations extending from local communities at home to migrant communities abroad. The fifth province is to be found, if anywhere, at the swinging door which connects the 'parish' (in Kavanagh's sense) with the 'cosmos'.[7]

Overall, Field Day tended to approach the political situation obliquely, inviting audiences to interpret their plays, many of them versions of classical dramas, as allegorical. They also gained a reputation both within and outside Ireland as purveyors of high-quality theatre that functioned both intellectually and as entertainment; before that:

> I think no one was really addressing what our problems were; we had a very sparse repertoire that we were turning over again and again and the plays that we produced were not big plays. Friel was writing, [Tom] Murphy was writing; these individuals would always be thrown up but the collective power of a theatre wasn't really used to explore what was happening.[8]

Rea has insisted on the importance of producing plays that could be performed with equal impact in small rural venues in Ireland and on the London stage. At the same time, he has also spoken of his reluctance to speak with an accent other than his own:

> I found standard English difficult to work in. It seemed to cut me off from emotion, it seemed to cut me off from rhythm and everything that was real to me. And that southern English accent has been designed to conceal emotion and whatever happens all Irish accents reveal it in some way. And if you can't reveal it as an actor, where are you?[9]

Rea acted in all the early Field Day productions and also directed several of them, starting with Friel's *Three Sisters* (1981) and including Tom Paulin's *The Riot Act* (1984), a version of Sophocles' *Antigone*. One of his best-received performances was when he played both Brendan Bracken, an Irishman who served as

Churchill's Minister of Information during the Second World War, and William Joyce, the Irish Nazi radio propagandist, in Thomas Kilroy's *Double Cross* (1986). Brien Friel's decision to give his latest play, *Dancing at Lughnasa* (1990), to the Abbey rather than Field Day led to a falling out between him and Rea (Friel resigned from the company in 1994): 'I didn't feel that the Abbey deserved it. They hadn't done the work and we had done the work.'[10]

In 1983, Rea married Dolours Price, one of two sisters convicted along with six others of exploding two car bombs that killed one person and injured 200 more in London in 1973. Although Rea repeatedly warned the media not to confuse his and his wife's politics, it was inevitable that they would not heed him:

> I'm certain it affected my career in some way, not least that people perceived me to be perhaps more hard-line than I was, more rigid than I was. When in Field Day we did things that had a certain ambiguity about them, that ambiguity would be betrayed in some way by an image of me, which wasn't actually the case [...] It had an impact on films of course because I had done my first two films, playing the lead and that stopped. But that's OK, I stayed in theatre and this community of actors and theatre practitioners that existed in England were very, very loyal to me and it never became an issue.[11]

Although considerable academic attention has been paid to Field Day's plays and their pamphlets at a textual level, much less has been written about their performance. Marilynn Richtarik notes that David Rudkin was delighted to be commissioned to write a work for the company: 'Impatient with the slack, melodramatic strain he detected in much Irish acting, he wanted to write a play that would force Irish actors to adopt a more disciplined approach toward their roles.'[12] We can, of course, retrieve some sense of Rea's performance in the Field Day and other plays from their reviews; however, here I am more concerned with his screen career. In interview, he has spoken of his great admiration for Robert Mitchum:

> what it is I admire about his acting is that he's one of the great narrative actors. Nowadays everybody wants to 'show emotion'; everyone since the post-Brando Italian actors wants to scream the house down and show their innards, and Mitchum simply thinks. He must have been wonderful for a director because all you do is cut to Mitchum and he thinks something, and then you can take the movie in any direction you want.[13]

Like most post-Method actors, Rea does not subscribe to any particular acting technique; however, restraint is crucial to his character portrayal. Citing the opening sequence in *The Butcher Boy* (Neil Jordan, USA, 1997), where he is seen walking down a lane, Rea has said: 'I was pleased with the way that worked, and people said that the opening shot said everything about the guy. He's very drunk but walking, aggressively, but in as controlled a way as he could.'[14]

Very evidently, Rea and Jordan have a close, collaborative working relationship. According to Rea, he can concentrate on just playing the person, knowing that Jordan has taken care of the narrative. In other words, with less competent directors, Rea is always conscious of needing to impart information through his character about the narrative. From their first work together, *Angel*, Rea responded to Jordan's love of ambiguity by creating a continuum of characters who seem to drift through the films, often, it seems, unwilling or unable to comprehend just where their actions are leading them. Danny, in *Angel*, starts the film as a gregarious innocent, happy to play his saxophone and flirt with his co-performer, Dee (Honor Heffernan). Only after he has witnessed the bombing of the dance hall and the murder of the deaf-mute, Annie (Veronica Quilligan), does he become increasingly estranged from the everyday. Where his speech was once jaunty, now Rea delivers his lines disjointedly, addressing rhetorical questions to those he encounters. In particular, his conversations with Bloom have an elliptical quality about them, with neither actor quite catching the other's eye. 'There's a spell on you,' Dee remarks of her one-time lover, and there is indeed something dreamlike about Rea's Danny, as if he too died in the blast at the significantly titled Dreamland Ballroom. We do not need to go as far as his encounter with the prophetic seventh son of the seventh son to realise that Danny has moved from a real to a symbolic universe, one delimited by dream-logic.

The debate over how to interpret *Angel* has largely been defined by the contrasting perspectives of John Hill and Richard Kearney; the former has argued that Jordan's film is part of a cinematic inheritance that refuses to view the Troubles as arising from specific socio-economic conditions but instead sees them as an irruption of the atavistic tendencies of the Irish, the latter that the film is to be praised for exploring the psychical underpinnings of violence.[15] Kevin and Emer Rockett have written that *Angel* is imbued with Catholic religious symbolism while Brian McIlroy has wondered what the apparently Protestant Danny is doing killing violent paramilitaries of his own religious persuasion.[16] These ambiguities are made possible by Rea's performance. As he disengages from the characters around him so he retreats into an inner world to which the viewer is denied access; whether or not this is a rational state is not revealed. Rea has said that 'the camera likes to watch actors thinking' and much of *Angel* is given over to Jordan's camera holding his main actor in mid-shot, his face turned slightly away from the viewer, evidently doing just that.[17] The challenge to the audiences (and the film's many critics since then) is to guess what his thoughts are. Only once, after Annie's killing, does Danny seem suddenly to spring back to life, and this is when the woman in the farmhouse, Mary (Sorcha Cusack), commits suicide with his gun; he yells out, then walks away from the farmhouse, cradling himself and gagging.

Figure 7.1 'The camera likes to watch actors thinking'.
Stephen Rea and Ray McAnally in *Angel*

Much the same reaction occurs when Rea's Fergus realises that his lover has a penis, in his and Jordan's third collaboration, *The Crying Game* (GB, 1992). Pushing himself away from Dil (Jaye Davidson), he runs into the kitchenette off her room and throws up into the sink. Such extreme reactions mark crisis points in the film's narrative and contrast sharply with Rea's habitual languid, reflective movements. In both films, Jordan creates eddies of activity around his watchful central character. Rea may be the hero but not in any conventional sense;

'You're no pin-up. You're not handsome at all,' Jody (Forest Whitaker) says to him in *The Crying Game* and at this point in the film's early moments, he is right. Rea's long unkempt hair hangs over a pale face, its pallor rendered more obvious by an apparent lack of make-up. He has dark bags under his eyes and a look that moves between detached and resigned. Only subsequently, when he meets Dil, Jody's girlfriend, and has her cut his hair, does Jordan change both his camera angles and his lighting to de-accentuate Rea's funereal demeanour and give him a more open, less troubled appearance. Evidently, *Angel* and *The Crying Game* are companion pieces, their link emphasised by Rea's centrality to both. In the earlier film, his character follows a trajectory from carefree to troubled, in the later, his journey is reversed; as his relationship with Dil evolves, so he learns to slough off his inhibitions, and with them a narrow outlook associated with his Irish identity, replacing this with a cosmopolitanism and worldliness that comes with exchanging Northern Ireland for London.

The Crying Game remains the most-discussed of Jordan's films, with writers more divided over the nature of its gender politics than its commentary on the state of Northern Ireland. Rea has said of Fergus that he is definitely heterosexual, and that it was on his insistence that Jordan included a shot of him kissing Jude (Miranda Richardson).[18] Yet in a film where nothing is quite as it seems, it is hard to remain convinced that such absolutes pertain. As in *Angel*, Rea seems to be an innocent stranded in a world too complex for him to decode. He has, as Jody again says, a 'killer smile' and a 'baby face'. If the central question of *The Crying Game* is whether people can change, or whether, like the scorpion, their actions are always pre-determined, Fergus is the measure of that dilemma; on every occasion that he believes that he is in charge, external events throw his intentions off-kilter. Rea literally refuses to act decisively, abdicating his conventional positioning as the hero who propels the narrative forward, to the victim of the narrative's propulsion. He fails to save Jody who is then run over, in an early ironic twist, by a British army Saracen; in London he fails to notice that Dil is a transvestite or that he is in a gay bar; he is tied up on a bed when he ought to be preventing the assassination of the judge and he can only look on as Dil fatally shoots Jude. His one moment of decisiveness occurs off-screen, when he presumably turns himself in to the authorities and falsely confesses to the murder of Jude, thus protecting Dil. Even in the film's closing moments, he gives no indication that he is now in control.

Rea's performance style, his preference for thinking over doing, has been so closely tied in with Neil Jordan's own filmmaking practices that it has been hard for him to play more conventional hero roles. Furthermore, as he has himself conceded, his marriage linked him to a specific political ideology even if he did not in fact subscribe to it. Subsequent to that, he again ran into controversy for providing the voice-over for an interview with Sinn Féin leader, Gerry Adams, when the latter was prevented by censorship restrictions from speaking on television. Rea has also worked with Mike Leigh on three projects. In 1979, Rea took a part in Leigh's stage play, *Ecstasy*. He also worked with him on the television play, *Four Days in July* (GB, 1984), about two families, one Catholic, the other Protestant, set around 12 July as both women wait to have their first babies. In these performances, Leigh brought out Rea's comic ability, having him act in a self-deprecatory manner that suddenly shifts into unexpected bombast. His window cleaner, Dixie, in *Four Days*, with his garrulous reflections on the world, is in some ways closer to the conventional stage Irishman than his other parts, but re-inflected with a Northern Irish accent that divorces that character from his earlier Abbey roots and re-appropriates it for the North. In *Life is Sweet* (GB, 1990), he plays Patsy, whose name, though not his accent, suggests that he is Irish. Again, Rea's entrance as Patsy is as a drunk trying to keep his physical movements under control and his part consists of adding additional chaos to the lives of the English couple Wendy (Alison Steadman) and Andy (Jim Broadbent) when he persuades Andy to buy a rusting chip van. Appearing in a Leigh project means adopting an improvisatory approach to the part, although, as Rea has noted, by the time Leigh is ready to shoot, 'it's as tightly scripted as a script of Neil Jordan's'. Such a high degree of improvisation, however, leads to complete subjectivity, as you must always be in character – 'but you don't have an overall vision of the piece, which I believe you should have, because acting is a conscious art, as well as using areas of instinct and the unconscious'.[19] Despite what he says, Rea's performance as Gerry McAllister, a Belfastman married to a Dubliner, Ellie (Sinead Cusack), and living in London, in *Bad Behaviour* (Les Blair, GB, 1992) must count as one of his most engaging performances outside his work with Jordan. Although much of his filmmaking is for television, Blair's directorial style is often compared to Leigh's for whom he once worked as editor and producer. He favours improvisation and the domestic drama and cast several of Leigh's regular collaborators in *Bad Behaviour*; as well as

Rea, these include Phil Daniels (as the Nunn brothers) and Phillip Jackson as Howard Spink. If it wasn't so determinedly mundane, we might consider the McAllisters' North London terraced house as existing within the Fifth Province; reference is never made to the North–South divide that marks the marriage of Gerry and Ellie and any differences they have as a couple are more to do with her frustrations within the home and his frustrations at work – in the local council's planning office – than a political situation that is never mentioned. Apparently divested of the responsibility of bearing the freight of a traumatic national identity, Rea is able to produce a finely detailed study of a middle-aged man overwhelmed by the smothering trappings of domesticity and the intrigues of public service employment. Peering through round glasses and secretly composing a cartoon about a character named 'Paddy Plan-it', Rea seems to burrow into himself as the prevailing conditions of his life up their tempo. As much as he is resigned and cynical, he can summon up an energy and fluency of invective, a lesson in Belfast abuse, to throw at Spink when he tries to con them over a building job. Gone is the mannered, stylised vocal delivery that is so essential to his work with Jordan, to be replaced by an understated realism that is particularly effective when playing to Cusack's Ellie.

Although he has consistently turned down offers from Hollywood to play IRA men, Rea was himself involved in the pre-production of *A Further Gesture* (Robert Dornhelm, GB/Germany/Japan/Ireland, 1996), an attempt to exploit and develop his baby-faced killer persona. *A Further Gesture* was scripted by Ronan Bennett, who was himself imprisoned at the age of 18 for the murder of an RUC man during an armed robbery of a bank. The conviction was quashed on appeal after Bennett had spent thirteen months in jail, during which time he attempted to escape by posing as a remand prisoner. Bennett remained under suspicion for subversive activities for a number of years. Then a member of the Black Flag anarchist group, he has since turned to novel and scriptwriting. His work moves between generic gangster films and political thrillers and he has retained an interest in international conflict.

A Further Gesture was originated by Rea and, once Bennett's script was completed, it was intended that the film should be directed by Arthur Penn. Subsequently, Robert Dornhelm, who had been initially supposed to direct *Into the West* (Mike Newell, Ireland, 1992), was appointed as director. Just where the responsibility lies for the film's failure to meet the expectations attached to it is impossible to decide, though after its release, critics tended to blame Dornhelm. In a particularly frank interview with *Film Ireland*, Dornhelm suddenly remarked: 'You know what I discovered now, talking to you, why they hired me? Because I'm so totally naïve, and because I'm not part of this IRA/Irish conflict. Because it's better not to have someone who knows the nuances and the differences.'[20] As the interviewer, Ted Sheehy, suggested, the film's success hinged on understanding the motivations of Rea's character, Dowd, yet Rea's performance was so inscrutable that those motivations were always opaque. The film opens with a thrilling set-piece prison break (its US title was *The Break*), in which Dowd has to decide abruptly to join the other inmates in an escape bid. He and another prisoner, Richard (Brendan Gleeson), as well as a number of others make it, and Dowd removes himself to New York where he assumes a new identity. After intervening in a domestic dispute in his tenement, he is stabbed and nursed back to health by a Guatemalan brother and sister, Tulio (Alfred Molina) and Monica (Rosana Pastor). Dowd and Monica become lovers and, realising that they are amateurs who plan to shoot the torturer, Ramon (Esteban Fernandez), Dowd helps them to organise the assassination. In the final scene, he is surrounded by FBI agents and, as they close in on him, he smiles, shrugs and raises his weapon, to be gunned down by them and die instantly.

Was the film advocating the necessity of blood sacrifice, Sheehy wondered. 'I was warned against this sacrifice characteristic that the Irish have, they like to suffer...' Dornhelm informed him.[21] With comments like this, it is evident that the film's director was not in tune with the script's intentions. Yet, neither Rea nor Bennett seem to have been clear on what motivated Dowd, other than that he was a Camus-type existential loner. Of Dowd, Bennett has said:

> Stephen Rea's character is trying to leave idealism and commitment behind and isn't doing well – he's ambivalent about the struggle but he's also ambivalent about giving things up so when he is saved by these people, by Monica and her brother, Dulio [*sic*], he re-discovers people who are committed and who have this drive to right a wrong that has been done. It re-awakens his idealism and he can't just walk away from it. In this case though the motives are mixed – he's also in love with the woman, and his life had been going nowhere in any case, so there are many other motives involved but I wouldn't say it's an attempt to salve his conscience – it's a way to re-discover something he once had and now feels the absence of.[22]

Rea too has suggested that the film is about the redemption of his character: 'In the film, Dowd has lost this innocence, he is used up by the cause. He has allowed himself to become a person he did not want to be. Then he meets these people and he remembers his own innocence.'[23] Redemption is thus – as Sheehy reads it, but apparently Dornhelm does not – tied into blood sacrifice, a problematic and arguably regressive ideology. With such a high level of confusion informing the film's production, Rea seems stranded in the narrative. As he has said in interview, he likes direction; he evidently also needs a script. With little of either, he performs in *A Further Gesture* as if he were in a Jordan film. Yet, in *The Crying Game*, Jordan does not cut Rea loose until he has developed his character through his conversations with Jody and his reactions to his IRA colleagues. Jody humanises the conflict that Fergus has participated in, challenging his commitment; when Fergus is speaking to his superior, Maguire (Adrian Dunbar), the tensions between them suggest that Fergus has a history of minor insubordination. As Fergus moves through the London world that Dil inhabits, so he must constantly react to his new circumstances; brief moments with figures such as the barman, Col (Jim Broadbent) and the workers on the site allow the viewer to build up a complex picture of Fergus' character. Most particularly, Fergus is marked by a tenderness that informs Rea's best parts. This tenderness is conveyed by a look, a characteristic glance upwards and a slight softening of his facial expression that is almost imperceptible. With little dialogue, and few moments of sustained interaction between Dowd and the other characters in *A Further Gesture*, the keys that will unlock Dowd's persona are missing. Further, in *Angel* and *The Crying Game*, Rea was participating in films that were aesthetically non-realist. Although both these Jordan films referenced the real, they have, as we have seen, a dreamlike quality that is expressed through dialogue as well as being cued visually. Both Danny and Fergus deliver their lines in a slightly abstract, mechanistic fashion that distances them from emotion and suggests something ritualistic in their behaviour. We could say that they are being propelled by the rituals of the unfolding narrative rather than by any intentionality of their own. Dowd, on the other hand, is modelled to a far greater extent on the classic disenchanted Hollywood hero and bears the expectation of agency.

The release of *A Further Gesture* confirmed Rea's screen persona as that of the reluctant gunman, although he had only played that role in three films. Interviews with him, particularly in the American press, drew parallels between his performances and his performance of national identity: 'Shaping his moods, if not also his character, are the vagaries of Northern Ireland's troubles, which Mr. Rea feels all the more acutely because he is a Protestant who sympathizes with the historic plight of the province's Roman Catholics and is married to Dolours Price, a former I.R.A. militant who once served time in prison.'[24] Just as Barry Fitzgerald's wrinkles spelled Ireland, so Rea's lugubrious features have become metonymic for his country's ancient sufferings. As Ireland's landscape has become a measure of its historical identity – dark and brooding or bright and welcoming – so too the national actor's face is allegedly imprinted with the nation's history.

The expectation that Rea was both physically expressive of the cartography of the Troubles, but also spokesman for the political situation, was further enhanced when he took the role of the Irish journalist, Edward, in Frank McGuinness' 1992 play, *Someone Who'll Watch Over Me*. Set in Lebanon, Edward is one of three men held hostage by terrorists. The other two are the Englishman, Michael, and the American doctor, Adam. In interview, Rea has insisted that only an Irishman could play the part and that he drew on his own background to express Edward's 'politics, that glib irony which seems to suit Northern Irish people; his truculence about the English'.[25] McGuinness' play gently unpicked the construction of the national stereotype, so that each character at first appears to conform to expectation and gradually is revealed to add up to more, or less, than we might assume. *Someone Who'll Watch Over Me* opened on Broadway to modest reviews and a particularly negative response from the influential critic of the *New York Times*, Frank Rich. However, shortly afterwards, *The Crying Game* arrived on American screens, elevating Rea to the status of cult celebrity and drawing audiences to the play. He was then nominated for a Tony award (as was Liam Neeson for *Anna Christie*) as well as for an Academy Award (ultimately winning neither).

Working with Jordan and McGuinness as well as in the various Field Day productions allowed Rea to develop a performance style that moved beyond the stereotype of the stage Irishman; where the classic Abbey actors developed that character in a direction that underlined its constructedness, Rea more radically abandoned it to create a new type of performance: 'He raises two fingers to an audience's expectations of a part. He refuses to hide behind any notion of his country's national characteristics.'[26] At the same time, as we have just seen, popular media discourse, particularly in the

United States, strained to read national characteristics into Rea's persona and performances. Since *A Further Gesture,* Rea, like Jordan, has moved on to explore different narratives. Actor and director have continued to collaborate, though Jordan's Hollywood work has seen him substitute his former leading man with actors who it might seem are more suitable for parts such as Lestat (Tom Cruise) and Louis (Brad Pitt) in *Interview with the Vampire: The Vampire Chronicles* (USA, 1994). In *Michael Collins* (USA, 1996), Rea played Ned Broy in a role again designed to support the film's more conventional Hollywood-style hero (Liam Neeson). During this time, alongside his work with Jordan, he performed in a number of Hollywood productions, for instance *feardotCom* (William Malone, GB/Germany/Luxembourg/USA, 2002), appearances that we have to assume were financially motivated. Unlike his peers, although Rea now regularly participates in Hollywood productions, he has made little impression on Hollywood cinema, outside of those films, such as *Interview with the Vampire*, that were directed by Jordan. Although he has spoken of his pleasure in working with Robert Altman, it is perhaps regrettable that the film in question should have been *Prêt-A-Porter* (USA, 1994). His Milo O'Brannigan, a sleazy fashion photographer, was an unusual role for the Field Day founder but one that provides Altman's film with some of its more coherent and amusing moments.

Those who know him insist that there are two sides to Rea's personality, the maudlin brooder and the lively wit. After his seminal earlier films with Jordan, it was quite a different side of Rea's performance style that irrupted into *The Butcher Boy*, the production that marked Jordan's revisiting and reworking of his surreal vision of Ireland and the Irish. Here Rea plays Benny Brady as a manic reinvention of the traditional Irish father. Jordan's ability to render the tone of the originating novel (by Patrick McCabe, 1992) on screen was reliant on his use of heightened, surreal visuals and on the performances of the cast. It was equally important that this cast should work as an ensemble, without slipping into a realist acting style. Much has been written already about *The Butcher Boy* as a text, and particularly as a commentary on Ireland's history, and history of representation, yet little attention has been paid to the significance of performance in realising that effect.[27]

One of the many pleasures of watching *The Butcher Boy* lies in actor recognition. In particular, the casting of Milo O'Shea as the paedophile, Father Sullivan, creates a link to an older generation of Irish performers and functions, as much as the playing of ballads and enumeration of artefacts from the past (comics and flash bars), as a signifier of historicity. More than any of Jordan's other films, *The Butcher Boy* is also a showcase for the current generation of Irish screen actors – appearing alongside Stephen Rea are Brendan Gleeson, John Kavanagh, Sean McGinley, Gerard McSorley, Fiona Shaw and Birdy Sweeney. Ardal O'Hanlon plays Mr Purcell and Sean Hughes, Rosaleen Linehan, and Gina Moxley, all actors better known for stand-up and cabaret performances, take various roles. Sinéad O'Connor as the Virgin Mary easily accounts for the most mischievous casting, and the novel's author, Patrick McCabe, plays Jimmy the Skite. In the title role, the young Eamonn Owens represents a rising generation of Irish performers. Between them these older actors have played together in so many films and so often on television that they could be with justification considered a national repertory company. Just as in *Trojan Eddie*, in which Rea takes the lead, and which shares many actors with *The Butcher Boy*, they evidently perform to each other's strengths. Gleeson, Kavanagh, McGinley and McSorley all alternate between heroes and villains and Gleeson too moves with regularity between Irish and Hollywood parts.

Figure 7.2 Performing to each other's strengths. Brendan Gleeson and Stephen Rea in *Trojan Eddie*

In both *Trojan Eddie* and *The Butcher Boy*, there is a virtuosity of performance on display, an environment in which Rea is evidently at ease. His Benny Brady is, as he has said, an underplaying of what could have been a stock Irish type. His drunkenness erupts in sudden moments of violence, such as the scene that ends the party the family has held to mark the return of Uncle Alo (Ian Hart). Roaring at his brother-in-law, he then strikes his wife and clutches his hair, bemoaning the way his life has turned out. Yet Benny is not all bad. When he visits Francie in the industrial school, he suddenly says: 'I loved you like no father ever loved a son, Francie.' As he speaks, Rea turns slowly from the mantelpiece and reaches out towards the back of Francie's chair, without quite touching him, the summation of his failure and longing as a father.

The Butcher Boy is highly performative, emphasising its non-realist aesthetic and, in doing so, distinguishing it from *Trojan Eddie*. The latter gains its effect from its gentle and unobtrusive observations of its characters; *The Butcher Boy* moves from one set-piece to another, like a never-ending variety act that adds up to a narrative continuum. Its brief moments of tenderness, mostly occurring between Francie and Benny, allow the action momentarily to slow down, offering the audience a sanctuary from the feverish momentum of the forwards narrative drive.

Rea has also played smaller roles or cameos in a number of films, including the garrulous taxi driver in *The Last of the High Kings* (David Keating, Ireland/GB/Denmark, 1996), the priest, Father Quinn, in *This is My Father* (Paul Quinn, Ireland/Canada, 1998), the Irish emigrant in *I Could Read the Sky* (Nicola Bruce, GB/Ireland, 1998) and Dr Figure in *On the Edge* (John Carney, Ireland, 2001). These roles seem to have allowed him to free himself of the burden of carrying the plot and to give rein to his pleasure in performance.

By the end of the 1990s, Rea was speaking of being bored with the 'paraphernalia' of acting, of the waiting around on set. Only Neil Jordan, he said, was stimulating to work with: 'Neil keeps it going, because he loses his creative edge when it slows down, and that's why I love working with him.'[28] He was also becoming disillusioned with the direction Irish cinema was taking:

> I think that theatre and films at the moment coming out of this country tend to be films that say to the outside world: 'Relax, you have nothing to fear from the Irish. We are not a dangerous species.

There was a period when, of course, all the imagery of this country was that we were dangerous, threatening and guns and everything, and now it's all a bit more reassuring. Maybe this is a transitional period; I hope it is because it's not good enough, we have to be a bit harder with ourselves. We are a society in a state of flux so there are questions there to be asked clearly about immigration, but I don't know what dramatic form it will find. But, whatever it is, you can't reassure people.[29]

Perhaps in the hope of excavating new talent that would rescue Irish cinema from its current stasis, Rea has lent his name to new productions by emerging directors, notably *Bloom* (Sean Walsh, Ireland, 2003), *The Halo Effect* (Lance Daly, GB/Ireland, 2003) and the short film, *Fluent Dysphasia* (Daniel O'Hara, Ireland, 2004). The first is perhaps most interesting for demonstrating how Rea can switch from lugubrious to exuberant within the space of one narrative; here he plays Leopold Bloom in an adaptation of James Joyce's *Ulysses* (1922). The film is hampered by rendering a contemporary film as a period piece, an effect highlighted by the reverent orchestral score. A decision to have the action play in a realist manner, save for the extended fantasy sequence, and keep Joyce's dialogue and free-flowing prose for voice-over, creates a disjuncture between word and image that militates against any fidelity to the spirit of the original. Rea is trapped in the midst of this, forced to pass through scene after scene looking put-upon while accompanied by his own voice-over. Yet, even here, in the fantasy sequence as he parades as a king, a naked man, and other personae, his joy in performance lights up the screen, inviting the audience to relish the absurdities of his capering, clowning Bloom. *The Halo Effect* was low-budget director, Daly's, follow-up to *Last Days in Dublin* (Ireland, 2001) and like the earlier film, is an amiable, episodic ensemble piece that required of Rea that he turn in not so much a star turn as a performance that would anchor the troupe of ancillary players. The film is essentially a character study, structured around a week in a Dublin chip shop, whose owner, the ironically named Fatso (Rea) is on the brink of disaster as a result of his gambling compulsion. The café acts as a sanctuary for a disparate collection of individuals, played by several generations of what I have already termed the national repertory company – here including Simon Delaney, John Kavanagh, Mick Lally, Gerard McSorley and Fiona O'Shaughnessy. Again, in *Fluent Dysphasia*, the central character, Murph (Rea), is deliberately played by Rea against the grain of the virtuoso star performance. Here Rea is a dishevelled, single father who has little to say to his 15-year old daughter, Jane (Jayne Stynes), particularly when it comes to helping her with her Irish homework. However, after a night out watching an Arsenal game, he receives a knock on the head and comes around to find that he only speaks Irish. The remainder of the film sees Jane assist him in communicating his problem and finding a solution that leads to the film's ironic conclusion.

The thrust in the latter two films is to divest Rea's persona of the expectations of stardom; meanwhile, in his Hollywood productions he is cast and filmed on the assumption of that stardom. That some of Rea's best Irish films have seen him play as part of an ensemble reinforces an impression that interviews with him convey, that the concept of stardom is not one with which he is comfortable. That the actor should be a collaborator in the production is an under-standing that has underpinned Rea's career. On the other hand, the actor as auteur is not a position he willingly occupies. Despite the (primarily American) media's determination to elevate him to a symbol of troubled Irishness, in fact Rea's performance style and his persona have been devoted to rethinking the essentialism that mobilises that kind of facile attribution of national identity. His most successful performances have broken the mould of the stage Irishman, just as the most successful films in which he has appeared have been committed to the exploration of new cinematic forms and narratives for Irish film. Whether Irish cinema can continue to offer him the kind of challenging parts that he so evidently relishes remains to be seen.

NOTES

1   C. Morash, *A History of Irish Theatre* (Cambridge and New York: Cambridge University Press, 2002), pp. 258–9.
2   See also Barton, *Irish National Cinema*; M. McLoone, *Irish Film: The Emergence of a Contemporary Cinema* (London: British Film Institute, 2000).
3   *In My Life – Stephen Rea*, RTÉ Radio One, broadcast 8 January 2002.
4   M. Richtarik, 'The Field Day Theatre Company', in S. Richards (ed.), *The Cambridge Companion to Twentieth-Century Irish Drama* (Cambridge, New York etc.: Cambridge University Press, 2004) pp. 191–203, p. 192. See also, M. Richtarik, *Acting between the Lines* (Oxford, New York: Oxford University Press, 1994).
5   Morash, *A History of Irish Theatre*, pp, 234–5.
6   Richtarik, 'The Field Day Theatre Company', p. 195.
7   R. Kearney, *Postnationalist Ireland* (London and New York: Routledge, 1996), p. 100.

8   *In My Life – Stephen Rea.*
9   Ibid.
10 Ibid.
11 Ibid.
12 Richtarik, *Acting between the Lines,* pp. 192–3. Field Day subsequently rejected the play, *The Saxon Shore.*
13 C. Zucker, *In the Company of Actors* (New York: Theatre Arts Books/Routledge, 2001), p. 109.
14 Ibid., p. 116.
15 J. Hill, 'Images of violence', in Rockett, Gibbons and Hill, *Cinema and Ireland,* pp. 147–93, R. Kearney, *Transitions* (Dublin: Wolfhound Press, 1988), pp. 175–83.
16 E. and K. Rockett, *Neil Jordan: Exploring Boundaries* (Dublin: Liffey Press, 2003), pp. 17–35, B. McIlroy, *Shooting to Kill* (Trowbridge: Flicks Books, 1998), p. 57.
17 Zucker, *In the Company of Actors,* p. 116.
18 Ibid., p. 114.
19 Ibid., p. 117
20 T. Sheehy, 'Into the gesture', *Film Ireland,* 59 (June/July (1997), pp. 16–21, p. 20.
21 Ibid.
22 A. Crilly, 'More than just a writer', *Film Ireland,* 62 (December/January 1997/8), pp. 26–9, p. 28.
23 A. Riding, 'Cast in the middle of the long conflict in Northern Ireland', *New York Times,* 15 February 1998, pp. 11, 20, p. 11.
24 Ibid., p. 20.
25 A. McFerran, 'A star in another language', *Independent on Sunday,* 23 September 1992, p. 22.
26 Irving Wardle, quoted in McFerran, 'A star', p. 22.
27 See McLoone, *Irish Film,* pp. 213–23 and Rockett, *Neil Jordan,* pp. 179–203.
28 Ibid., p. 123.
29 *In My Life – Stephen Rea.*

8

Gabriel Byrne

Gothic traveller
(1950–; film career: 1978–)

ANOTHER PRODUCT of the revitalised Irish theatre scene, Gabriel Byrne's screen persona marks a return to and a reconfiguration of an earlier literary tradition. With his dark looks and a demeanour most frequently described as 'brooding', first British, then Hollywood cinema found in Byrne a new vision of the Gothic outsider-hero, a figure who, as we will see, found his hour with the advent of the millennium. At the same time, as it responded to shifts in ethnic representation, American filmmaking rediscovered in old generic forms new representational possibilities. Here, once again, it turned to Gabriel Byrne, this time to re-animate another outsider-hero, the Irish gangster.

Byrne's professional Irish acting career began with an invitation to join a small Dublin theatre, the Focus, run by Deirdre O'Connell:

> She was a brilliant actress steeped in the Stanislavski method and had taught some of the country's best actors, like Tom Hickey and Johnny Murphy and Tim McDonnell. Her gentle demeanour belied her extraordinary energy and her commitment to giving Dublin alternative classical theatre [. . .] Anything I ever learned about acting this woman taught me. If the Irish theatre has a heroine it is she, who taught me that passion and commitment and love of the work were more important than any technique.[1]

From the Focus, Byrne moved to an institution that was to provide the locus for a new generation of Irish actors, the Project Arts Centre, established by Jim and Peter Sheridan to provide Dublin audiences with an alternative to the tradition encapsulated by the Abbey. A response to the disillusionment of the 1970s, the Project confronted head-on the social issues of a society marked by personal disempowerment and institutional repression. Byrne was a cast member in *The Liberty Suit*, the 1977 production based on Mannix

Flynn's experiences in prison, written by Flynn in collaboration with Peter Sheridan, and directed by Jim Sheridan. A critical success at home and in Britain, the play broke new territory with on-stage nudity and an intense exploration of male bonding and brutality.[2] Byrne initially played the role of Grennell, taking over the lead, Curly, from Mannix Flynn when the production moved to the Royal Court Theatre in 1980. In 1982, Byrne moved to London with his partner, Áine O'Connor, where he worked at the National Theatre and the Royal Court before breaking into cinema with his role as the investigative journalist, Nick Mullen, in *Defence of the Realm* (David Drury, GB, 1985) and as Lord Byron, in Ken Russell's *Gothic* (GB, 1986).

Peter Thorslev has charted the evolution of the romantic hero, from noble outlaw and man of sensibility, to a darker more rebellious figure who shares many of the traits of the gothic villain. The latter is 'always striking, and frequently handsome. Of about middle age or somewhat younger, he has a tall, manly, stalwart physique, with dark hair and brows frequently set off by a pale and ascetic complexion.'[3] Most notable are his dark, piercing eyes. The later romantic hero inherited many of the traits of the gothic villain, with the important exception that he was capable of redemption. Such heroes are solitary by nature and 'adjustment to society as it exists is impossible for them; they either go down to glorious defeat, cursing God and dying, or they commit their lives to transforming the world'.[4] The shift from one type to the next within the Romantic movement signified a transformation 'from conformism in large social patterns of conduct or thought, to radical individualism; from humble right reason, common sense, and the proper study of mankind, to a thirst to know and experience all things, to encompass infinities; from acquiescence before God and the social order, to heroism and *hubris*'.[5] The two most distinctive traits of the romantic hero were 'their sensibility and their Satanism', and their legacy was 'total rebellion because it is a rebellion not only on a political level, but also on the philosophical and religious level – and sometimes, in nihilistic extremes, against life itself'.[6]

In *Gothic*, Byrne first played the part that was to define his film persona in fin-de-siècle Hollywood. His Lord Byron is a characteristically flamboyant Russell creation – limping, demonic, energetic and sensuous. Byron's first appearance, at the top of the stairs in the Villa Diodati, brocade robe swinging dramatically from his shoulders as he greets his guests, Percy Shelley (Julian Sands), his mistress, Mary Godwin (Natasha Richardson) and her half-sister, Claire (Myriam Cyr), is an entrance worthy of the London stage of Bram Stoker and Henry Irving. 'Tolerance is a virtue,' he will shortly declaim. 'I have no virtues.' Fuelled with laudanum and alcohol, he and his guests spend their evening pursuing each other, and each other's fantasies, through corridors and into bedrooms; a dead knight's face erupts with maggots, an automaton dances to thrusting sexual rhythms before playing the piano and, as morning dawns, an unborn baby is shown lying just below the surface of Lake Geneva's waters, its head gently mutating into the features of Boris Karlov's Monster, a nod to the film's ostensible exploration of the creation of Mary Shelley's *Frankenstein*.

Figure 8.1 Romantic hero, gothic villain. Gabriel Byrne in *Gothic*

As the *Monthly Film Bulletin* reviewer remarked: 'it is a Russell habit, much cherished by his admirers, that having done his biographical homework he has no hesitation in embellishing the bits of history that appeal to him and discarding the rest, and it would be irrelevant to condemn *Gothic* for being so embellished that the biographical aspects are worthless'.[7] In the place of fact, Russell substitutes affect, overturning British cinema's conventional realism, and its elegant literary adaptations, for a delirious sensuousness and disregard for the primacy of the written word. His is the kind of Gothic horror that Julian Petley celebrates in his early excursion into what has since become a wholesale reclamation of that cinema's '"deviant", non-realist strands'.[8] Achieved primarily at the level of image – the burning trees, the leeches, the dead children – and through its fast-paced editing, casting is also key to Russell's effect. On a straightforward level, the blonde Julian Sands and Natasha Richardson are counter-pointed by the dark Cyr and Byrne. Sands' most recent films before *Gothic* were *The Doctor and the Devils* (Freddie Francis, GB, 1985) and *A Room With a View* (James Ivory, GB, 1985) and, like Richardson, he is closely associated with a Britishness that is often less stable than it initially seems. Both were established actors by the time of their appearance in Russell's film, yet Byrne's only significant release had been *Defence of the Realm*. Although Byrne's performance is highly theatrical, in the tradition that we have seen, say, Laughton play, he is also the film's outsider, at the time a virtual unknown. 'Tell them the truth,' Claire exhorts Byron, 'you are the devil.' And so he is, a dark figure infiltrating Mary Godwin's mind and Claire's body, caressing the hysterical Shelley and assuring him that 'we have all been weaned on blood.' Byrne's Byron drives the film, springing, in terms of British cinema, from nowhere to do so.

In his essay, 'Ireland, America, and the Gothic Memory: Transatlantic Terror in the Early Republic', Luke Gibbons has argued that the American Gothic, pioneered at the close of the eighteenth century by Charles Brockden Brown, was informed by a fear of 'destructive Irish interlopers on American soil'.[9] In the same period, John Robinson's *Proofs of a Conspiracy Against all the Religions and Governments of Europe, carried on in the Secret meetings of Free Masons, Illuminati and Reading Societies* (published in Edinburgh and London in 1797 and Philadelphia in 1798) found Catholic secret societies infiltrating the uppermost echelons of European politics and connections were soon made by, amongst others, Brown between these and the Irish political underground.[10] That these might travel across the Atlantic and so undermine the American pastoral, Gibbons sees as an analogy for the Irish gothic's own journey across the ocean, where it 'materialized . . . in the form of the American gothic'.[11]

That these dates might have another significance becomes more evident if we move forward in time to the writings of another popular American author who shares a surname with his literary progenitor. Dan Brown's phenomenally successful *The Da Vinci Code* (2003) was written on the coat tails of a fusion of American cultural anxieties set in motion by the advent of the millennium and formalised by the events of 9/11. Revelling in Catholic secret societies and the corruption of American innocence by European decadence, it only omits the Irish element. This, however, was supplied by two earlier expressions of millennial anxiety, the films *End of Days* (Peter Hyams, USA, 1999) and *Stigmata* (Rupert Wainwright, USA, 1999).

Of these two films, the first point that needs to be made is that neither is a work of intelligence. *End of Days* opens in 1979 with the birth of a baby who will, in twenty years time – December 1999 – be reclaimed by a satanic cult whose master is determined that she will bear his child and hasten the apocalyptic end of days. Coming between the young woman, Christine York (Robin Tunney) and her nemesis, simply called the Man (Byrne), is an avenging bodyguard, Jericho Cane (Arnold Schwarzenegger), with most of the film devoted to an extended special effects showdown between the two. Another triumph of production design, *Stigmata* follows the fortunes of hairdresser, Frankie Page (Patricia Arquette), after she receives a gift of a rosary from Brazil. Soon afterwards, she begins to display signs of stigmata and the Vatican dispatches Father Andrew Kiernan (Byrne) to conduct an investigation. Priest and unbeliever are attracted to each other, Frankie's sufferings increase and it emerges that she is witness to a new gospel that the Catholic Church has been trying to conceal. Kiernan has to defend her against this well-connected secret society and save her from death by stigmata.

Both films were met with derision by critics, though in each case Byrne escaped most of the vitriol. In both he plays liminal characters; in the former he is part-human, part-Satan, his body that of the Wall Street banker that is now possessed by the demon; in *Stigmata* he is the representative of a corrupt Catholic Church who must abandon one conspiracy for another in order to save his lover. It may not be common enough knowledge that Byrne himself spent four years in a seminary, leaving him a 'failed priest at fifteen', to argue for biography being meaning-making in this case, or that he has since spoken of being sexually abused in that English seminary.[12] However, his character in these two millennial films brings with it a tradition of representation that draws on a sense of the gothic as a dark history that will not go away. In common with Thorslev's romantic hero, he must either go down to glorious defeat, cursing God and dying, or commit his life to transforming the world. Although Byrne can, as he demonstrated in *Gothic*, ham up an English accent, he has never quite managed to shake off his native Dublin tones and learn to pass as American. Thus, his Hollywood characters bear lingering traces of an Irish identity. This has implications both for how we read films such as *End of Days* and *Stigmata* but also how we understand the workings of his alternative gangster persona, discussed later.

Postmodernism, Paul Coates has argued, is drawn to 'negative theology'.[13] Religion, with its assertion of the triumph of good over evil, has fallen victim to the fate of other grand narratives, its place taken by an indeterminate spirituality. Further, the reluctance of most contemporary Western representational forms to imagine what God is like has meant that: 'a cloud of unknowing, spirituality, inserts itself between ourselves and the divine. What we perceive when the cloud disperses, however, may be a god or a monster.'[14] That Byrne could be cast as Satan and as a seeker-hero priest in two films made contemporaneously is symptomatic of Hollywood's, and beyond it popular culture's, undecidedness as to the intentions of the divine and the relationship between institutionalised religion and spirituality. The Irish immigrant's historic association with Catholicism (even if many immigrants were in fact from the Protestant denominations) allows for a nexus of connections to determine Byrne's double characterisation – as a figure of religion, with connotations of pastness, and as a tormented Byronic hero. Of the films, *End of Days* is by far the most conventional. Here, Satan is a classic gothic seducer in Thorslev's formulation of the type – having been penetrated by the demon's spirit in the men's bathrooms, the Man returns to his dinner table, grabs his fellow diner's breast and kisses her passionately, all the time glowering at her male companion so threateningly as to reduce him to a state of powerlessness. Throughout the film, he is defined by his libidinal energies and a cynical humour, leaving his interpreter with little to do other than invest his Satan with a theatricality that is reminiscent of his earlier Lord Byron.

Where both films climax with the victory of good over evil, both associate Catholicism with a world of conspiracy, secret societies and cabbalistic mysticism. The church building in *End of Days* is styled on the European gothic, with Byrne's Satan as the interloper come to destroy American society. Both films locate the source of threat within the Vatican enclaves and define Byrne's character as an emissary, in the one of evil, the other good. Abandoning his native accent for his best effort at sounding American made little difference for, by the time of the release of *End of Days*, the actor was firmly established in the public eye as Irish. Gone are the kindly Irish priests of Barry Fitzgerald and Bing Crosby's times, with only *Stigmata*'s Father Kiernan left to salvage the reputation so assiduously fostered by those performers and others of their day. That priests make problematic Hollywood heroes was evident in *The Bells of St Mary's* where Crosby's Father O'Malley would, had he had an alternative profession, have been romantically attracted to Ingrid Bergman's Sister Mary Benedict, had she had any other calling. *Stigmata* solves this narrative dilemma by signalling from early on that Father Kiernan will fall for the uncomprehending stigmata victim, Frankie Page whom the Vatican has sent him to investigate. Until he meets Frankie, Father Kiernan has been something of a Vatican enforcer, travelling around the world investigating (and disproving) miracles. Whereas a love affair between Father O'Malley and Sister Mary Benedict would have been heretical, in *Stigmata*, Father Kiernan's attraction to Frankie is symptomatic of his dwindling allegiance to the Church as an institution; as he says, 'I love Jesus. I don't need an institution between him and me.' Rather than provoking a crisis in his faith, this enables his embrace of a spirituality that is denied those who remain in Church orders.

As Coates discusses, the substitution of spirituality for religion, combined with a sense of alienation from controlling Churches, is the ultimate trajectory of the Protestant critique of priestly mediation.[15] *Stigmata* employs the Gospel of St Thomas' exhortation to believe that God 'is with you and all around you, not in buildings of wood or stone' as the basis for its exposé of the Catholic Church and its corrupt hierarchy of priests.[16] Within this hierarchy, Father Kiernan is a lone seeker of truth; a former organic chemist, he was inspired by the inexplicability of creation to join the Jesuits but now finds himself caught up in a web of conspiracies, since, if it is to retain its position, the Church must suppress this Gospel. Within a film that is wildly over-burdened by signifiers – Frankie's apartment is filled with burning candles and a mysterious source of dripping water; sinister priests and nuns clutching crucifixes materialise in the subway as she experiences the piercings of the stigmata; doves rise over and again in slow motion from Pittsburgh's city squares – Byrne's habitual underplaying of his role provides *Stigmata* with its few moments of calm. Similarly, given the production's reliance on suggestion over narrative coherence, his screen persona imbues his character with the trappings of the outsider as romantic hero, while his Irish accent connotes both devotion and rebelliousness.

In both these films, Byrne is the bearer of a series of extra-textual meanings whose origins can be located at the intersection between his screen history, his national identity and his off-screen persona. Most often, he plays a man with an unresolved past, torn between ego and id, conscience and temptation. In interview, he has said that: 'acting is about having the courage to become yourself, and the great challenge of acting is to put your emotions at the service of the storyteller, to use your private pain to express emotions that other people can identify with'.[17] His often troubled figures exhibit none of the debonair qualities of his contemporary, Pierce Brosnan, or the insouciant masculinity of the younger Colin Farrell. Instead, his acting style and the characters he plays link Byrne directly to the representational history of the Irish on screen, while allowing him to update and re-negotiate that history. We have already seen how this is worked through via his evocation of the devil and the priest; we can see it equally in his alternative persona, that of the Irish screen gangster.

The classic American screen gangster was marked by his ethnicity; whether Irish-American or Italian-American, his failure to achieve upward mobility through legitimate channels resulted in his embrace of crime as the only route to wealth. Robert Warshow has influentially argued that the gangster was a 'tragic hero', doomed to be destroyed by the very system that created his dreams of wealth and success.[18] As we have seen earlier in this book, Irish characters in the classic era were allowed little leeway within the confines of their stereotyping; once a poor priest, a struggling boxer or a loyal foot soldier, they were offered few if any opportunities to transcend class barriers. Hollywood's narrative containment of its characters reflected a wider sense of class immobility so that, as Jonathan Munby has argued, the screen gangster allowed for an expression of ethnic America's frustration over its right to move up through the social system.[19] The higher the gangster tried to climb, the more laughable his attempts to appear 'classy' were shown to be; yet the films' makers were adept at opening up a space for identification with their victim-heroes before supplying the inevitable punishment for such transgression. The coming of sound re-emphasised the gangster's origins, allowing audiences to hear his unadulterated ethnic accent, that proclamation of his hyphenated identity.[20]

This was the voice of James Cagney, the most unstable and the most charismatic of the Irish screen gangsters.[21] Cagney's balletic movements, his expressive hands, whether delivering a quick jab at a friend or an enemy, and his quickfire verbal delivery were an inheritance from his days in vaudeville and defined his performances. By contrast, when he came to play Tom Reagan in *Miller's Crossing* (Joel Coen, USA, 1990), Byrne's still, often unreadable presence is essential to his reworking of the iconic figure of the Hammett gangster. *Miller's Crossing* is not an adaptation of any one Hammett novel but more an interweaving of *Red Harvest* (1929) and *The Glass Key* (1931), borrowing elements from both to create a work that is at once homage and identifiably an auteur production. The Coen Brothers' characters tend to deliver their lines as non-sequitors and to appear to be somewhat adrift in complex plots that barely hang together at the point of resolution. Reagan is in this sense a classic Coen creation; yet played by Byrne he is never a comic figure nor does he seem unsure of his own position within the labyrinthine plottings of the American gangster fraternity. We first see Reagan as an out-of-focus figure walking towards and then to the side of the camera while Johnny Caspar (Jon Polito) pleads with Leo (Albert Finney) to have Bernie Bernbaum (John Torturro) killed for profiteering. As the two men square up to each other, Reagan sits quietly to one side, observing them. This is to be his position, both metaphorically and figuratively, throughout the film, an onlooker to the other characters as they lose their cool over money and power. If he is interested in either, it is not a defining reason for any of his actions. Just what does motivate Reagan is the film's enigma, but it gradually becomes evident that it is he who is driving the narrative, and that he is behind much of the violence that is so lavishly treated on screen. With his slight physique, his dark hair and his luminously white skin, Byrne's Reagan is a shadowy figure; in his final moments with Bernie, the latter begs Reagan to look into his heart. 'What heart?' Reagan responds before finally shooting dead the man whose life he so recently saved. What he says bears little relationship to what he does and he often seems to be delivering his lines for iconic effect rather than explication. The camera favours him alone, sitting smoking a cigarette or in his bare, virtually unfurnished room. In a typical exchange, Verna (Marcia Gay Harden), the lover Reagan shares with Leo, sashays away from an argument with the comment: 'I suppose you think you raised hell.' 'Sister,' Reagan replies, 'when I raise hell, you'll know it.' At this point the camera steadicams giddily backwards from him as if startled by his threat. If he refuses to trade in metaphor, insisting that the hat in his dream is just that, his actions suggest hidden motivations, emanating from a past to which the viewer is denied any access.

Figure 8.2 Onlooker and outsider. Gabriel Byrne in
Miller's Crossing

It is this ability to suggest that there is a depth to Tom Reagan's character that moves Byrne's performance beyond pastiche. With his laconic delivery and hard-boiled dialogue, Reagan could have been little more than a stylish reconstruction of the corrupt film noir hero; as it is, there is much here to recall a classic Hammett adaptation, John Huston's *The Maltese Falcon* (USA, 1941), another film with an Irish subplot and a fat man, this time called Kaspar (for the benefit of those who miss the connection, Caspar comments to Tom, 'I guess you could be useful in spades'). Byrne's Reagan is both of the moment and historical, referencing and reinvigorating the Hammett hero. His moral ambiguity constantly deflects the film from veering into nostalgia while, arguably, speaking to the ethical morass of the second Reagan administration.

It is also an updating of the character of the classic Irish gangster. The part was originally written as Jewish but altered on Byrne's behest, adding to the film's referencing of Irish ethnicity, otherwise most strikingly expressed in the sequence where Leo turns his weapon on the assassins sent to kill him and guns down one of them to the tune of *Danny Boy* (sung by Frank Patterson), to which he had been listening on the gramophone. After the scene had been shot, Patterson recorded the song in studio while watching the scene play on monitor in order to match the cadences of the ballad to the on-screen slaughter; the film's main theme is a re-arrangement of the harp tune, *Limerick's Lamentation* or *Lochaber No More*, suggested by Byrne. As the authors of the article, 'The Combination of Music and Film in Miller's Crossing', argue:

> the material being used is by no means Irish traditional music, having more to do with early Twentieth Century American music culture than Irish, even though the Irish elements can be heard clearly throughout. Carter Burwell (the composer/arranger for the film) used aspects of his own musical culture – which through reasons of history have become part of our own musical heritage – in his preparation of this score.[22]

Thus, the musical score becomes metonymic for the place of the Irish immigrant in American culture, part-integrated, part a reminder of an older tradition. The crucial distinction between Byrne's Irish gangster and Cagney's is the issue of agency. Where Cagney is a victim of his environment, 'not the real city, but that dangerous and sad city of the imagination, which is so much more important, which is the modern world', Reagan controls his; he may be punched about by his superiors, and most of *Miller's Crossing*'s scenes end with Reagan being assaulted, but these are only distractions.[23] In the Coens' early 1990s revisioning of power and politics, to be on the outside is to be in a position of strength. With an accent now altered from Cagney's second-generation urban ethnicity to a distinct Dublin working-class intonation, Byrne also benefited from the associations of Irishness and cool that would in turn so influence Colin Farrell's rise to fame. Even before he took the part of Tom Reagan, Byrne had enjoyed much press attention for his outsider status, a reputation cemented by his appearance as the investigative journalist, Nick Mullen, in the British thriller, *Defence of the Realm*. Initially cynical and unmotivated, Mullen is drawn into a newspaper story that he gradually realises involves top British politicians in an American nuclear scandal. A small, downbeat film that ends with

Mullen causing his own death in the interests of exposing the corruption, *Defence of the Realm* was critically well received and Byrne widely touted as having, 'all the makings of a romantic leading man, a rarity in British cinema'.[24] Unhappy in England, Byrne moved to America, initially to New York with his then wife, Ellen Barkin, and their two children; after their divorce he moved to Hollywood before returning to New York to be closer to his children. He has always insisted that he does not belong in the Hollywood mainstream, and his most successful work has been in the independent sector.

Formulating his concept of 'an accented cinema', Hamid Naficy has argued that accent differentiates exilic from dominant culture; in this case 'accented' does not just denote vocal delivery but rather describes a cinema that is syntactically other – 'exilic and diasporic accent permeates the film's deep structure: its narrative, visual style, characters, subject matter, theme, and plot'.[25] *Miller's Crossing* is evidently not an example of exilic or diasporic filmmaking yet we can understand Byrne's accent here, and in the later *The Usual Suspects* (Bryan Singer, USA, 1995), as the mainstream's recognition of the place that the exilic has historically held within it. Naficy here also reminds us that:

> people make use of accents to judge not only the social standing of the speakers but also their personality. Depending on their accents, some speakers may be considered regional, local yokel, vulgar, ugly, or comic, whereas others may be thought of as educated, upper-class, sophisticated, beautiful, and proper. As a result, accent is one of the most intimate and powerful markers of group identity and solidarity, as well as of individual difference and personality.[26]

Part of Barry Fitzgerald's achievement in Hollywood was to retain his accent and still play characters outside of the ethnic working class that being Irish so often connoted; George Brent, on the other hand, lost all trace of his Irish accent as part of a strategy of passing as other, in his case, as American. Even in the 1980s, as we shall see in Chapter 9, Pierce Brosnan adopted the tones of English theatre in order to play the type of sophisticate on which he built his reputation. Byrne's retention of his accent, therefore, like Stephen Rea's, was an assertion of the validity of the exilic persona and a refusal to be marginalised because of it. This and a new perception of Irishness must have recommended him to the makers of *The Usual Suspects*, a film whose cult status is a validation of its embrace of cool.

Like *Miller's Crossing*, Singer's film recalled the detective fiction of Hammett and Chandler and the style of post-war film noir; at the same time, it reminded us that narrative is a construction, a matter of perspective. Here, two perspectives clash, that of the narrator, Verbal Klint (Kevin Spacey) and the police interrogator, Detective Kujan (Chazz Palminteri). The latter believes that the raid on the docked ship that opens the film was an elaborate scheme devised by Dean Keaton (Gabriel Byrne) to allow him to disappear from police attention; the former tells a tale that revolves around the machinations of a fabled master criminal, Keyser Soze, whom he asserts is behind the plan. In the now famous ending, Klint is revealed to be Soze and Keaton, we assume, has indeed died. Of the assembled criminals that form the gang, only Keaton's past is significant and is (depending on the narrative perspective) a determining factor in the plot. Byrne plays Keaton as a man for whom the lure of transgression is in constant competition with the virtues of going straight. Only when he concedes that he cannot throw off his past and settle down with a decent woman can the action truly start. Irish again, Byrne's Keaton references back to *Miller's Crossing* and further to an association of Irish ethnicity and pastness, which, in both cases, is defined by the attraction of evil.

With his dark looks and brooding demeanour, Byrne is that traveller from across the Atlantic that unites Gibbons' Irish gothic with Thorslev's rebelliousness 'against life itself'. If he re-inflected the screen Irishman with the accent of an originating ethnicity, so too he brought to his local Irish roles a sense of a corrupting but alluring past. In 1992, Byrne formed his own production company, Mirabilis Films, and acted as Executive Producer on *Into the West*, also taking the role of the one-time Traveller king, Papa Riley. In 1993, he executive produced *In The Name of The Father* (Jim Sheridan, Ireland/GB/USA, 1993). Although this project was initiated by Byrne, who acquired the rights to Gerry Conlon's account of his false imprisonment as one of the Guildford Four, the actor has since spoken of his disappointment over the liberties the film took with the facts of the case and of the decision to cast Emma Thompson as the solicitor, Garth Pierce. These differences of opinion led to a falling out with Jim Sheridan and Byrne's subsequent withdrawal from involvement with the making of the film.[27] With Áine O'Connor, he made the Irish-language television film, *Draiocht*, in 1996. He co-wrote *The Last of the High Kings* and played the part of 'Da', father of Frankie Griffin (Jared Leto), the teenager whose right of passage forms the core of the narrative; he co-produced *The Brylcreem Boys* (Terence Ryan, GB, 1998), an Irish prisoner-of-war drama in which he played Sean O'Brien. In 1997 he formed Plurabelle Films and executive produced *Mad About Mambo* (John Forte, Ireland/GB, 2000), a teenage love story. He has also co-produced a number of minor American releases including *Somebody is Waiting* (Martin Donovan, USA, 1996) and directed and wrote *The Lark in the Clear Air* (USA, 1996). In 2000, Byrne's television series for ABC, *Madigan Men*, was launched. A sitcom revolving around three generations of Irish fathers and sons, Byrne executive produced and took the lead role of Ben Madigan, a New York architect. As the *New York Times* forewarned, the actor, 'with his hangdog good looks and idiosyncratic charm', was an unconventional lead for a sitcom; nor did the series promise the kind of camp humour that fuelled much of prime-time American television.[28] With a poor audience response, *Madigan Men* folded after one season.

Byrne has frequently referred to his sense of his own liminality. One such remark prefaces the 'Introduction', or as he has said: 'Since I've left Ireland I won't ever belong there again, yet I won't ever really belong in America.'[29] His best Irish roles have exploited that liminality, creating a persona who is positioned on the outside of his own culture. For audiences in Ireland over a certain age, Byrne remains Pat Barry, first in 'The Riordans' (RTÉ, 1965–79) and then in the follow-up series, 'Bracken' (RTÉ, 1980–2). In an era when many households only had access to the national broadcaster, 'The Riordans' has been widely considered to have played an influential part in Ireland's rapid process of modernisation, particularly with regard to the rural community. The casting of Byrne as Pat Barry, towards the end of the series, introduced a leather-clad rebel into the cast: 'he was the only male character in the whole run of "The Riordans" to have developed as such an obvious sex symbol. Indeed he soon replaced Benjy [Riordan], not only in the work of the farm, but also in Maggie's affections in the most noteworthy adulterous affair in the history of Irish television drama.'[30] When 'Bracken' succeeded 'The Riordans', Pat Barry was retained as one of the central characters. 'Bracken' differed from 'The Riordans' 'in foregrounding the lone individual [Pat Barry] over against [sic] both community and family'.[31]

Less widely seen was his threatening businessman/drug baron in *The Courier* (Joe Lee, Frank Deasy, Ireland, 1987), a locally produced genre-based thriller exploring the underside of Dublin's rapidly modernising culture. Pre-empting Byrne's later Irish-American gangster roles, the film suffered from weak casting in several other parts and an unconvincing romantic sub-plot. On the other hand, Byrne's Val is a genuinely menacing character with no redeeming features. By the time he returned to Ireland to play Papa Reilly in *Into the West*, he brought a performance history to the part that resonated with those Irish audiences familiar with his earlier, local career and with his move to America. Although Byrne has participated in a number of Irish productions, notably *The Last of the High Kings*, where, despite being married with a family, he is a rootless actor, *Into the West* remains his most fully realised indigenous role.

An erstwhile romantic figure – King of the Travellers – Papa Reilly is out of work and trapped in a derelict high-rise block of apartments where he seeks escape in alcohol. In order to rediscover the romance of the road and the values of his outsider status, Reilly is forced to make a journey 'into the west' that is both figurative (in pursuit of his two sons) and symbolic (back to the 'real' Ireland). In an additional layering of biographical detail, he is aided in his quest by a female tracker played by Ellen Barkin.[32] In Sheridan's screenplay, Traveller life is portrayed as representative of an authentic Irishness that has been pushed into near oblivion by the encroachment of a modernising capitalism. Viewed with a much greater measure of sentimentality than in, say, *Trojan Eddie*, its symbolic value overwhelms any sense of its contemporaneity. Within this schema, Byrne's Traveller King is a link to an earlier culture that is suggested as much by his dark looks as by any historical accuracy, namely the 'Black Irish'. A term that originates, by common consent, with the survivors of the wreckage of the Spanish Armada, it loosely describes those Irish with dark colouring and blue eyes who formed an earlier wave of ethnic outsiders. Here, I would suggest, is the genesis of the romantic/Gothic Irish hero, a figure that has defined Gabriel Byrne's screen career. Travelling through Irish popular memory, redefined in Gothic literature, reviled in Victorian caricature, and revitalised in late-twentieth century screen culture, the Black Irishman could be said to act as a test of mainstream culture's positioning of the Irish as outsiders. 'There is an archaic weight of history with which English society has become entangled, and which is threatening to drag it down, and its name is Heathcliff, or Ireland', Terry Eagleton has written in his provocative reinscription of Irishness into *Wuthering Heights*. 'Better surely to shuck it off and face the future. But Heathcliff, like the Irish revolution itself, is archaic and modern together – a mournful remembrance of past wrongs which then unleashes a frenetically transformative drive to the future.'[33] Noel Ignatiev, in turn, has persuasively argued for the history of Irish emigration to America as one of becoming 'white'.[34] In one sense, with the success of actors such as Gabriel Byrne, Pierce Brosnan and Colin Farrell, they have now become 'black' again. In Byrne's career, particularly in independent cinema, we can trace popular culture's burgeoning romance with the dark other of Irish history.

NOTES

1   G. Byrne, *Pictures in My Head* (Dublin: Wolfhound Press, 1994), p. 77.
2   See also R. Barton, 'Jim Sheridan', in A. Roche (ed.), *The UCD Aesthetic* (Dublin: New Island, 2005), pp. 190–8; pp. 191–2.
3   P. Thorslev, *The Byronic Hero* (Minneapolis, MN: University of Minneapolis Press, 1962), pp. 53–4.
4   Ibid., p. 66.
5   Ibid.
6   Ibid., pp. 188 and 197.
7   P. Strick, 'Gothic', *Monthly Film Bulletin*, 54, 637 (1987), pp. 47–8, p. 48.
8   J. Petley, 'The lost continent', in C. Barr (ed.), *All Our Yesterdays* (London: British Film Institute, 1986), pp. 98–119, p. 100.
9   L. Gibbons, 'Ireland, America, and gothic memory: transatlantic terror in the early republic', *Boundary 2*, 31, 1(2004), pp. 25–47, p. 30.
10 Ibid., pp. 39ff.
11 Ibid., p. 47.
12 Byrne, *Pictures*, p. 56; M. Ross, 'The angel in Gabriel', *Sunday Times* (*Culture*), 8 August 1999, pp. 4–5.
13 P. Coates, *Cinema, Religion and the Romantic Legacy* (Aldershot and Burlington: Ashgate, 2003), p. 17.
14 Ibid., p. 17.
15 Ibid., p. 4.
16 The 'lost' Gospel of St Thomas is the basis for a proliferation of conspiracy theories, many directed at the Catholic Church. The reader can find any number of them on various dedicated websites.
17 Ross, 'Pictures', p. 4.
18 R. Warshow, 'The gangster as tragic hero', in *The Immediate Experience: Movies, Comics Theater, and Other Aspects of Popular Culture* (New York: Doubleday, 1969), pp. 127–33.
19 J. Munby, *Public Enemies, Public Heroes: Screening the Gangster from Little Caesar to Touch of Evil* (Chicago, IL: University of Chicago Press, 1999).
20 Ibid., p. 44.
21 See L. Fischer, 'Mama's boy, filial hysteria in *White Heat*' in S. Cohan and I.R. Hark (eds), *Screening the Male* (London and New York: Routledge, 1993), pp. 70–84.

22 S. Joyce and N. Keegan, 'The combination of music and film in Miller's Crossing', *Film West,* 21, (Summer 1995), pp. 32–3, p. 33. See also, S. Levy, 'Shot by Shot', in P. A. Woods (ed.), *Joel and Ethan Coen* (London: Plexus, 2000), pp. 74–7.
23 Warshow, 'The gangster as tragic hero', p. 135.
24 W. Russell, 'Irish charmer on his way to stardom', *Glasgow Herald,* 28 January 1986, p. 4.
25 H. Naficy, *An Accented Cinema* (Princeton, NJ and Oxford: Princeton University Press, 2001), p. 23.
26 Ibid.
27 R. Bennett, 'Let down by a dangerous woman', *The Observer* (Arts section) 8 May 1994, pp. 4–5.
28 P. Marks, 'A leading man tries TV in a show about men', *New York Times,* 8 October 2000, pp. 30, 39, p. 39.
29 J. Oppenheimer, 'Home is Where the Art is', *L.A. Village View,* 25–31 August 1995, pp. 14, 16, p. 14.
30 H. Sheehan, *Irish Television Drama* (Dublin: Radio Telefís Éireann, 1987), p. 342.
31 Ibid., p. 345.
32 See also Barton, *Jim Sheridan,* pp. 123–37.
33 T. Eagleton, *Heathcliff and the Great Hunger* (London and New York: Verso, 1995), p. 21.
34 Ignatiev, *How the Irish Became White.*

9

Pierce Brosnan

The bonds of authenticity
(1953–; film career: 1979–)

IN HIS 1975 essay 'Travels in hyperreality', Umberto Eco distinguishes in West Coast America the abandonment of the 'real' for the 'authentic copy'. More perfect than the real, the copy replaces flaws with flawlessness, so much so that the viewer or participant in the spectacle will no longer feel any need for the original. America, he suggests is 'a country obsessed with realism, where, if a reconstruction is to be credible, it must be absolutely iconic, a perfect likeness, a "real" copy of the reality being repre-sented'.[1] The 'real', in Eco's formulation, has not disappeared entirely; it is still to be found in the Old World and occasionally – the old Creole city of New Orleans is an example – in the New. This assumption, of Old World authenticity versus New World fakery, underpins both popular and academic discourse; here I would like to explore its implications for an analysis of Pierce Brosnan's career in Hollywood and in Ireland, and how it informs his best-known cinema role, that of James Bond.

Born in Ireland, Brosnan moved to London in 1964 at the age of 11 to join his mother who had emigrated when he was an infant, having been abandoned by Brosnan's father, Tom.[2] He was initially brought up by his grandparents but, on their death, passed from one family member to another. Exchanging a tiny school in Navan for a huge comprehensive in Putney forced Brosnan to develop a Cockney accent 'to sound like one of the lads – all my mates were from Clapham Junction – and so I became one of the lads. But that felt uncomfortable; it wasn't me, wasn't my soul, wasn't who I was spiritually.'[3] Only through theatre, which he discovered at the Oval House theatre club in Kennington, did Brosnan find the medium to express himself: 'That's where my education truly began as an actor, as an artist – as somebody who had found a voice to express all the pain, all the angst of my childhood, and all the anger towards the community, towards people who had hurt me, shamed me.'[4] Brosnan then went on to study at the London Drama Centre and enjoyed a brief theatre career before being cast as Rory O'Manion in the mini-series, 'The Manions of America' (ABC, 1981).

'The Manions of America' was one of a series of historical family melodramas produced by ABC Television that dealt with issues of origins and ethnicity, of which the prototype was the British 'The Forsyte Saga' (BBC, 1967) and the most commercially successful 'Roots' (ABC, 1977). A later Irish-emigrant-themed series was 'The Thornbirds' (ABC, 1983). In 'The Manions', two members of an impoverished Irish family, Rory and Deirdre (Linda Purl), fall in love with a sister and brother, Rachel (Kate Mulgrew) and David Clement (Simon MacCorkindale), who are the offspring of the English landlord. The famine strikes, Rory is framed for murder and accidentally kills his own brother and all variously emigrate to America, where due to a flow of mishaps and unfortunate coincidences, they are separated, lose children, take on lovers and engage in Fenian plots. Brosnan plays Rory as the classic passionate Irishman, losing no opportunity to declare his love for Ireland and Irish freedom while building up a fortune in America. Shot to accentuate his swarthy looks, with a lock of hair falling over his face, convinced that there is a curse on him, Rory is also a doomed romantic who can only be redeemed by absorption into the New World. In the end, he is forced to abandon any active participation in the struggle for Irish freedom and settle down to be an upstanding American businessman (the series concludes with the confirmation of his family line via the birth of a son, even if this is at the expense of Rachel's life). With its theme of reconciliation through marriage – the symbolic Irish–English love affairs – its reliance on coincidence and its opposition of passion and reason, 'The Manions'' lineage runs directly back to Boucicault. Brosnan's interpretation of Rory is also very much in the tradition of the theatrical melodrama, relying on gesture and an exaggerated display of emotion to engage the viewer with his character. An Old World man of passion, he must learn the art of containment if he is to flourish in the New.

For the media, Rory's trajectory was also Brosnan's:

> When Mannions [*sic*] of America begins, the year is 1848 and Rory O'Mannion leaves his home and the family he loves in Ireland to make a new life for himself in another land – American [*sic*], a land where he can find work with dignity and bring that family to join him.

That was a long time ago, and things change. Slightly over 100 years later, in the 1950s, Pierce Brosnan's mother left Ireland and the baby son she loved to make a new life for herself in another land, England, where she could study to become a nurse and bring that son to join her [. . .]

And so Pierce Brosnan, who found a new home in England, becomes Rory O'Mannion, who found a new home in America as part of the wave of determined men and women we now see as our honoured forebears.[5]

Cast, no doubt, for his looks as much for his Irishness, the actor's authenticity in the part is complicated by his accent. Here and subsequently he literally speaks his hybridity; for Brosnan has never managed to acquire a convincing local Irish accent. Although the actor has recalled the frustration he felt in his early career at being typecast as Irish or American, and of being refused roles in BBC productions because of his 'lilt', his speaking voice at the time of 'The Manions' must have been that of the London-Irish, a hyphenated intonation that bespoke a hyphenated identity.[6] Offered the role of Remington Steele in the series of the same name, Brosnan and his wife Cassandra Harris moved to Hollywood, transforming not only the Irishman's career, but also his accent. From the first episodes of 'Remington Steele' (NBC, 1982–7), Brosnan's tones are those of the British theatre, only rendered slightly more proletarian by the occasional flat Irish vowel. The strategic importance of this adopted accent was made clear during a 1999 episode of 'The Simpsons', ('The Simpsons' Hallowe'en Special XII: House of Whacks'); Marge, prompted by memories of 'Remington Steele', chooses Pierce Brosnan as the voice of their new household computer. In a parody of *2001: A Space Odyssey* (Stanley Kubrick, GB, 1968) the computer takes over the Simpsons' home, spies on Marge in the bath and threatens to kill off Homer. As Homer dismantles the cybertronic ultrabot's circuitry, the voice begs: 'don't take out my British charm unit. Without that I'm just a boorish American clod.'

Marge is quite correct in returning to 'Remington Steele' to locate Brosnan's defining persona. As the former thief hired by private investigator, Laura Holt (Stephanie Zimbalist), to act the role of her boss so that prospective clients are not put off by the idea of a female-led detective agency, Brosnan swiftly traded his rebel Irish role for that of the sophisticate: '*Remington Steele* has become *the* series for people who don't like to admit they watch TV, and

Brosnan, the hunk with brains,' the *Washington Post* enthused, finding little to distinguish between the actor and the role. 'Warm him up a bit, and there's Remington in the flesh, huggable, inviting, funny and yes, *ooohh* so vulnerable.'[7] The same *Washington Post* article speaks of the actor as 'a matinee idol of yuppie America' and a 'new genre of male sex symbol'.[8]

Figure 9.1 'A new genre of male sex symbol'. Pierce Brosnan and Stephanie Zimbalist in *Remington Steele*

In the consumer-driven society that Fredric Jameson has famously defined as being in a state of late capitalism, Brosnan was himself a pastiche, that is, his on- and off-screen persona were identifiably constructed via 'the imitation of a peculiar or unique style, the wearing of a stylistic mask, speech in a dead language' but, as Jameson's critique continues, 'it is a neutral practice of such mimicry, without parody's ulterior motive, without the satirical impulse, without laughter, without that still latent feeling that there exists something normal compared to which what is being imitated is rather comic'.[9]

The point that Jameson misses is that re-inventing yourself as someone else, or as a pastiche of a 'real' character type, permits for a sense of self-control in a world that no longer respects the naturalness of bourgeois individualism. The theoretical concept that better describes Brosnan's self-positioning, both on-screen and off, via his now permanent Remington Steele accent, is that of the masquerade, the wearing of a mask as 'a challenge to categories of identity'.[10] The philosophy of the mask, Tseëlon argues, 'represents two approaches to identity. One assumes the authenticity of the self (that the mask – sometimes – covers). The other approach maintains that through a multitude of authentic manifestations the mask reveals the multiplicity of our identities.'[11] Returning to the quotation from Naficy in the 'Introduction', Brosnan's identity performance locates him within that 'slipzone of unfitting' that distinguishes the exilic persona.[12]

Brosnan's most notable performances are defined by the theme of fakery. These are also bound up, through the tensions between his public/private persona, with a discourse on national identity that acknowledges its malleability. Since he became an American citizen (in 2003) and even before then, it has obviously been important for his public image to insist on his Irish identity and to remind those who might doubt it that he is not English, or indeed, a boorish American clod. Yet, if being Irish is the actor's 'real' identity, for Brosnan Ireland is not automatically the locus of immigrant nostalgia; instead, as he has commented, it is a space he associates with a childhood of pain, anger and angst. In recent years, however, he seems to have become more at ease with the idea of Ireland as home, saying that:

> one plays it up and I'd be the first to admit that myself, but that I should be pulled back to Ireland in adult life fascinates me, I feel I am Irish, born an Irishman, lived an Irish life, celebrated it and endured it from an early age. You have to acknowledge that, you can't reject it, you have to put some kind of perspective on it.[13]

Certainly he has been aided in this by a more nuanced concept of Irishness, one that acknowledges trauma as part of its inheritance. A consequence of this has been his new eagerness to play Irish roles, many created for, and we may assume by, him via his production company, Irish Dreamtime (discussed below).

Brosnan's strategy of masquerade allowed the actor to play the 'both/and' game; his Remington Steele was both British and other, the lingering traces of his Irish accent allowing the series to suggest that part of Steele's mysterious early life may have been spent in Ireland. His imputed British identity further permitted Brosnan to access connotations of sophistication and cosmopolitanism that being Irish in the 1980s, and prior to that, did not permit. At the same time, the public knowledge that he was not, in fact, British but Irish, and that his background was one of disadvantage, allowed the actor to engage in a simultaneous process of disavowal; under the mask there was an authentic self, but the mask also expressed his multiple selves.

In Remington Steele, Brosnan developed a character that had its roots in the culture of the 'swinging sixties', a post-imperial Britishness that re-invented the English gentleman as a figure of style but little political or moral substance. Most like the debonair of the 1930s, Remington Steele was an attractive cad, whose smart suits were funded by dubious activities. He was also, importantly, a creation of the 1980s, a response to the increasing empowerment of the career woman. In the earlier episodes, Holt is the brains behind the outfit, and Steele simply provides the charm factor that the series creators obviously felt a career woman might lack. Due, however, to Brosnan's increasing fan base, his part was gradually developed to the point that it was often he who called the shots, leaving Holt (with Zimbalist protesting loudly) to become the assistant that she was never intended to be.

Steele's Britishness is carefully constructed to combine the suave good manners of the aristocrat with a proletarian toughness that will recommend him to an American public raised on an ideal of political democracy tempered with an admiration for Old World privilege. In keeping with the tenor of the show, Zimbalist and Brosnan play their characters for laughs, with the audience's complicity in concealing Steele's true identity (as a thief) crucial to this. That Steele is not the well-bred Englishman he appears to be is the basis for a number of sub-plots. In 'Sting of Steele' (1983), Holt meets Steele's old friend and mentor, the conman Daniel Chalmers (played by Stephanie Zimbalist's father, Efrem Zimbalist, Jr). She presses him to tell her more about his protégé's background. 'When I found him', Chalmers remembers, 'he was an educated, unsophisticated, unwanted young man filled with hostility and violence [...], there he was on the streets of London, hustling for a quid...'. Chalmers took the young man under his wing: 'The years were good to us, then Harry...'

'Harry?', Holt interrupts, 'his name is Harry?' 'That's what I finally wound up calling him in self-defence. He had a bagful of names. I doubt even he knows which was real and which were the product of his fertile imagination,' is the reply, 'but eventually he became gripped with wanderlust and moved on. We kept in touch as best we could. Our paths crossed occasionally and I marvelled at the élan he acquired along the way.' By the final double-episode, 'Steeled With a Kiss' (1987), Chalmers is dying and finally admits to Steele that he is in fact his birth father. Whether or not the episode's play on paternity was meant to be read as a nod to Brosnan's failed reconciliation with his own birth father, it now knowingly fuses his Irish identity with his still unrealised Bond persona. This episode takes place in Ireland and plays as a parody of *The Quiet Man*, with Steele and his entourage stepping off the ferry and asking the way to Glencree. 'Glencree, is it?' the porter responds, 'Ah, yous must be after a spot of trout fishing. 'No, we're trying to get to Ashford Castle,' Steele replies. A dockhand steps forward: 'Ashford Castle, now that's a wee bit north of Glencree.' 'Not by way of Glencarren,' the porter asserts, cuing the entry of a second dockhand: 'did someone say 'Glencarren?'' The scene continues for a while along these lines until an elderly man wearing a bowler hat and green scarf around his neck introduces himself: 'Glencree? This way. Mikeleen O'Flynn, major domo, head factotum, chief of staff at your service, your lordship.' Once at the castle that Steele has inherited, one of the maids introduces herself as Mary Kate O'Danaher before the episode veers off into Bond territory taking in Russian spies, double agents and Iron Curtain manoeuvrings.

That Remington Steele is a fake (his real name remains a secret to the end of the series) was as important in establishing Brosnan as the future Bond as was his invented accent. In many ways, Remington Steele was a dry run for Bond, a lesson in the acquisition of élan; indeed, such was Brosnan's suitability for the role of the well-dressed British master spy that he was offered it in 1986. As was widely reported at the time and since, NBC revived a clause in his contract that prevented him from accepting the part and shot an extra, unplanned season of the series to exploit the Bond connection, and it was not until 1995 that Brosnan was eventually successfully cast in *GoldenEye* (Martin Campbell, GB/USA, 1995).

In the interim, keeping the Bond cycle in touch with trends in cinema had become increasingly problematic for its makers. As James Chapman has demonstrated in his study of the films, this was a recurrent crisis and they, like any other generic product, were forced to adapt and modify themselves according to 'various industrial, political and cultural determinants'.[14] The films are also, to an unusually high degree, identified via the actor who plays the title role, with comparisons inevitably being made between any new incumbent and the defining interpretations of Sean Connery and Roger Moore. The introduction of a new Bond is one of the markers of generic change and rumours of who that might be serve to fuel interest in the cycle between releases. That Pierce Brosnan would eventually find himself in the role was taken for granted in the media after 1986; in fact his casting as the Russian spy, Major Petrofsky, in *The Fourth Protocol* (John MacKenzie, GB, 1987) seems like a deconstruction of his Bond before it had even happened, with Brosnan posing as a suave Englishman as he awaits instructions from Moscow before he can detonate the nuclear missile that will wipe out an American airbase, taking several thousand civilians with it (MacKenzie also has Brosnan pass himself off as a gay pick-up in black leathers as he had in his earlier *The Long Good Friday* [GB, 1979]). In the event, the nine years that passed between the original offer and its renewal in 1995 were notably fallow ones for Brosnan's career, his only roles of note being Dr Lawrence Angelo in the science fiction release, *The Lawnmower Man* (Brett Leonard, GB/USA, 1992) and Stuart Dunmeyer in *Mrs Doubtfire* (Chris Columbus, USA, 1993). Opinions as to his appropriateness to play Bond also wavered, with more than one columnist questioning the measure of his masculinity; James Chapman's assessment of Brosnan as a 'more lightweight persona' is in much the same vein.[15]

Also during these years, Brosnan's wife, Cassandra Harris, developed and, in 1991, died of ovarian cancer, and he took time out from screen acting to care for her. Since then, the actor has openly discussed the trauma of his loss in the media and used his public persona to generate a substantial revenue for cancer-related and other charities with which he is associated. That he, unlike Bond, is a devoted family man, eventually marrying his new partner, and mother of their two children, Keely Shaye Smith, in 2001, is the other consistently reported-on facet of his private life.

The new Bond of *GoldenEye* thus arrived in the role, trailing none of the playboy image that had accompanied Connery or Moore in their day or, as we shall see in the next chapter, that was to become the defining persona of Brosnan's younger contemporary, Colin Farrell. On screen, he has, as the genre requires, been paired with the

'Bond girl' of the moment although this relationship has been, at least nominally, reconfigured to accommodate gender sensibilities. James Chapman has discussed the strategic release of studio publicity material that suggested in advance of *GoldenEye* that the sexism of the Bond films to date had been replaced with a new commitment to portraying 'intelligent and highly independent [female] characters', concluding that, in fact, *GoldenEye*'s 'strategy for incorporating feminist discourses is not to alter Bond's attitude towards women, but rather to alter the attitudes of the women around him to Bond himself. Indeed, the film presents Bond as being beleaguered by women in positions of power and authority.'[16] As he notes, the most quoted line in this respect belongs to the new female M (Judi Dench) when she calls him 'a sexist, misogynist dinosaur, a relic of the Cold War whose boyish charms, though wasted on me, obviously appealed to that young woman I sent out to evaluate you.'[17]

Much of the media coverage surrounding the latest Bond focused on Brosnan's 'new man' masculinity. Reviews of the film itself, both in Europe and the United States, were mixed, reinforcing the series' 'critic-proof' status as *GoldenEye* became the highest grossing Bond film ever to be released, with a worldwide box-office take of $351,500,000.[18] Where some reviewers welcomed Brosnan into the role, others saw him as a pale shadow of his predecessors, inevitably Connery and Moore. Yet, it was not in the regular review slots, mostly occupied by male critics, but in the lifestyle columns and in articles written by and for women, that the most intense discussion of Brosnan's Bond took place. Although opinions were again divided, the consensus was that Brosnan had re-invented Bond as a response to 1990s gender politics. Within this discourse considerable agency was awarded to the actor as the 'author' of his character and most writers were happy to allow for a high degree of slippage between Brosnan's on- and off-screen personality. Interviews with Brosnan tended to focus on his love for Cassandra Harris and subsequently on his burgeoning relationship with Keely Shaye-Smith; his closeness to his children was also mentioned with approval. That these added to his universally acknowledged sex appeal was the foundation for most, although not all, reporters:

> Famously widowed by his late wife, Cassie, Brosnan has not one shred of anxiety about wearing his heart on his sleeve, or about expressing his pain at the passing of one so precious to him. Now he seems to be settled with a new partner, Keely. And because this is a man who

combines the best of both machismo and gentleness, all one can say is
– lucky her.

As the new Mr Bond comes to life, it will be interesting to see
whether some of Brosnan's sensitivity begins to peek out. If it does,
then women will only find him all the more devastating, and men the
more enviable.[19]

Vulnerability, sensitivity, femininity – all these qualities were
variously detected in the new Bond and greeted with approval. Only
occasionally did the odd dissenter suggest that Bond had an issue
with virility, one that, it was implied, Brosnan shared. Evidently riled
by the *Daily Telegraph* writer in question, the actor responded: 'I
certainly don't think I have taken away his virility. I like women – a
lot. In any case, Bond deals with the villainess in the end.' Reasserting
'I *have* virility' did little to convince his interviewer who pronounced
that: 'It is, however, the polite, unthreatening virility of a Sunday
school teacher; in other words, New Bond always *asks* first.'[20]

Arguments as to whether Brosnan/Bond is or is not virile need to
be tempered with a wider discourse articulated within this apparently
woman-to-woman debate as to the redefinition of desirable
masculinity. Much of this bears out Sally Robinson's observation that
exploring newer models of masculinity has tended to enforce the
binaries of 'traditional' versus 'alternative': '"Traditional"
masculinity always means distant, cold, insensitive and/or violent
masculinity; "alternative" means anything and everything else.'[21] For
the majority of these writers, Bond had changed and for the better,
and 'asking first' was part of that improvement. Certainly, there is
less sexual cruelty in Brosnan's Bond – in *GoldenEye* his despatch of
the 'perverse' Xenia Onatopp (Famke Janssen) is perfunctory and his
comment, as he looks at her dead body pinned to a tree, that 'she
always did enjoy a good squeeze', seems more like a line borrowed
from Connery than one written for him. On the other hand, in an
idyllic moment out of the action, Bond is found by Natalya Simonova
(Izabella Scorupco) sitting contemplating the ocean. Realising that
Bond's most pressing dilemma in the film is that he must assassinate
Alex Trevelyan (Sean Bean), the former 006 and his companion in
innumerable and unrecorded missions, she wonders out loud how he
can act like this, how he can be 'so cold'. 'It's what keeps me alive',
Bond replies. 'It's what keeps you alone,' Natalya pronounces before
they make cathartic love in an interior scene lit and filmed to
accentuate its romanticism. Although Bond seems otherwise to

ignore Trevelyan's challenges to him to question whether 'all the vodka martinis ever silence the screams of all the men you killed', on the beach in Cuba he reveals the vulnerability that so appealed to so much of his female viewership. That he is indirectly responsible for the death of his old lover, Paris Carver (Teri Hatcher), in *Tomorrow Never Dies* (Roger Spottiswoode, GB/USA, 1997) provides a subtext of regret for the life he has led that haunts the second of Brosnan's Bonds and allows for at least a partial acknowledgement of Trevelyan's words, as well as hinting at a more mature relationship than the standard transitory sexual encounter that is the marker of Bond's regular involvement with women.

In Brosnan's third outing as Bond, *The World is Not Enough* (Michael Apted, GB/USA, 1999), this vulnerability is expressed, unusually for this series, as loss of physical potency. In the opening sequence, Bond chases a female subversive through the London docklands, finally catching up with her as she takes off in a hot-air balloon. When this explodes, he throws himself onto the roof of the Millennium Dome, yelling out in pain as he lands. The ruptured shoulder that he suffers as a consequence becomes a recurrent motif in the film. He has to seduce the MI5 doctor, Dr Molly Warmflash (Serena Scott Thomas), so that she will declare him fit for action and, after he and Elektra King (Sophie Marceau) have first made love, he is alerted to her treachery when the villain, Renard (Robert Carlyle), uses his knowledge of the injury to overcome him. That Bond hurts is a measure of his humanity, contrasted here with Renard's inability to feel pain since a bullet lodged itself in his nervous system. As Martin Willis has discussed, Brosnan's Bond is distinguished by his mastery of technology, linked quite specifically at the end of this film by R (John Cleese) to fear of the millennium bug:

> Brosnan's Bond differs from the others. He indulges in what has become known as 'the disappearing body', where the 'masculinist dreams of body transcendence' become focused on the 'phallic excesses' of technological objects. Brosnan's Bond is not simply extending his sexuality through technology, he is transferring that sexuality from his own body onto the hardware itself. That Bond imbues the technology he uses with his own sexual potency serves to increase the power of that technology, and by extension the power of Bond himself.[22]

Bond can compensate for his depleted and vulnerable body via his mastery of sexy technology, to the extent, as Willis suggests, that the boundaries between him and that technology are erased. 'What do I need to defuse a nuclear bomb?' he asks Christmas Jones (Denise Richards), the American nuclear scientist. 'Me,' she replies. Yet when the race against time (nuclear destruction) is underway, it is Bond who is evidently in charge, leaving Jones to do little more than be rescued. Although as Willis and others recognise, Bond films have historically been identified by their excessive display of gadgetry; only with Brosnan has the use of technology superseded physical prowess. Hence the need for Bond to hurt; otherwise it would be too easy to confuse him with the man/machine villains that have populated Bond films from the earliest days of Oddjob and Jaws.

Bond's relationships with women are also circumscribed by technology. At the beginning of *The World is not Enough*, he sits alone watching old television footage of Elektra King's release from captivity. She is in tears, causing the voyeur Bond to caress her cheek on the screen with his finger. Here her image is under his control, but subsequently she will play on his attraction to her by seducing and finally torturing him, remarking as she turns the screws of the device: 'I've always had power over men.' Determined to disprove her taunt that he could not kill a woman he loved, he then shoots her, and repeats, as M (Judi Dench) looks on, the gesture of touching her now dead face. The film swiftly moves on, replacing this near necrophilic moment with more fast action until Bond can close the picture by making love to the considerably more wholesome Christmas Jones.

Brosnan's final outing as Bond, *Die Another Day* (Lee Tamahori, GB/USA, 2002), marked the fortieth anniversary of the series, providing the occasion for a proliferation of intra-textual references.[23] It also was the first of Brosnan's Bonds to feature an extended torture sequence, one that runs from the pre-credit sequence, through the opening titles and into the main action. It begins with Bond being captured by the North Koreans, continues over fourteen months and ends with him emerging from the underground bunker with Christ-like long hair, an unkempt beard and moustache, blood-streaked skin and dirty, ripped clothing. Subsequently he is disowned by M (Judi Dench) and only readmitted to the service when he has proved his integrity in a lengthy fencing duel with the villain, Gustav Graves (Toby Stephens). The film moves from the steamy, hot and primitive terrain of North Korea via a forgotten Victorian underground station in London in which Bond is readmitted to MI5, to the futuristic ice palace where Graves is putting the final touches to his Icarus project (guaranteed world domination). *Die Another Day* is a film obsessed with temporality; aware of the series' own history, it also propels Bond between place and time, reinserting him into visually cued historical moments – the birth of Christianity with the resurrected Christ, the age of the British swordsman, the heyday of Victorian technology and on into a future that he too can control by eliminating the threat posed by Graves. This is Bond as virtual time-traveller, history's Everyman, a project aided by Brosnan's chameleon-like presence. That there may be multiple Bonds at any one time is also given consideration. As the story unfolds, the agent learns that Graves is in fact Colonel Moon, whom he believed he had killed and who has had his face reconstructed to look like Bond. Similarly, in the film's opening sequence, Bond takes the place of a diamond trader whom he closely resembles in order to infiltrate Moon's headquarters.

'While you were away, the world changed,' M tells Bond. 'Not for me,' he replies. Presumably, while he was 'away' (being tortured in North Korea), 9/11, the ultimate Bond nightmare, took place. Hence, the film's desperate concern to emphasise Bond's ubiquity even if, in 2001, he was not around to save Western civilisation. Just as it struggles to reassert the cult of the super-hero, evidence of his disempowerment seeps into the narrative – as the *Variety* reviewer observed of the opening sequences up to Bond's arrival, still in Christ garb and bearing the marks of his torture, at the Hong Kong Yacht Club: 'the net effect of the entire interlude is unsettling, at least for Bond veterans of long standing; while it's daily routine for Bond to be thrown into immediate jeopardy, never in memory has the character effectively been neutralized, or put in a similar position of not being able to control his own fate.'[24] The discursive significance of torture as a plot device is further discussed in Chapter 10; however, the sense of powerlessness that the writer detects in Bond is reflective of a wider unease with his representation of conventional masculinity.

Vulnerable to doubt, to pain and to women, Brosnan's Bond is challenged in his first three outings as much by the conditions of being male in the late twentieth century as by the villains he is up against. The altered circumstances of the dawning twenty-first century threw his character once more into crisis, one that could only be worked through via a return to traditional masculine competencies (the duel).

As we have seen in the context of Sean Connery's career, being best known as James Bond can pose problems for actors with ambitions to play other types of roles. In fact, Brosnan has astutely managed his career since *GoldenEye*, capitalising on the Bond persona to play variations on it, including Andrew Osnard in *The Tailor of Panama* (John Boorman, USA/Ireland, 2001) and, most successfully, Thomas Crowne in *The Thomas Crowne Affair* (John McTiernan, USA, 1999).

The latter was produced by his Irish Dreamtime company, which has become a means both to control his own Hollywood career and to fund the highly personal Irish films that he has turned to in recent years. Formed in 1996 with Beau St Clair, Irish Dreamtime's policy seems to be to alternate between producing commercial Hollywood fare that exploits Brosnan's reputation as Bond and low-budget, Irish-themed works that reflect on his own somewhat traumatic relationship with the country of his birth. In certain instances, notably *Laws of Attraction* (Peter Howitt, Germany/USA/Ireland, 2004), the clash of two filmmaking cultures has expressed itself in a return to an older, more simplistic image of Ireland and the Irish. Since the success of the Bond films, Brosnan has been careful to remind interviewers that he should not be confused with his most famous role: 'I am perceived as this rather suave sophisticate,' he explains, 'but that ain't me. I make a living being something that I'm not.'[25] The formation of Irish Dreamtime has offered him the opportunity to take roles and have parts created for him that, we may assume, are closer to what he is, or what he feels himself to be; in other words to achieve that authenticity that Eco detected in Old-World representations and institutions. That this has not been quite as straightforward as Brosnan might have wished it to be is the subject of the final section of this chapter.

Barry King has defined the two most commonly practised acting techniques in mainstream cinema as 'impersonation' and 'personification'. The former describes the kind of performance that entails the person undergoing significant transformation in order to 'become' that role; in the latter an actor does not greatly change persona but remains largely 'themselves' across a number of parts.[26] Richard Dyer, however, proposes that what fascinates us about actors is exactly their personalities and their individuality. Thus, when an actor presents a consistency of character type across a range of roles, when they engage in personification, this allows us to feel that we are closer to them:

People often say that they do not rate such and such a star because he or she is always the same. In this view, the trouble with say, Gary Cooper or Doris Day, is that they are always Gary Cooper and Doris Day. But if you like Cooper or Day, then precisely what you value about them is that they are always 'themselves' – no matter how different their roles, they bear witness to the continuousness of their own selves.[27]

In Brosnan's case, this distinction has been complicated in part by his strategy of 'masking', of foregrounding the fakery that acting demands to the extent that there is a misfit between his character type and his 'self', that slipzone of unfitting. Second, for his Irish films, he has attempted to redefine his persona so that he is no longer playing variations on his Remington Steele prototype but Irish characters that the audience is expected to interpret as authentic. In addition, his persona now bears the weight of some considerable longevity, begging the question: how long can he continue to play the romantic lead, given that his only alternative to date has been that of the (often mad) scientist (*The Lawnmower Man, Dante's Peak* [Roger Donaldson, USA, 1997], *Mars Attacks!* [Tim Burton, USA, 1996])? These latter roles exploit that chink in the romantic lead armour that the media have variously detected as lack of emotional engagement/virility, or the triumph of looks over talent. The function of Irish Dreamtime is therefore both to provide Brosnan with the platform to exploit his persona for commercial gain and to prove that there is more to him than being a 'man who fully expects to be called back at any moment and told to model sweaters for the rest of the day'.[28]

The Thomas Crowne Affair signalled to financiers and the media that Brosnan was now a top box-office draw in his own right.[29] A remake of the earlier film of the same title (Norman Jewison, USA, 1968), Brosnan's Thomas Crowne updated Steve McQueen's in a number of ways, most significantly for the purposes of this argument by substituting the bank robbery with the theft of a painting and then complicating this crime with a proliferation of forgeries; the part also shares many of the traits of his Stuart (Stu) Dunmeyer in *Mrs Doubtfire*. The latter film was a multi-layered articulation of the anxieties around gender roles and the family that circulated in the early 1990s. In it, Brosnan plays a playboy millionaire who starts to date Miranda Hilliard (Sally Field) after her split-up with her husband, Daniel (also Mrs Doubtfire), played by Robin Williams.

The film's strength is its refusal either to demonise Miranda, the workaholic career woman, or the smoothly handsome Stu. As much as Daniel in his re-incarnation as British nanny, Euphegenia Doubtfire, lampoons his competitor and belittles his manly attributes, so the film suggests that what Miranda may well need in her life is a rich, good-looking man who can treat her and the children to a lavish day out in the country club.

Because of her family circumstances, Miranda also requires a Mrs Doubtfire to run the house and serve candlelit dinners, which is essentially what Daniel must continue to do if he is to stay in his children's lives. Without children, career woman Catherine Banning (Rene Russo) in 1999's *Thomas Crowne Affair* only needs the rich, good-looking man. Confident in this thesis, the film proceeds to shoot Brosnan in a multiplicity of poses that set his looks off against a background of lavish acquisitions, relocating him and Banning finally to the tropical paradise that sees their relationship fully realised. More importantly for Brosnan's reputation, McTiernan filmed the key lovemaking sequence between him and Russo on the staircase of his mansion as a carnival of lust. *The Thomas Crowne Affair* is about fakery, at the level of plot through its narrative of forging old master paintings, but equally in its characterisation of its principal character who confesses to Banning over dinner that he got from Glasgow to Oxford on a boxing scholarship – 'the hard part was learning to talk'.

The success of *The Thomas Crowne Affair* led to another heist movie, *After the Sunset* (Brett Ratner, USA, 2004), and to the marital caper, *Laws of Attraction*, the latter co-produced by Irish Dreamtime. *After the Sunset* added little to its prototype other than admitting that Brosnan was ageing via shots of a slightly less toned body and greying stubble; it did, however, identify its protagonist as Irish. In an early exchange, investigator Stan Lloyd (Woody Harrelson) advises Brosnan's worldly Max Burdett that 'Just because you're English, doesn't mean you need to hide your emotions.' 'I'm Irish,' Burdett replies. 'We let people know how we feel. Now, fuck off.'

This identification with a new, cosmopolitan version of Irishness, one that remains emotionally spontaneous while permitting a high level of sophistication, has been one facet of Brosnan's most recent self-projection. It is crucial to *Laws of Attraction*, and provides the opportunity for a bizarre subplot that sees him, as wealthy divorce lawyer, Daniel Rafferty, return to Ireland with Audrey Woods (Julianne Moore) to assess the value of divorcing rock star couple's,

Serena (Parker Posey) and Thorne (Michael Sheen) castle. Once in Ireland Daniel and Audrey become caught up in a local *feis* (festival), losing their inhibitions under the influence of a wild Irish dance and much alcohol before inadvertently, they believe, marrying. Later they discover that the wedding was only part of the revelry whose theme is the celebration of romance and thus has no legal standing; by this stage they have realised that they want to marry anyway.

It is perhaps unfair to blame Brosnan's influence too much for this regressive, clichéd representation of contemporary Ireland, populated as it is by wily rogues and other stage Irish caricatures; nor should it be forgotten that another of the film's co-producers was Hell's Kitchen, the company formed by Jim Sheridan and Arthur Lappin primarily to make Irish films. Maybe both parties believed that this was the image of Ireland that still appealed to American audiences. In the event, this was far from the case, with the film drawing consistently poor notices, if less for Brosnan's performance than for Moore's.

For the *Irish Times* critic, *Laws of Attraction* was the occasion for an excursion into hilarity induced by viewing the film; the review begins: 'Jesus, Mary and Joseph will ye look who it is. It's that James Bond fella, so it is, so it is. No, not him, the other one – the English lad who thinks he's from Naas or Newbridge or wherever.' It concludes:

> Well, let me tell you, don't they [Brosnan and Moore] then head off to a castle in this fair Emerald Isle and doesn't the whole thing become the greatest load of fertiliser ye've seen since Jimmy Doyle's goat ate aul Mrs Brady's medicine and did his business in the priest's window box? And, sure that's why I'm writing in this fierce annoying style.
>
> Though I'll tell ye, it isn't a pincheen as annoying as the jigs, reels, twinkly blarney and – may the Lord strike me down if I tell a lie – porcelain leprechauns ye'll have thrown at ye if ye allow James Bond's wild horses to drag ye to *Laws of Attraction*.[30]

Glib as the above may be, it articulated many of the difficulties of popular perception Brosnan would face in his efforts to be taken seriously as an Irish screen actor, let alone as an authentic Irishman.

When Irish Dreamtime turned its attention to Brosnan's two most personal projects, *The Nephew* (Eugene Brady, Ireland, 1998) and *Evelyn* (Bruce Beresford, Germany/USA/Ireland, 2002), the influence of the actor/producer's own ambiguous attitude to the country of his birth became the prism through which Irish society, particularly of the past, was viewed. In fact, neither of these two films was Brosnan's first major indigenous Irish role – in *Taffin* (Francis Megahy, GB/USA, 1987), he played another pre-Bond character, this time a professional debt collector, who has been hired by the local villagers to protect them against the encroachment of the big business consortium that is planning to build a chemical plant on the local playing fields. *Taffin* is a genre film that speaks to Ireland's problematic process of modernisation and owes much to the tradition of the low-budget British television thriller. *The Nephew* and *Evelyn* belong to a more recent cycle of productions that address in various ways the sense that representations of the Irish past must bear witness to a history of frustrated sexuality and institutional abuse.[31] Both films also attempt in some way to negotiate the Irish-American narrative of return 'home'. This is the central theme of *The Nephew*, which opens with a young man, Chad (Hill Harper), arriving in the island of Inis Dora to scatter his mother's ashes and stay with her brother, Tony Egan (Donal McCann). Once there, Chad finds that he must work through a family history that hinges around Egan's opposition to his sister's relationship with the local publican, Joe Brady (Pierce Brosnan), a trauma that caused her to emigrate. That Chad is himself mixed-race forms a minor sub-plot concerning the acceptance by the 'old' Irish of the new. He in turn falls in love with Brady's daughter, Aislín (Aislín McGuckin), a relationship opposed by her father. One of the privileges of stardom that Brosnan has usefully exploited in his new role as producer has been his ability to cast leading Irish actors in his films. In *The Nephew*, Donal McCann, one of the most intense stage and screen performers of his day, dominates the screen with his depiction of Egan as a man consumed by his need to control both himself and others, yet endowed with enough understanding to sense his own fallibility.[32] In a support role, Sinéad Cusack as Egan's old flame, Brenda O'Boyce, plays the calm to McCann's storm. Both actors bring to their roles a theatricality that, particularly in McCann's case, is at odds with the more naturalistic, understated screen-acting techniques of the other lead players. Brosnan, in particular, seems often to be little more than the foil for McCann's outward battle with his inner demons, while the American Harper appears quite unaware of the weight of emotional history his character's arrival exposes. These clashes of casting and interpretation are not ameliorated by the inclusion of an array of stage-Irish secondary roles, mostly taken by the villagers. A tendency to film the island as a pre-lapsarian Celtic homeland, with dolmens standing in barren countryside lit by the rays of the setting sun, added to its freight of cultural baggage, with a further layer of meaning entering the frame via the use of a number of Phil Lynott's songs on the soundtrack.

To blame Brosnan uniquely for the production of a film that was mired in its own signifiers is probably unjust; if he has continued to speak of *The Nephew* with the fondness of a personal project, then the making of *Evelyn* has been widely understood as an exorcism of his own childhood traumas: 'Insiders have suggested the story of Desmond Doyle, fraught with missing parents and unhappy, abandoned children, is a suitably cathartic project for Brosnan, connecting greatly with his past, without actually replicating its minutiae.'[33] Based on real events of the early 1950s, *Evelyn* recounts the events surrounding Desmond Doyle's (Brosnan) efforts to force the Irish legal system to recognise his parental rights and to have his three children restored to him after they have been taken into care when his wife leaves home. Surrounding himself again with pre-eminent stage and screen actors – Stephen Rea and Alan Bates as his legal team of Michael Beattie and Tom Connolly, alongside Aidan Quinn as the returned Irish-American, Nick Barron, and John Lynch as Senior Counsel Mr Wolfe – Brosnan here plays the lead, a Dublin working man who must first overcome drink and a tendency towards impetuosity that leads him into violent confrontations before he can confront the legal system that will ultimately grant him his rights. Brosnan has said of the film that he wanted it to be more graphic but that he was restrained by Beresford who preferred an understated approach to the material so that 'this is a mild interpretation of what happened to Doyle and his children.'[34]

Again, it is impossible to establish the parameters of Brosnan's authorial control over *Evelyn*, yet his portrayal of Doyle suffers from a reluctance to give full rein to his character's emotions. His Doyle is too sanitised, Brosnan's performance too demure, particularly given the acting tradition of which he is part and the intense historical trauma that this film addresses. Compared, say, to Aidan Quinn's own performance in *Song for a Raggy Boy* (Aisling Walsh, Ireland/GB/Denmark/Spain, 2003) or Peter Mullan's cameo in his own *The Magdalene Sisters* (GB/Ireland, 2002), both films that attempt to cover similar ground, Brosnan seems hamstrung by his own acting history, that layering of inauthenticity and irony that have so distinguished his cinema roles. Nor does his accent help: 'Pierce sounds like an American actor making a bags of the Irish

Figure 9.2 Surrounded by pre-eminent stage and screen actors.
Aidan Quinn, Pierce Brosnan and Stephen Rea in *Evelyn*

brogue,' one critic typically remarked.[35] Others suggested that the film, like *Laws of Attraction,* was an anachronism: 'Just when we thought we had left behind the barrage of films that painted Ireland as little other than a nation of booze-swilling, God-fearing, hard-up paddys, along comes Evelyn.'[36] *The Nephew* met with a similar response: 'frequently and uncomfortably stereotypical, *The Nephew* appears contrived rather than organic, focusing as it does on images of Ireland which might have been challenging thirty years ago.'[37] The unspoken consensus was that Brosnan, decent fellow that he was universally acknowledged to be, was out of touch with today's Ireland and its priorities.

Searching for authenticity in a postmodern era of scepticism may seem futile. Yet Brosnan's history of identity performance describes a trajectory that has led him from masquerade to unmasking. Now apparently reconciled to his own Irishness, flawed and traumatic as he recognises it to be, he seems to wish not just to act out, to impersonate, his identity of origin, but to personify it. This process has challenged him to engage in a new mode of performance that abandons ironic disengagement in favour of an exploration of his 'real' self; equally, it has challenged the local Irish critical establishment to understand the nature of a hyphenated identity. That neither has fully managed to do this is at least partially attributable to the vehicles, the films, Brosnan has selected to express himself through. As Irish cinema belatedly abandons the exploration of the real in favour of the embrace of postmodern representational modes, obliterating along the way the distinction between sincerity and sentimentality, it may be that the Old World authenticity of Eco's imagination has become too compromised for Brosnan's purposes. How he negotiates any future Irish roles he takes will ultimately be the measure of his transformation.

NOTES

1   U. Eco, 'Travels in hyperreality' in *Faith in Fakes* (London: Martin Secker & Warburg, 1986; trans. William Weaver), pp. 3–58, p. 4.

2   For a biography of Brosnan, see Y. Membery, *Pierce Brosnan* (London: Virgin Books, 2002).

3   In Á. O'Connor, *Leading Hollywood* (Dublin and London: Wolfhound Press), p. 125.

4   Ibid., p. 126.

5   'Ireland's Greatest Export', *TV Week* (27 September – 3 October 1981) (Pierce Brosnan file, AMPAS).

6   Ibid., p. 128.

7   L. Romano, 'Pierce Brosnan, Man of Steele', *Washington Post*, 14 May 1985, pp. E1, E3.

8   Ibid., p. E1.

9   F. Jameson, 'Postmodernism and Consumer Society', in E. Ann Kaplan (ed.), *Postmodernism and its Discontents* (London and New York: Verso, 1988), pp. 13–29, p. 16.

10 E. Tseëlon, 'Reflections on mask and carnival' in E. Tseëlon (ed.), *Masquerade and Identities* (London and New York: Routledge, 2001), pp. 18–37, p. 1.

11 Ibid., p. 25.

12 See p. 6.

13 S. Caden, 'The spy who came in from the cold', *Sunday Independent*, Review section, 14 November 2004, p. 11.

14 J. Chapman, *Licence to Thrill: A Cultural History of the James Bond Films* (London and New York: I.B. Tauris, 1999), p. 200.

15 Ibid., p. 247.

16 Ibid., p. 256.

17 Ibid., p. 257.

18 imdb.com (accessed 23 August 2005).

19 S. von Strunckel, 'What the stars say about him', *Sunday Times*, Section 9, 19 November 1995, p. 35.

20 P. Wyatt, 'Don't mention Connery', *Daily Telegraph*, 23 November 1995, p. 15.

21 S. Robinson, 'Pedagogy of the opaque: teaching masculinity studies', in J.K. Gardiner (ed.), *Masculinity Studies and Feminist Theory* (New York and Chichester: Columbia University Press, 2002), pp. 141–60, p. 144.

22 M. Willis, 'Hard-wear: the millennium, technology and Brosnan's Bond' in C. Lindner (ed.), *The James Bond Phenomenon* (Manchester and New York: Manchester University Press, 2003), pp. 151–65, p. 156.

23 For a listing of many of these, see Kim Newman's review of the film, '*Die Another Day*', *Sight and Sound*, 13, 1 (2003), pp. 41–2.

24 T. McCarthy, '*Die Another Day*', *Variety*, 18 November 2002, pp. 6 and 20, p. 20.

25 V. Cohen, "'I love Bond, but there's more to life. You must take risks"', *Evening Standard,* 18 August 1999, p. 23.

26 B. King, 'Articulating Stardom', *Screen*, 26, 5 (September/October 1985), pp. 27–50, pp. 41–2.

27 R. Dyer, *Heavenly Bodies* (London and New York: Routledge, 2004, 2nd edition), p. 10.

28 T. Shone, 'The gilt-edged Bond', *Sunday Times*, 19 November 1995, S-10, p. 67. But see also Andrew Spicer's analysis of Brosnan as a 'hero of consumption' in A. Spicer, *Typical Men* (London and New York: I.B. Tauris, 2001), p. 186.

29 The worldwide gross box office takings were $124,305,181 (imdb.com, accessed 23 August 2005).

30 D. Clarke, 'Rules of repulsion', *Irish Times* (*The Ticket*), 6 May 2004, p. 8.

31 See also Martin McLoone's discussion of *This is My Father* (Paul Quinn, Ireland/Canada, 1998) in *Irish Film, The Emergence of a Contemporary Cinema*, pp. 188–95.

32 Donal McCann died in July 1999.

33 N.P. Walsh, 'Brosnan confronts childhood demons', *The Observer*, 14 October 2001, p. 11.

34 P. Brosnan, *Evelyn*, DVD (region 2) commentary.

35 C. Dwyer, 'Pierce Unshaken but Stirred', *Sunday Independent* (accessed via Newsbank, 9 September 2005).

36 H. Boylan, '*Evelyn*', *Sunday Business Post*, 30 March 2003, p. a7.

37 J. Hayden, '*The Nephew*' (review), *Film West*, 34 (1998), p. 60.

10

Colin Farrell

Very f***in' Irish!
(1972–; film career: 1997–)

ONE OF THE enduring myths of stardom has been that of the 'meteoric rise to fame'. Star potential within this discourse is innate, not acquired; it is there to be discovered, usually by an older director, producer or fellow actor. Although star athletes are often compared with star actors, in this aspect of their occupations there is a marked divergence. Athletes are expected to train rigorously, to have displayed exceptional talent since youth and to have built on that through years of physical self-development. 'Overnight' film stars appear from nowhere, routinely professing their wonderment at their sudden fame and in doing so contributing to the notion that there is a magical quality to screen success. In the discourse of fandom, itself motored by a mixture of speculation and the drip-feeding of 'hard facts' by the star and his or her publicists, looks, body, sex appeal, alongside talent, are all invoked to account for instant celebrity.

The corollary to this unmediated rise to fame is the instability of success. Accompanying such star discourse is a secondary anxiety, even excitement, about an actor's equally inexplicable fall from grace. The media is on the alert as much for failure as success, stripping stars of their magical powers as gleefully as they award them. Colin Farrell's transformation into a major Hollywood star is illustrative of the 'phenomenal' aspect of stardom just outlined; though at the time of writing, despite his participation in a number of notably unsuccessful films, there is little sign that his career is in any danger of decline.

After one or two small film roles, Farrell came to attention locally when he played the romantic outsider, Daniel McCarthy, in the RTÉ/BBC(NI) co-production of Deirdre Purcell's 'Falling for a Dancer' (1998). A small-time poacher, McCarthy falls for older, unhappily married woman, Elizabeth Sullivan (Elizabeth Dermot-

Walsh) and, in a tussle, shoots her husband, Neeley (Dermot Crowley). In the mini-series Farrell is presented as a classic outsider-hero, his hair worn shoulder length, the lighting enhancing his swarthy looks, and his demeanour suggesting pent-up emotion, which, under pressure, will explode. This part was followed by that of Danny Byrne in the long running BBC series, 'Ballykissangel'. Here he played a working-class kid who, believing that the police want to impound his horse, escapes from Dublin to live on his uncle Eamonn's (Birdy Sweeney) derelict farm. Farrell's involvement spanned the two final series (four and five) and heralded a new type of storyline for the show. Introduced in the autumn 1988 season as one of five new characters intended to revitalise the series after the departures of Father Peter (Stephen Tompkinson) and Assumpta (Dervla Kirwan), Farrell represented a new urban characterisation that provided an antidote to the dominance of the series' investment in rural heritage nostalgia.[1] Farrell as Danny, along with Lorcan Cranitch and Kate McEnery as Sean Dillon and his daughter, Emma, played city blow-ins who were ambiguous about whether they wished to be accepted by the established inhabitants of Bally-kissangel. The latter two were returning from England where Dillon, having left Ballykissangel and his overbearing father twenty years earlier, had made his fortune. Emma, in particular, resented the claustrophobia of village life and was soon set up as a potential love interest for fellow rebel, Danny.

Danny was an obvious continuation of Farrell's persona in 'Falling for a Dancer', only exchanging a rural character for an urban one and trading his shoulder-length haircut for his now trademark designer stubble and quiff. His romantic appeal was as 'rough trade' with a warm heart: 'He may look like a bad boy, but Danny Byrne, Eamonn's young nephew, isn't all leather and aggression,' a feature writer in the *Radio Times* enthused, in language that was to be commonly applied to the Irish actor, adding that, 'gorgeous, brooding Danny looks set to become a new teen heart-throb'.[2]

Compared later in the same article with Brad Pitt, Farrell seemed on course to become the new Gabriel Byrne or Pierce Brosnan, with concomitant roles that combined romance and threat. For Irish audiences, his was not a meteoric rise to fame but one that was taking the more conventional route of accruing television and small film roles until experience and opportunity lead to more prominent parts. For global audiences, however, or at least those unfamiliar with the last two seasons of 'Ballykissangel', Farrell burst onto the scene with his star role in *Tigerland* (Joel Schumacher, USA, 2000). This was followed by leading parts in *American Outlaws* (Les Mayfield, USA, 2001), *Hart's War* (Gregory Hoblit, USA, 2002), *Phone Booth* (Joel Schumacher, USA, 2002), *The Recruit* (Roger Donaldson, USA, 2003), *S.W.A.T.* (Clark Johnson, USA, 2003), *A Home at the End of the World* (Michael Mayer, USA, 2004) and *Alexander* (Oliver Stone, USA/GB/Germany/Netherlands, 2004). In addition, he played investigator, Danny Witwer, opposite Tom Cruise in *Minority Report* (Steven Spielberg, USA, 2002) when Matt Damon became unavailable. In all of these films, bar *Alexander* and *Daredevil* (Mark Steven Johnson, USA, 2003), Farrell was cast as American characters with no Irish connection. During this time, Farrell also took lesser parts in films with Irish narratives and, in some cases, Irish directors: predating his stardom in *Ordinary Decent Criminal* (Thaddeus O'Sullivan, GB/Germany/ Ireland/USA, 2000) and subsequent to it in *Veronica Guerin* (Joel Schumacher, USA/Ireland/GB, 2003) and *interMission* (John Crowley, GB/Ireland, 2003).

Colin Farrell established both his name and his star persona in Joel Schumacher's study of military training camp mores, *Tigerland*. As the rebel, Bozz, he becomes the bearer of the film's critique of the hyper-macho ethos of boot camp training, yet as a closer look at the film demonstrates, it ultimately validates an unproblematic and relatively traditional masculinity. This low-budget, anti-war film was one step in Schumacher's transition from directing blockbusters such as *Batman & Robin* (USA, 1997) and *8mm* (USA, 1999) to a new independent-type profile that saw the release of *Tigerland*, *Phone Booth* (also starring Farrell) and *Veronica Guerin* (in which Farrell played a cameo). Both *Tigerland* and *Phone Booth* place Farrell in roles that question aspects of masculinity both historically (in the war movie) and in the present, while *Veronica Guerin* is primarily concerned with interrogating the consequences for the individual and the family when women enter a conventionally male space, in this case that of the investigative journalist threatened by gangster violence. All three films signal their director's new status as 'indie' filmmaker via a number of conventional strategies, including the casting of non-American leads, a reliance on performances rather than costly special effects to carry the narrative, and ensemble acting. The casting of an unknown as the lead in *Tigerland* was therefore an important statement, Schumacher publicly turning his back on the Hollywood mainstream.

As the charismatic and intelligent Bozz in *Tigerland*, Farrell played a part that required him to display exceptional if subversive leadership qualities; his heterosexuality was established through casual pick-ups although overall the film substitutes the company of the all-male group for romantic attachment. Farrell's acting style in this, as in his subsequent films, is naturalistic, adhering to the conventions of what James Naremore terms 'expressive coherence' – 'a formal logic that operates as rigorously in ordinary life as in professional theater'.[3] In other words, the actor (re)produces a character that seems to have 'real life' qualities even though these are created artificially. This is achieved here through employing an understated set of mannerisms and, even though the part is associated with a high degree of physicality, reserving excessive body movements for moments of emotional intensity. To take an example, in one scene Bozz, Paxton (Matthew Davis) and Cantwell (Thomas Guiry) are alone, late at night, peeling potatoes around a table. Already sharing a common sense of grievance for having to undertake this punishment/task, the three open up to each other. Cantwell, who has been earmarked as a victim, delivers a somewhat stagy monologue in which he professes his awe at the 'big shiny moon' before going on to tell the others about his disadvantaged background and the wife and child he has left behind. The film cuts to Paxton and Bozz who sit quietly listening. Only after Cantwell has ended does Bozz suddenly leap out of his seat, kicking over chairs and tables in an unexpected movement that illustrates his own reaction of frustration and anger at Cantwell's tale of hardship.

In a series of showdowns between him and Sergeant Thomas (James McDonald), the older actor's movements are physically threatening and very mobile. In contrast, Farrell as Bozz appears to be calm, his energies in reserve, his temper under control. This sense of naturalism is heightened by the film's camerawork (by Matthew Libatique) and as a consequence of shooting on 16mm in order to create a sense of freewheeling documentary making.[4] *Tigerland*'s construction of its central character illustrates just how Farrell has inserted himself, or been inserted, into a nexus of discourses around masculinity in mainstream cinema. *Tigerland*'s boot camp setting and study of male rivalries immediately invokes *Full Metal Jacket* (Stanley Kubrick, GB, 1987) and *Platoon* (Oliver Stone, USA, 1986). Kubrick and Stone's Vietnam films, alongside others such as *Apocalypse Now* (Francis Coppola, USA, 1979) and *Casualties of War* (Brian de Palma, USA, 1989), form a canon of works that have come to typify a post-Vietnam critique of the war formulated by a generation of directors influenced by the 1960s' anti-war movement. Although a first wave of criticism analysed the Vietnam war film for its accuracy and its political sentiments, much of the later work has focused on the films' gender politics, and particularly, on their interrogation of masculinity. John Newsinger, for instance, argues that Hollywood has failed to confront the politics of the war and that, instead, 'what we have are a number of films that portray the War as a crisis of American masculinity'.[5] The young American male, not Vietnam's ravaged villages or raped women, as both he and Michael Selig argue, has consistently been seen as the prime victim of the war, a discourse encapsulated in the title of de Palma's film.[6] In boot camp and in combat, these young men undergo a rite of passage that ultimately enhances their individuality: 'most of the Vietnam films present a humanistic, life-affirming veneer which values individual subjectivity above all else'.[7] These films are often related by a disenchanted narrator, one of whose functions is to remind us that the war (and by extension the film being viewed) does not conform to the classical heroic mode of the Second World War film; this is a dirty war, carried out in a kind of primeval swamp where the hero is ultimately reborn. Blame for the corruption of the war is usually filtered through the figure of an obsessive, sadistic commanding officer, reducing it to a dogfight between might and right, rather than a consequence of decisions taken by identifiable American political figures. Part of the films' critique of the kind of obsessive masculinity displayed by these commanding officers is expressed through their language, which tends towards misogynistic sloganising. The men are harangued in terms that equate them with homosexuals and prostitutes; conversely, when their bonding looks like verging on the homoerotic, they are strategically blown asunder.

Schumacher's contribution to the genre replicates many of the paradigms of the Vietnam war movies of the 1980s discussed above. As an ensemble piece, it charts the responses of a cadre of recruits to life in training camp, in particular the notorious Tigerland, on the way to the war in Vietnam. It is ostensibly narrated by one of these, Jim Paxton, although he is not present in all the film's scenes. Paxton is the squadron's only volunteer and is further demarcated from the group by being a 'college boy'. From the beginning he is taunted by the film's and his book's subject, Bozz, who suggests that his friend is creating typical characters, stereotypes, who respond in a conventional manner to a conventional war situation. Clearly, the

Figure 10.1 Displaying a humanistic individualism.
Colin Farrell in *Tigerland*

film is positioning itself as unconventional, if, in fact, it is far from
so. The minor roles – the psychopathic sergeant, the understanding
sergeant, the sergeant as cynic, the recruit who conforms, the recruit
who rebels, and so on – are stock characters of the genre. Even Bozz
conforms to an extent to a pattern of masculinity idealised by many
other and similar works; offset against Sergeant Thomas, he displays
a humanistic individualism that is expressed through opposition to
the irrationalities of command and his championing of lesser men's
causes. If Bozz has any wider critique of the political situation, he
does not express it, nor is it proposed to him by his friend, the more
educated and therefore more potentially politically aware Paxton.
When Sergeant Landers (Afemo Omilami) puts the rebel in charge of
the squadron, the film's trajectory becomes completely transparent –
Bozz is in fact the ideal soldier as well as being the ideal male – loyal,
physically powerful, intelligent and with exceptional leadership
qualities. By the film's conclusion, Bozz has faced up to his true
nature – after arranging for his own escape from the camp, he
returns to save Paxton from being sent to the war, and in the final
moments we see him leave for Vietnam.

Where Bozz differs from the earlier boy/heroes of the Vietnam war
film is in the high degree of mastery he displays throughout the

narrative. Unlike his predecessors, he does not undergo the rituals of initiation and humiliation that mark the passage from innocent boy to hardened man. Compared with, say, Matthew Modine in *Full Metal Jacket*, Charlie Sheen in *Platoon* or Sylvester Stallone in the various Rambo films, Farrell does not suffer or lose control either physically or mentally. Other characters in the films such as Cantwell, Miter (Clifton Collins Jr) and Paxton are subjected to extreme brutality at the hands of the other men; Miter, like Bozz, is awarded a privileged moment in which he too outlines to Bozz a 'white trash' background that, like Cantwell, leaves him too weak psychologically to deal with the rigours of army apprenticeship. In both cases, Bozz orchestrates the men's discharge from the army on technicalities which he has gleaned from familiarising himself with army regulations. Of Bozz's own background we learn very little other than that he comes from Texas. If the Vietnam films of the 1980s provided a rite of passage for their actors that mirrored the progression of their characters (Modine, Sheen and also Michael J. Fox in *Casualties of War* were all associated with youthful roles at the time of taking their parts in these films), *Tigerland* produces a young male lead that has apparently sprung from nowhere, either diegetically or in real life. That the test of his physicality amounts to little more than having his head ground in the mud or being forced to carry out extra press-ups seems to indicate that Farrell/Bozz's manhood does not need to be proven – it simply exists. Moreover, the viewer, particularly the male viewer implicit in the war genre, is not to be punished for enjoying the spectacle.

Writing on the action films of the 1980s, Yvonne Tasker sees productions such as *Die Hard* (John McTiernan, USA, 1988), *Die Hard 2* (Renny Harlin, USA, 1990), *Lock Up* (John Flynn, USA, 1989) and *Tango and Cash* (Andrei Konchalovsky, USA, 1989) exemplifying:

> a tendency of the Hollywood action cinema toward the construction of the male body as spectacle, together with an awareness of masculinity as performance. Also evident in these films is the continuation and amplification of an established tradition of the Hollywood cinema – play upon images of power and powerlessness at the center of which is the male hero.
>
> Within this structure suffering – torture, in particular – operates as both a set of narrative hurdles to be overcome, tests that the hero must survive, and as a set of aestheticized images to be lovingly dwelt on.[8]

The central characters of these films, played by Bruce Willis and

Sylvester Stallone, both foreground their physicality and undergo extremes of bodily humiliation and abuse during the course of the narratives. They are not, however, emasculated by this process; rather, by overcoming torture, they confirm, as Jeffrey Brown argues in the context of Mel Gibson's films, their status as tough guys.[9] Defining the gendered gaze in the context of the stripped-bare male body, particularly when the viewer is placed in a sadomasochistic/masochistic viewing position (as in Richard Harris' 'Horse' cycle or Sergio Leone's use of Clint Eastwood as a suffering, silent hero) has led Steve Neale to propose that:

> the spectatorial look in mainstream cinema is implicitly male: it is one of the fundamental reasons why the erotic elements involved in the relations between the spectator and the male image have constantly to be repressed and disavowed. Were this not the case, mainstream cinema would openly have to come to terms with the male homosexuality it so assiduously seems either to denigrate or deny.[10]

Farrell's unproblematic display of the male body in *Tigerland* forms part of a new discourse on masculinity that has moved closer to accepting that male-on-male look, and differentiates less between the male and female gaze in cinema. In so doing, it opens up an opportunity to break down the gender binaries that structure older discourses around 'looking'. In part this is achieved through a more outward-looking performance style. Farrell engages with the other characters and, by extension, with the viewer, through eye contact and facial gestures, generally by smiling. If charisma is in any way explicable, and Farrell is frequently written about as charismatic, this acting outwards may in part account for that aspect of his reputation. It also allows for his films to portray a more relaxed, less introspective form of contemporary manhood, one defined by Mark Simpson as 'metrosexuality'. In an analysis of English footballer, David Beckham's persona, Simpson announced the arrival of the metrosexual, a man primarily defined by his narcissism and by his love of being looked at. The metrosexual delights in consumerism and the display of men's fashion. Generally urban, they may be gay, straight, either or both and have largely been responsible for the mainstreaming of gay culture.[11]

Off-screen, Farrell has reinforced this image with the collusion of the media. To a much greater extent than his Irish screen forbears, Farrell has taken an active part in constructing his persona, cornering the fashion and lifestyle magazine market with interviews and photo shoots appearing in all the major magazines, including *Vanity Fair* (July 2002); *Playboy* (March 2003); *Esquire* (September 2003); *GQ* (November 2003) and *Vogue* (September 2004). They in turn have lapped up his projected identity: 'Why We Love Him: Unapologetically un-PC, this gregarious rogue is up for anything. His idea of group therapy? Happy hour. His motto? "Life's too short." Diet? "All the salads in L.A. get on my nerves."'[12]

Just as Hollywood cinema embraced Richard Harris' Celtic iconoclasm and his devil-may-care outspokenness nearly half a century earlier, so the same institutions seized on Farrell as the bearer of a new energy that would put paid to an instability in the contemporary star system. The studios seem to believe that the machismo of the older generation of male actors is now outdated, if also an object of nostalgia for audiences. At the same time, they appear to recognise that there is something bland and inter-changeable about those actors' successors. Publicity and its mirror image, media coverage, both fasten with something like panic on any new face that may offer a way out of this acting hiatus:

> Colin Farrell is Bozz in *Tigerland* is Marlon Brando in *On the Waterfront* is James Dean in *Giant*. He is an instant American icon, and a menacing, brooding vision of heroism. Which makes him a rarity in Hollywood, especially amid the avuncular comfort of Tom Hanks, the puerile passivity of Adam Sandler, the arthritic antics of Mel Gibson and the post-pubescent posturing of every anonymous teen idol. Instead, the feral, dark-eyed, 24-year-old Farrell is a Hollywood orgasm waiting to happen.[13]

This process is intensified by having Farrell cast in a series of roles in films that are either remakes of older works or recall older works. As we have seen, *Tigerland* is a late Vietnam film, *American Outlaws* is a reworking of the Jesse James legend and, like *Young Guns* (Christopher Cain, USA, 1988) before it, a showcase for an ensemble of rising male stars. *Hart's War* is a combination of the courtroom and prison camp dramas, touted in the trade press at the time as the new *Bridge on the River Kwai* (David Lean, GB, 1957), *S.W.A.T.* is a spin-off from the 1970s TV series and *Alexander* is one of a sequence of films to try to recreate the glory days of the historical epic. Casting Farrell opposite Bruce Willis (*Hart's War*), Tom Cruise and Al Pacino (*The Recruit*) may be further seen as Hollywood openly renewing itself, the old heralding the new.

Can we then see in the less problematic representation of Colin Farrell's body in *Tigerland* and in his subsequent films a greater sense of ease with a sexualised masculinity? Within *Tigerland*'s narrative, Farrell appears naked (in his only heterosexual encounter – having sex with a prostitute) and the film makes much of his physique although it denies the viewer any explicit view of his genitals. While not obviously pumped up in bodybuilder fashion, Farrell/Bozz enjoys a physicality that is represented as superior to that of many of the other men. In this and in two other of his films (*The Recruit* and *S.W.A.T.*), this is efficiently established by showing his character shoot a succession of bulls-eyes on a firing range. Nor does he exhibit symptoms of the kind of narcissistic, pre-oedipal silence that Neale identified in the Eastwood/Leone collaborations. This ease with Farrell/Bozz's physicality chimes with Hollywood's increasing awareness of gay culture's crossover into the mainstream, already an issue, as we have seen, for Gabriel Byrne.

Farrell's potential appeal to a cross-gender audience was swiftly taken up by the press and, in a special issue on rising actors, *Interview* magazine devoted its October 2000 cover to an image of Farrell, shot by Bruce Weber, in which the actor is posed naked from the waist up holding a ball and looking with slightly raised eyebrows towards the camera. With the promise of 'hot photos' to come, the cover announces that 'Cover boy Farrell brings his Irish charm to *Interview* magazine'. The hot photos include Farrell and Russell Richardson, the latter with his left arm reaching across Farrell's T-shirt and holding his back while he draws him to his chest with his right (both men have their eyes shut) and a full page spread of Farrell, again semi-naked, holding a rabbit against his torso. In the centrefold, Farrell poses in a loose satin robe amongst pink cushions, a cascade of hearts falling across his bare chest.

The magazine contains two interviews with Farrell in which he talks about filming *Tigerland* and about his own background. The interviews are typical of any amount of other ones carried out as Farrell was being 'discovered', in so far as they fasten on what is perceived as rebelliousness: a flow of expletives, usually rendered on the page as Irish brogue (shite, fuckin', etc.); identification with Bozz as a character; alongside personal charm, a recognition of the hard work that goes into making a film and an ironic and humorous take on his own instant fame. Here Farrell, as in other interviews, is clearly playing to the interviewer – when asked who his Valentine is, his response is: 'Marlon Brando. Me and Marlon over a nice candlelit dinner and a nice bottle of wine.'[14] Farrell also plays heavily on his Irishness and is proposed by the interviewers and himself as representative of and spokesman for a new Ireland:

> EH: [*Ordinary Decent Criminal*] sounds different from all those Irish movies about shamrocks, thatch cottages, and diddly-eye farmers in Connemara.
> CF: That's the American concept of Ireland – they love the idea of Ireland because it's so small and it's green and people drink so much – but that's the exception and not the rule. Walk down O'Connell Street…on a Friday night and you'll get stabbed within ten minutes.[15]

Farrell's Irishness is linked in this attendant publicity to his rebelliousness and to his spontaneity; being Irish he can see through the falsity of Hollywood. In a different interview, Schumacher underlines this:

> 'Okay,' he said, 'I'm gonna "out" Colin Farrell for you. You're gonna get an exclusive.' He takes a deep breath. 'Here goes: Colin smokes… He drinks…He likes to have sex with women…And he says "fuck".'
> And with that, Schumacher burst into laughter. 'I guess people don't know any 26-year-old men,' he shrugged. 'I mean, even the girls are like that in Dublin!'[16]

These interviews cannily locate Farrell with the new commercialisation of gay culture while simultaneously insisting on his macho credentials. Two subsequent films, *A Home at the End of the World* and *Alexander*, attempted to take this further by having him play parts that suggested bisexuality without quite committing to it. Before those, the Irish actor starred in a succession of roles that were distinguished by their star's increasing salary and their own lack of critical and sometimes commercial success. During this period, his pay packet increased from $100,000 for *Tigerland* to $2m for *Minority Report*, and $8m for *S.W.A.T.*[17] *Tigerland* grossed $139,500 in the USA on its theatrical release with *S.W.A.T.* taking in a more respectable $116,643,346.[18]

As in *Tigerland*, Farrell portrayed a character who came from nowhere and who was significant for his immediacy rather than his history. In *American Outlaws*, he was again a romantic and

charismatic outsider, a part he repeated in *The Recruit* and *S.W.A.T.*
A somewhat pointless pastiche, *American Outlaws* plays fast and
loose with the Jesse James legend. Most obviously, it dispenses with
James' early death by the cowardly Bob Ford; more generally it
treats the escapades of the gang members as a youthful lark with few
social or moral consequences. The actor clearly could do little with
a part that required him to gambol in a saddle and smile with
alternating menace and charm, depending on whether he was taking
his revenge on mercenary Easterners or wooing the doctor's
daughter. The same might be said about Farrell's role in *The Recruit*,
a film that recalled the conspiracy thrillers of the 1970s and where
he played another role that required him to be cool, subversive and
quick-thinking in order to outwit the mastermind behind the
infiltration of the CIA's intelligence operation. In *Hart's War*,
another box office failure, Farrell is required to display the same
virtues, this time as a rookie officer who must defend a black soldier
in a rigged courtroom within a German prisoner-of-war camp.[19]

Farrell's second production with Schumacher, *Phone Booth*,
offered Farrell the opportunity to extend his screen persona beyond
action films. Another low-budget piece, again filmed in hand-held
cinema verité style, the narrative concerns a smug advertising
executive, Stu, played by Farrell, who is being stalked by an
obsessive voyeur (Kiefer Sutherland). The stalker traps Stu in a
phone booth in central Manhattan and challenges him to recant his
sleazy lifestyle and confess his alleged infidelities to his wife, Kelly
(Radha Mitchell). The film is at its most effective in its gradual
stripping down of Stu's confidence, bringing him to a symbolic point
of rebirth when, cowering in the booth, his faced streaked with
blood and wet with perspiration, Stu realises that he cannot talk his
way out of this one and that the sniper will not give up his position
in return for a place on prime-time television. Again, the film is most
interesting for its dialogue with opposing models of masculinity:
'Stand up and be a man!' the sniper challenges his captive. His
mantra hinges on Stu's betrayal of conventional male values: 'Take
responsibility for what you have done. Be a man!', a position the
film seems in danger of sympathising with. As an advertising
executive, with all its connotations of superficiality and deception,
Stu is an easy target not just for the gunman but the film's viewers.
Under these circumstances, it is not surprising that *Phone Booth*'s
release was delayed from December 2002 to April 2003 as a
consequence of the activities of the Washington sniper. Although the

film never suggests that the (fictional) sniper is justified in assassinating people he considers corrupt and corrupting, it is still in sympathy with his critique of Stu as a representative of contemporary masculinity. To redeem himself, Stu must find a new sincerity and a new commitment to morality and probity.

Ironically, Farrell himself met, married and divorced fellow actor, Amelia Warner, in the period July to November 2001. Since then the gossip columns have linked his name with a number of top celebrities, adding womanising to a list of positive attributes for the emerging male Hollywood star. At the same time, Farrell began to ease into roles that played on his sexuality, notably, as we have already mentioned, *A Home at the End of the World* and *Alexander*. The former is an adaptation of Michael Cunningham's 1990 novel of the same title and traces the relationship between two boyhood friends, Bobby (Farrell) and Jonathan (Jonathan Glover) and their *ménage à trois* with the bohemian Clare (Robin Wright Penn). Jonathan is gay, while Bobby's sexuality is ambiguous. Although he has sex with Clare, he also has a close, potentially homoerotic relationship with Bobby, who develops AIDS. Clare becomes pregnant and the film closes with her leaving the two men so that she can live her own life with the child, away from the shadow, the film implies, of their unresolved relationship.

Mayer's film only achieved a limited theatrical release and mixed reviews. Some, such as the *Los Angeles Times*, found much to praise in the story and acting:

> It is rare in a movie that four people — including Alice [Jonathan's mother, played by Sissy Spacek] — are so completely captivating, thanks to their honesty, strength and vulnerability. Mayer and Cunningham, author of the Pulitzer Prize-winning 'The Hours', inspire their actors to take one risk after another and challenge the full measure of their intellect and perception in a way that seems to reach beyond their formidable talent. Charged by a passion for life, *A Home at the End of the World* is a major achievement.[20]

Others such as the *Chicago Tribune* argued that the filmic adaptation came too late:

> In its time, 'Home' the novel succinctly captured the ethos of a certain brand of twentysomethings grappling with the '80s: gay life, bisexuality, Reagan-era New York bohemia and the hunger to forge an ad hoc, extended family.

[...]

But since the novel, we've had not only 'Angels in America,' but scads of movies and TV films dealing with these topics. Youthful, extended families today are as familiar as 'Friends', while AIDS as a dramatic topic has evolved, thanks to medical advances and the shifting face of its victims.[21]

Most praised Farrell's acting and his ability to move from action roles to intimate drama. Internet message boards have since hosted innumerable discussion groups, largely led by young contributors who have used the forum to relate their own sexuality to Bobby's. The film also bears out Peter Lehman's theory that Hollywood has become concerned to re-negotiate an older machismo that represented itself via the penis, to the extent that, under certain circumstances, 'big penises pose a deadly threat to their possessors'.[22] Or, in the parlance of the zeitgeist, size doesn't matter. *A Home...* strategically intimates that Farrell's penis is worthy of display, but that to do so would be untoward: 'Colin Farrell's full-frontal nude scene in *A Home at the End...*' was so hot, it was cut from the film! [...] In test screenings, "people felt [his penis] was too distracting from the emotional moment in the scene," director Michael Mayer tells *Us.*'[23]

A Home... is certainly compromised by its own hesitancy; at the same time its love triangle suggests a new twist in this key narrative device. Eve Sedgewick's seminal study of the dynamics of this three-way relationship posited that in it the female becomes the object of exchange that facilitates a homosocial relationship between two men.[24] Subsequently, Judith Halberstam has analysed a series of late 1990s Hollywood releases, notably *As Good as it Gets* (James L. Brooks, USA, 1997), that position a gay man or lesbian as the competitor for the heterosexual woman's affections. These 'heterosexual conversion fantasies' see the woman fall for the gay man, cherishing his domesticity and sensitivity, until she meets the straight alpha male who will displace the gay best friend while 'articulating his rage in protracted bouts of loud homophobic reaction followed by loud sexist outbursts'.[25] The films predictably end with the woman either accepting the boorish new man after she has reformed him, or moving on to a more sensitive but heterosexual substitute for the gay best friend. *A Home...* seems like a conscious reworking of both these paradigms, allowing as it does for Farrell to function as a bisexual object of desire. It makes manifest the homosexuality that Sedgewick detects as latent in homosocial bonding, but it also problematises this by 'punishing' Jonathan (with AIDS). Nor can it fully embrace bisexuality, rupturing as it does the relationship between Clare and both men.

More controversially, Oliver Stone attempted to unite Farrell's action-hero persona with his projected metrosexuality by casting him as the bisexual Alexander in his film of the same name. *Alexander* was so universally derided that it is hard to escape its reputation, or the fact that much of the criticism was deserved. The film could at best be described as an honourable failure; it is undoubtedly too long and poorly structured, while its potential as an allegory for US imperialism is undermined by its embrace of orientalism. Farrell, it seems to me, but not to many of the production's critics, does his best to invest his characteristic energy into the part. He has since been quoted as saying: '"It's pretty amazing that, in this day and age, people can't handle the idea of a little sexual diversity in their heroes."'[26] Certainly, Alexander's bisexuality is unexpected, but rather than updating the epic's generic conventions, it just seems misplaced and even opportunistic in an otherwise machismo-driven narrative. More to the point is that today's acting styles fit poorly into the heroic mode of the historical epic. The same was evident in the (mis)casting of Brad Pitt as Achilles in *Troy* (Wolfgang Petersen, GB/USA/Malta, 2004). Unlike Peter O'Toole (King Priam) in the latter, neither Pitt nor Farrell can summon either the regality or the theatricality that their roles demand of them. Only Russell Crowe in the more earthy role of *Gladiator*'s Maximus has been able successfully to mine the genre's potential.

More startling again are the many Irish accents in the cast. Apparently Stone had decided that the Macedonians and Greeks enjoyed a relationship similar to that between the Irish and English, hence the use of so many Irish actors and accents, and the forced adoption of Irish accents by others such as Val Kilmer (as Philip). To a local audience, the effect of hearing Mick Lally deliver his lines as the horse-seller in tones unchanged from his best-known role as Miley in the long-running rural soap opera, 'Glenroe', caused much hilarity. Both these issues – the casting of Farrell and the use of Irish accents – highlight wider issues that permeate this book, namely the expectation that Irish actors will re-invigorate a moribund film culture and that, ethnically, they represent the vicarious appeal of the underdog who bites back.

Like the late-life Harris and, since then, Stephen Rea, Gabriel Byrne and Pierce Brosnan, Colin Farrell has appeared in a number of low-budget Irish films, playing in each case young, working-class Dubliners. The last of these, *interMission,* was made in the wake of Farrell's stardom and very explicitly connects the actor's off-screen persona to an egregious version of Irish masculinity. Influenced by the director's background in Irish theatre, and by Irish cinema's tendency towards ensemble playing, the presentational style is collaborative and neither Farrell nor Colm Meaney (as detective, Jerry Lynch) is required to deliver star performances. The pre-credit sequence opens with Lehiff (Farrell) engaged in an inconsequential conversation with a young Dublin shop assistant, played by Kerry Condon. As he banters about the nature of love, she evidently feels that a date with this tough-but-sensitive guy might be on the cards. Abruptly he changes tone, punches her in the face and robs the till. The ensuing chase sees him being pursued by the store detectives whom he taunts – 'Come on, youse humpy cunts!' – before the scene leaves him astride a car bonnet, threatening the driver with a shovel. Throughout the film, this propensity to sudden violence remains a threat as he organises the kidnapping of a bank manager that will form one of the strands of a narrative that is discursive and playful, moving between a number of subplots. Farrell's character is by far the most intense of the ensemble, and his acting style is here a combination of bodily swagger, a kind of side-to-side roll that connotes defiance, and a range of facial gestures, in particular a way of hanging his mouth open, that announces a pleasure in being uncouth. Farrell's portrayal of Lehiff locates an energy in being urban working-class that is simultaneously attractive and dangerous and it is not surprising that at least one critic compared his on-screen role with the real life Roy Keane.[27]

The film's opening scene is one that in mainstream Hollywood, with its circumspect attitude to casual violence against women, Farrell would be unlikely to play. In other ways, however, it belongs squarely within his image of wild Irish lad. His most developed of these roles is in Crowley's film, though this bears much in common with his cameo in *Veronica Guerin*. In the latter, Guerin (Cate Blanchett) is walking down a street at night when she comes across a young man shouting abuse at a shop window television screen. Joining him as he watches the game, she exclaims that this is 'real poetry'. When he explains to her that Eric Cantona is putting in a poor performance for Manchester United, Guerin surprises the

Figure 10.2 Locating an energy in Dublin working class culture.
Colin Farrell in *interMission*

youth by reeling off Cantona's biography and telling him that she has met the footballer. 'Well fuck me pink!' comes the reply, followed by an optimistic request to join him for a pint. Throughout, Farrell's performance is one of relaxed earthiness. Again, he is evidently acting outwards, engaging Guerin and, outwards further, the audience. Compared to the menace of the gangsters and the uselessness of the male authority figures with which Guerin is dealing, Farrell's brief interlude in the film hints at a new take on Old World authenticity, here linked to the disruption of capitalist endeavour.

Farrell does not in fact come from an inner-city background. His own creation of this myth and Irish cinema's need to see him as such represent a shift towards the embrace of a new kind of working-class urban chic.[28] At the same time, he is identified by a freewheeling garrulousness that draws on long-existing associations between Irish acting and the oral tradition. The difference is that this is now seen as being sexy; according to one newspaper report: 'As smooth-talking actor Colin Farrell already knows – if you want to woo the ladies then there's no beating the Irish accent. For the Celtic brogue has been voted the sexiest in Britain and Ireland – beating off competition from the Scots, Welsh, Geordies, Brummies, West Country and posh English contenders.'[29] Where Barry Fitzgerald most often played a kind of ageing leprechaun, the current generation of male Irish actors have refashioned that image to one of dark Byronic romanticism and an aura of sometimes dangerous sexuality concealed behind the beguiling soft tones of the national brogue. An episode of the surreal hospital drama, 'Scrubs', entitled 'My Lucky Charm' (NBC 2005), encapsulated Farrell's positioning within a contemporary discourse on Irishness that acknowledges the anachronism of its old stereotypes and the commercial reasons for preserving them. As we hear that a patient has been admitted with his Irish brother, a leprechaun briefly pops up on the screen, dancing and laughing. Wondering whether he is an Irish 'brother' (i.e., African-American) or an Irishman who is the guy's brother, J.D. (Zach Braff) goes into the ward with Turk (Donald Faison). There they are greeted by Billy (Farrell) who assures them first of all that he is from Texas (in an American accent) and then that he is only joking, that he is really Irish (in an inner-city Dublin accent). The acid identity test is passed when he can recite: 'Pink hearts, yellow moons, orange stars, green clovers', the slogan from the (American) Lucky Charms cereal. The series' two central male characters, J.D. and Turk, have become increasingly disenchanted with life's possibilities, and now spend evenings in their apartment playing 'Go Fish'. Billy takes one look at them and diagnoses their ailment; they need to get out and meet more women. The next moment, Turk signals to J.D. that Billy is kissing Elliot (Sarah Chalke). Mistily she tells them that he has just whispered to her that her eyes look like the Irish countryside after a soft rain. Much the same happens when he tells Carla (Judy Reyes) that her hair is curly, leading to all-out war in the canteen. Once J.D. and Turk discover that in fact Billy is not related to the unconscious man in the bed and that he only met him the night before when he knocked him out, they realise that he has committed a felony. 'Where I come from,' Billy assures them, 'you knock someone unconscious, you stay around to make sure they're OK, so guess what, I won't be leaving.' The arrest of Billy causes a furore among the staff, who insist that: 'You have one day to get us another gorgeous Irishman.' All is finally resolved and, thanks to Billy, a sense of well-being briefly permeates the Sacred Heart Hospital. J.D. realises that it is important not to take life for granted, while the chronic patient, Jerry (Michael Bunin) sighs that: 'When I was alive, I wish I had lived one day like he lives every day of his life.'

Charming, good looking, in touch with Irish values of friendship and spontaneity, Farrell's Billy acknowledges the commercial environment his character has emerged from while enacting it all over again, as if it were new. Dispensing with the rebel politics that created George Brent's persona, Farrell can now exploit his position within the domain of personal politics, where rebellion is now about refusing to eat health foods. Embedded in this new man metrosexuality are traces of an Old World identity that is rooted in values of home and hearth and seen to be unavailable in the lifestyle of the New World. Or, as Farrell puts it: "'I'm a total mummy's boy. She's my best pal in the world. [...] I really adore and respect women and it comes from just loving my mother all my life.'"[30]

NOTES

1   See R. Barton, 'The Ballykissangelisation of Ireland', *Historical Journal of Film, Radio and Television*, 20, 3 (2000), pp. 413–26.

2   T. Ogle, 'Life After Assumpta', *Radio Times*, 19–25 September 1998, pp. 24–5, p. 24.

3   Naremore, *Acting in the Cinema*, p. 68.

4   Libatique had already shot Darren Aronofsky's *Pi* (USA, 1998) and *Requiem for a Dream* (USA, 2000).

5   J. Newsinger, '"Do you walk the walk?": Aspects of masculinity in some Vietnam war films', in P. Kirkham and J. Thumin (eds), *You Tarzan: Masculinity, Movies and Men* (London: Lawrence & Wishart, 1993), p. 135. For an earlier academic approach to the Vietnam war, see A. Auster and L. Quart, *How the War was Remembered: Hollywood and Vietnam* (New York, Westport, CI and London: Praeger, 1988).

6   M. Selig, 'Genre, gender, and the discourse of war: the a/historical and Vietnam films', *Screen*, 34, 1 (1993), pp. 1–18.

7   Ibid., p. 3.

8   Y. Tasker, 'Dumb movies for dumb people', in S. Cohan and I.R. Hark (eds), *Screening the Male* (London and New York: Routledge, 1993), pp. 230–44, p. 230.

9   For a discussion of torture as affirmative of masculinity see, J.A. Brown, 'The tortures of Mel Gibson', *Men and Masculinities*, 5, 1 (October 2002), pp. 123–43.

10 S. Neale, 'Masculinity as spectacle', in *The Sexual Subject*, pp. 277–87, p. 286.

11 M. Simpson, 'Meet the metrosexual', *Salon.com* (http://www.salon.com/ent/feature/2002/07/22/metrosexual/, accessed 5 September 2005).

12 '50 hottest bachelors', *People*, 28 June 2004, Colin Farrell file, AMPAS.

13 (http://www.colinfarrell.ie/interviews/misc-The Face.htm, consulted 22 April 2004)

14 E. Helmore, 'Colin Farrell', *Interview* (February 2000), p. 148.

15 Ibid.

16 *Empire*, 171 (September 2003), p. 21.

17 A. Billen, "It doesn't take much to be a bad boy", *The Times*, 25 March 2003, pp 14–15, p. 15.

18 imdb.com (accessed 28 June 2005).

19 *Hart's War* took $19,076,815 on an estimated budget of $70,000,000, ibid.

20 K. Thomas, 'A *Home at the End of the World*', *Los Angeles Times*, July 23, 2004 (available at: http://www.calendarlive.com/movies/reviews/cl-et-home 23jul23,2,3970184.story, accessed 28 June 2005).

21 S. Smith, 'Movie review: A Home at the End of the World', *Chicago Tribune*, (available at: http://metromix.chicagotribune.com/movies/mmx-040728-movies-review-ss-home,0,659059.story, accessed 28 June 2005).

22 P. Lehman, 'In an imperfect world, men with small penises are unforgiven', *Men and Masculinities*, 1, 2 (October 1998), pp. 123–37, p. 136.

23 E. Andersson, *Us*, 12–17 July 2004, Colin Farrell file, AMPAS.

24 E.K. Sedgwick, *Between Men: English Literature and Male Homosocial Desire* (New York: Columbia University Press, 1985).

25 J. Halberstam, 'The good, the bad, and the ugly', in J.K. Gardiner (ed.), *Masculinity Studies and Feminist Theory* (New York: Columbia University Press, 2002), pp. 305–67, p. 348.

26 Quoted in P. Byrne, 'Ice cold on Alex', *Sunday Business Post*, 16 January 2005, p. A5.

27 G. Macnab, '*interMission*' (review), *Sight and Sound*, 14, 1 (2004), p. 47. For an extended discussion of Keane as a national symbol and representative of a new masculinity, see M. Free, 'Preparing to fail: gender, consumption, play and national identity in Irish broadcast media coverage of the "Roy Keane affair" and the 2002 World Cup', in R. Barton and H. O'Brien (eds), *Keeping it Real* (London and New York: Wallflower Press, 2004), pp. 172–84.

28 See also R. Barton, *Irish National Cinema*, pp. 113–29.

29 'Irish accent voted sexiest in TV poll', *Irish Post*, 3 April 2004, p. 3.

30 Quoted in 'Farrell on Film', *TV Now*, 173, 23–29 August 2003, p. 12.

Conclusion

A troupe, a trope

In Evelyn Waugh's satire on Hollywood, *The Loved One*, Sir Francis lists his problems to his fellow expatriates; having made over his protégée, Baby Aaronson, as Juanita del Pablo, a refugee from Franco's Spain, the post-war League of Decency now wants 'healthy' films:

> So poor Juanita has to start at the beginning again as an Irish colleen. They've bleached her hair and dyed it vermilion. I told them colleens were dark but the technicolor men insisted. She's worked ten hours a day learning the brogue and to make it harder for the poor girl they've pulled all her teeth out. She never had to smile before and her own set was good enough for a snarl. Now she'll have to laugh roguishly all the time. That means dentures.[1]

She will also have to change her name again; though, to add to Sir Francis' difficulties, there are already two Maureens, no-one can pronounce Deirdre, Oonagh sounds Chinese and Bridget is too common.

Classic Hollywood was, as Sir Francis knew, relentless in its pursuit of the majority taste; when this was not consensual (if it ever is), then it unhesitatingly played both ends against the middle. The two Maureens soon learnt that this meant trading assimilation off against ethnicity, conjuring up good Catholic home lives and all-American values for the League of Decency while hinting at more exotic possibilities for the benefit of the less moralistic. Being Irish and white, and very evidently so, offered both actors opportunities in Hollywood that they used to their advantage. Constance Smith, in her turn, was able to ride the wave of their popularity and to exploit Hollywood's love for Irish feistiness, so long as it was played out on screen and not behind the scenes, on the studio lot.

The Irish popular press was little different, with women's magazines in particular titillating their readers with accounts of

Hollywood life and mores while firmly distancing themselves from the allure of the forbidden. Thus a profile of Clark Gable mused that: 'All this talk of complicated marriages and divorces – so foreign to our customs and beliefs – makes one wonder what kind of a place Hollywood really is...'[2] At the same time, tales of Hollywood excess, images of Hollywood fashion, and beauty tips from the stars offered wartime Irish women a temporary liberation from austerity, never more so than when one of their own 'made it':

> Her story is one that must thrill every woman in the country. A five-figure contract... the friendship and admiration of the world's most famous people... a thrilling career and the promise of stardom... these are the glamorous and exciting things that have come to Maureen Fitzsimons in the short space of four months.[3]

Why Irish female actors have so signally failed to attain stardom in Hollywood since then is a moot point. Certainly whiteness is part of the reason. Those very traits that caused Juanita to be displaced by the Maureens, have since, as Diane Negra has identified, come full circle.[4] Now the ideal of beauty is darker-skinned – Latina or mixed-race – tinged with a hint of submissiveness. There is perhaps something just too imperious about the Maureen O'Hara type, too castrating, to cut much ice in a studio environment dedicated to the pursuit of blockbusters aimed at teenage boys. We also need to look within indigenous Irish filmmaking to understand why Irish women are not enjoying the career opportunities of their male counterparts. As I have argued elsewhere, since the revitalisation of the Film Board in the early 1990s, Irish cinema has overwhelmingly favoured narratives dedicated to issues of masculinity; enabled by developments in digital production, and encouraged by an official policy of supporting such production, a new generation of young male filmmakers has emerged and with them a new wave of male-oriented dramas.[5] Although no satisfactory study of the gender issues at stake in contemporary Irish filmmaking has to date been published, received wisdom suggests that young men are more attracted to technology-driven industries than young women; nor does a woman behind the camera guarantee better roles for her counterparts on the screen. Still, I believe the connection is there be made. A vicious circle has emerged whereby the lead female roles in those few female-oriented dramas that have been produced of late, such as *About Adam* (Gerard Stembridge, Ireland/USA/GB, 2000), have been occupied by imported actors, thus denying rising indigenous performers the opportunity to play on the international circuit. The casting of Meryl Streep in *Dancing at Lughnasa* (Pat O'Connor, Ireland/GB/USA, 1998) is not the worst example of this practice, though Daryl Hannah in the earlier *High Spirits* (Neil Jordan, USA, 1988) might be.

Aside from the gender deficiency, the increasing levels of local Irish film and television production have meant that this generation of Irish actors has been able to make a living in Ireland, especially if they are prepared to move between theatre and filmmaking, as most do. As we have seen, the dark looks of the Irish male, with their dual appeal of threat and promise, have never gone out of fashion; on the contrary, they enjoy considerable currency in today's Hollywood. Increasingly, such actors can start out 'at home' and then move on to British theatre and cinema and/or Hollywood and Broadway; they can also move freely between the local and the international film production business. You may see Brendan Gleeson one week as a banjo-playing errant American father in *Cold Mountain* (Anthony Minghella, USA/GB/Romania/Italy, 2003) and the next as an Irish-accented King Menelaus in *Troy*. Or you can catch him with Cillian Murphy and Colin Farrell in *interMission* or in any number of locally produced Irish films. The opportunity to watch Irish performers working together in Irish narratives, rather than as isolated figures in non-Irish dramas, better allows us to address the question of whether an indigenous acting style exists. If there is one, then it is evidently not static. It is hard to imagine, for instance, the performances we have discussed in *The Quiet Man* being re-created today, unless ironically. Irish screen acting has very evidently evolved since its early roots in the twin traditions of vaudeville and the Abbey. Now, in line with international practice, it tends towards the understated and to operate within a new concept of realism. I do not believe that there is, in fact, a decodable form of Irish performance, visible to those versed in it, invisible to others. As I have argued, however, it does seem to me that the most consistent performative practice has been that of the ensemble. From those early Abbey screen outings through to any number of recent instances of Irish actors appearing together on film, collaboration has been a key identifying trait, so much so that I would suggest there exists a national troupe of Irish actors, accustomed to working collaboratively with each other, and constantly being replenished by rising new performers. This practice has a number of consequences;

for one, it does not foster a star culture. It still remains the case that if Irish actors wish to become and remain internationally recognised stars, then they must appear in overseas, mostly Hollywood, cinema; only Stephen Rea, as a consequence of his work with Neil Jordan, has proved otherwise. Conversely, they must be prepared to forgo the 'star performance' when appearing in local productions. In another way, ensemble acting reflects a commonly held perception of Irish culture as being cohesive and communal. Even when the diegetic community is under scrutiny and found to be lacking, as is common, it remains a core trope. This invocation of communality is effected via the communality of the Irish acting troupe, whose members play to each other with the ease of an equivalent social grouping. By extension, the ensemble may then be read as substituting for the national, for which the community is metonymic. In indigenous filmmaking of this kind, the performance of national identity is, however, less overt; the ensemble erases the emblematic individual, shifting the weight of representation onto the group, and complicating any single reading as it does.

The individual performance of national identity is decided largely by address. As this study has demonstrated, one of the greatest challenges facing those Irish actors who do pursue Hollywood careers has been to transcend national stereotyping:

> In American films (excepting a handful set in Britain and France which call for a wide range of social representation), British and French characters – or characters in some way coded as 'British or 'French' – are almost always aristocratic or quasi, and often cross-coded to dandyism, effeminacy. Irish, German or Italian characters, by contrast, can be coded to a kind of proletarian earthiness. In real life there are plenty of French proletarians (and in the cinema too, since Jean Gabin's career was almost entirely structured around a proletarian image). There are also a number of Irish dandies, beginning with Oscar Wilde. But in Hollywood movies there is a strong tendency to relate national stereotype to the stereotype of the immigrant. Since the English and French are not identified as belonging to the poor, the huddled masses, the stereotype of the English or French man or woman follows suit. You can't have English roughnecks, nor can you have Irish dandies; if Wilde is to remain a dandy, then scrub the Irishness.[6]

The most recent generation of Irish immigrant actors knows that to succeed they must still be prepared to scrub their Irishness – but to a far lesser extent than, say, George Brent ever did. The rise of multi-culturalism as the predominant ethos within American society has given official status to a practice that had hitherto enjoyed only unofficial existence. Irishness remains the most commercial of identities, appealing not only to the Irish-American population who, in any case, themselves boast multiple hyphenated ethnic allegiances, but to the wider American and non-American cinema viewer.[7] At the same time, it has been important for stars to function both as other and as white. Thus, in *The Shawshank Redemption* (Frank Darabont, USA, 1994), close to the beginning of the film, in a scene not as far removed as it might seem from that described in the 'Introduction', Andy Dufresne (Tim Robbins) asks the African-American prison 'fixer', Red (Morgan Freeman), how he got his name. The answer? 'I'm Irish'. How ridiculous, the film's subtext pronounces, he couldn't be.

The popular press, particularly in America, loves to attribute aspects of an imagined national identity to individual actors; some blatantly exploit it:

> Colin Farrell never leaves his trailer on the first day of film shoot without his lucky shamrock-covered underpants. The handsome Irish actor has confessed he always wears the patriotic boxer shorts when he starts making a new movie. He revealed: 'They have these Irish shamrocks on them and it says "Luck of the Irish" on the band, and I wear them on the first day of every film I do. They're my lucky charm. And if I don't have them with me I won't come out of the trailer – I'd shoot myself. They're starting to get a bit old now but I could never ever part with them.'[8]

The romance of the Irish rebel was not, as we have seen, invented by the fans of Colin Farrell, though its definition has changed since George Brent's times. This mode of address is one that is primarily directed outwards and is aimed at cementing identification between the emblematic individual and the exogenous community. The performance of Irishness is also, increasingly, played out ironically and self-consciously, and not necessarily by ethnic Irish stars. The most irony-laden of such displays is Brad Pitt's outing as the gypsy, Mickey One Punch O'Neil, in *Snatch* (Guy Ritchie, GB/USA, 2000). Sporting a stage Irish accent that is an echo of countless Barry Fitzgerald performances, Pitt plays the part with a knowingness that fully acknowledges his character's lack of authenticity. Mickey One Punch O'Neil's garrulous flow of stage-Irishisms is a tribute to, as well as an ironic reworking of, that tradition of the loquacious Irish trickster. Again, as we have seen, this archetype has not only offered Irish actors a niche within Hollywood but also within British theatre and on British screens. It has also functioned as a device to distinguish the actor from his (mostly) British counterparts. Where British acting has been characterised by emotional reticence, particularly in performances of what is now associated with white, middle-class English cinema, and British actors have remained defiantly aghast at Hollywood excess, Irish actors, and the characters they have played, have been embraced both in Britain, and outside of it, for their emotional impulsiveness. Performers such as Richard Harris have fulfilled very similar functions within British and American culture, of re-invigorating what is perceived as an atrophied tradition with a fresh Celtic spontaneity.

The Irish actor is a constituent part of a vibrant national cinema, in particular one that is recognisable to its home audience. It is also certainly the case that, in the long absence of an indigenous cinema, the Irish actor in Hollywood (and to a lesser extent British) cinema provided a link for Irish audiences to the cinematic mainstream, and by extension to the wider world. The Irish actor has been both emblem and embodiment of the greater Irish diasporic nation, a synecdoche for its history of emigration and exile. The actor also provided the link between the history and traditions of Irish theatre and cinema, validating the one through the other, and memorialising the transient moment of the stage performance within the celluloid museum. That we can now cast a locally produced Irish film with a roster of internationally recognised Irish stars is a tribute to the vibrancy of our diasporic culture. Liminality, for all its disadvantages, is an enabling position.

NOTES

1   E. Waugh, *The Loved One* (London, New York: Penguin, 2000, first published 1948), p. 11.
2   *Woman's Life*, 18 September 1937, p. 6.
3   Ibid., 19 February 1938, p. 6.
4   Negra, *Off-White Hollywood*.
5   See Barton, *Irish National Cinema*.
6   G. Nowell-Smith, 'The beautiful and the bad: notes on some actorial stereotypes', in G. Nowell-Smith and S. Ricci (eds), *Hollywood and Europe* (London: British Film Institute, 1998), pp. 135–41, p. 139.
7   For a detailed discussion of Irishness and ethnicity in the contemporary

American media, see, D. Negra, 'Irishness, innocence, and American identity politics before and after 11 September', in Barton and O'Brien, *Keeping it Real*, pp. 54–68.

8   http://www.femalefirst.co.uk/celebrity/5102004.htm (accessed 25 October 2005); my thanks to Diane Negra for updating me on Farrell's boxers.

Bibliography

Anderson, L. *Never Apologise*, ed. P. Ryan (London: Plexus, 2004).

Babington, B. (ed) *British Stars and Stardom* (Manchester and New York: Manchester University Press, 2001).

Barton, R. *Jim Sheridan: Framing the Nation* (Dublin: The Liffey Press, 2002).

—*Irish National Cinema* (London and New York: Routledge, 2004).

Barton R. and O'Brien, H. *Keeping it Real* (London and New York: Wallflower, 2004).

Behlmer, R. (ed.) *Inside Warner Bros.* (London: Weidenfeld and Nicolson, 1986).

Bernardi, D. (ed.) *Classic Hollywood, Classic Whiteness* (Minneapolis and London: University of Minnesota Press, 2001).

Bernstein M. and Studlar, G. (eds.) *Visions of the East* (London and New York: I.B. Tauris, 1997).

Burns-Bisogno, L. *Censoring Irish Nationalism* (Jefferson, North Carolina and London: McFarland, 1997).

Burroughs, E. R. *Tarzan of the Apes* (New York, Dover Publications 1997; first published 1914).

Byrne, G. *Pictures in My Head* (Dublin: Wolfhound Press, 1994).

Callan, M.F., *Richard Harris* (London: Robson Books, 2003).

Callow, S. *Charles Laughton, A Difficult Actor* (London: Methuen, 1987).

Chapman, J. *Licence to Thrill, A Cultural History of the James Bond Films* (London and New York: I.B. Tauris, 1999).

Coates, P. *Cinema, Religion and the Romantic Legacy* (Aldershot and Burlington: Ashgate, 2003).

Cohan, S. and Hark, I. R. *Screening the Male* (London and New York: Routledge, 1993).

Curran, J.M. *Hibernian Green on the Silver Screen* (New York, Westport, London: Greenwood Press, 1989).

Davis, B. *The Lonely Life* (London: Macdonald, 1962).

Doherty, T. *Pre-Code Hollywood, Sex, Immorality, and Insurrection in American Cinema, 1930-1934* (New York: Columbia University Press, 1999).

Dyer, R., *Heavenly Bodies* (London and New York: Routledge, 2004 2nd edition).

—*Stars* (London: BFI, 1998, new edition; first published 1979).

Eagleton, T. *Heathcliff and the Great Hunger* (London and New York: Verso, 1995).

Eco, U. *Faith in Fakes* (London: Martin Secker and Warburg, 1986; trans William Weaver).

Essoe, G. *Tarzan of the Movies* (Syracuse, N.J.: Citadel Press, 1979).

Fanon, F. *Black Skins White Masks* (translated by Charles Lam Markmann) (London: Pluto Press, 1986).

Fischer, L. and Landy, M, *Stars: the Film Reader* (London and New York: Routledge, 2004).

Friedman, L.D. (ed), *Unspeakable Images, Ethnicity and the American Cinema* (Urbana and Chicago: University of Illinois Press, 1991).

Gallagher, T. *John Ford: the Man and his Films* (London, Berkeley: University of California Press, 1986).

Gardiner, J.K. (ed.), *Masculinity Studies and Feminist Theory* (New York: Columbia University Press, 2002).

Gibbons, L. *The Quiet Man* (Cork: Cork University Press, 2002).

Glancy, H.M. *When Hollywood Loved Britain* (Manchester and New York; Manchester University Press, 1999).

Gledhill, C. (ed.) *Stardom: Industry of Desire* (London: Routledge, 1991).

Hardt, U. *From Caligari to California* (Oxford, Providence: Berghahn Books, 1996).

Hill, J. *Sex, Class and Realism* (London: British Film Institute, 1986).

Hogan, R., Burnham, R. and Poteet, D.P., *The Abbey Theatre: The Rise of the Realists, 1910-1915* (Dublin: Dolmen Press, 1979).

Ignatiev, N. *How the Irish Became White* (London and New York: Routledge, 1995).

Kasson, J. F. *Houdini, Tarzan and the Perfect Man* (New York: Hill and Wang, 2001).

Kearney, R. *Postnationalist Ireland* (London and New York: Routledge, 1997).

Kirkham P. and Thumin, J. (eds), *You Tarzan: Masculinity, Movies and Men* (London: Lawrence & Wishart, 1993).

Krämer, P. and Lovell, A (eds.), *Screen Acting* (London and New York: Routledge, 1999).

Krause , D. (ed), *The Letters of Sean O'Casey, 1910-41* (London: Cassell, 1975).

Lindner, C. (ed.) *The James Bond Phenomenon* (Manchester and New York: Manchester University Press, 2003).

Littlewood, J. *Joan's Book* (London: Methuen, 1994).

McBride, J. *Searching for John Ford* (London and New York: Faber and Faber, 2001/2003).

McGilligan, P. *Alfred Hitchcock: A Life in Darkness and Light* (London: Wiley, 2003).

McLoone, M. *Irish Film: The Emergence of a Contemporary Cinema* (London: BFI, 2000).

Macnab, G. *Searching for Stars: Stardom and Screen Acting in British Cinema* (London and New York: Cassell, 2000).

Mast, G. *The Comic Mind* (London: New English Library, 1973).

Mayne, J. *Directed by Dorothy Arzner* (Bloomington and Indianapolis, Indiana University Press, 1994).

Membery, Y. *Pierce Brosnan* (London: Virgin Books, 2002).

Mikhail, E.H. (ed.), *The Abbey Theatre: Interviews and Recollections* (London and Hampshire: The Macmillan Press, 1988).

Monahan, B. *Deconstructing the Nation: the Abbey Theatre and stage-Irishness on Screen, 1930-1960,* unpublished PhD thesis (Trinity College Dublin, 2003).

Morash, C. *A History of Irish Theatre* (Cambridge, New York etc.: Cambridge University Press, 2002).

Morley, S. *Tales From the Hollywood Raj* (London: Weidenfeld and Nicholson, 1983).

Murphy, R. *Sixties British Cinema* (London: British Film Institute, 1992).

Murray, C. *Seán O'Casey* (Dublin: Gill and Macmillan, 2004).

Naficy, H. (ed.) *Home, Exile, Homeland* (London and New York: Routledge, 1999).

—*An Accented Cinema* (Princeton and Oxford: Princeton University Press, 2001).

Naremore, J. *Acting in the Cinema* (Berkeley, Los Angeles, London: University of California Press, 1988).

Negra, D. *Off-White Hollywood* (London and New York: Routledge, 2001).

Nowell-Smith, G. and Ricci, S. (eds) *Hollywood and Europe* (London: BFI, 1998).

O'Casey, E. *Sean* (London: Gill and Macmillan, 1971).

O'Connor, A. *Leading Hollywood* (Dublin and London: Wolfhound Press, 1996).

O'Hara, M. (with John Nicoletti), *'Tis Herself*, (London, New York, Sydney, Toronto, Dublin: Simon and Schuster, 2004).

Parish, J. *The RKO Gals* (London: Ian Allan, 1974).

Parish, J. R. and Stanke, D.E. *The Debonairs* (New Rochelle, New York: Arlington House Publishers, 1975).

Pearson, R. *Eloquent Gestures* (Berkeley, Los Angeles, Oxford: University of California Press, 1992).

Penley, C. (ed.) *Feminism and Film Theory* (London and New York: BFI, 1988).

Pettitt, L. *Screening Ireland* (Manchester and New York: Manchester University Press, 2000).

Richards, J. *The Swordsmen of the Screen* (London: Routledge and Kegan Paul, 1977).

Richards, S. (ed), *The Cambridge Companion to Twentieth-Century Irish Drama* (Cambridge, New York etc.: Cambridge University Press, 2004).

Richtarik, M. *Acting between the Lines* (Oxford, New York etc.: Oxford University Press, 1994).

Rockett, K., Gibbons, L. Hill, J. *Cinema and Ireland* (London: Routledge, 1988).

Rockett, K. *The Irish Filmography* (Dublin: Red Mountain Media, 1996).

Roddick, N. *A New Deal in Entertainment, Warner Brothers in the 1930s* (London: BFI, 1983).

The Sexual Subject: A Screen *Reader in Sexuality* (London and New York: Routledge, 1992).

Schatz, T. *The Genius of the System* (New York: Metropolitan Books, 1996).

Sheehan, H. *Irish Television Drama* (Dublin: Radio Telefís Éireann, 1987).

Thorslev, P. *The Byronic Hero* (Minneapolis: University of Minneapolis Press, 1962).

Troyan, M. *A Rose for Mrs. Miniver* (Kentucky: The University of Kentucky Press, 1999).

Tseëlon, E. (ed.), *Masquerade and Identities* (London and New York: Routledge, 2001).

Vincendeau, G. *Stars and Stardom in French Cinema* (London and New York: Continuum, 2000).

Warshow, R. *The Immediate Experience: Movies, Comics, Theater, and Other Aspects of Popular Culture* (New York: Doubleday, 1969).

Waters, M. *The Comic Irishman* (Albany: State University of New York Press, 1984).

Welch, R. *The Abbey Theatre 1899-1999* (Oxford and New York: Oxford University Press, 1999).

Williams, W.H.A. *'Twas Only an Irishman's Dream* (Urbana and Chicago: University of Illinois Press, 1996).

Zucker, C. *In the Company of Actors* (New York: Theatre Arts Books/Routledge, 2001).

Index